the autobiography

the autobiography
john hartson

Copyright © Harte Promotions Limited 2006

The right of John Hartson to be identified as
the author of this work has been asserted by him
in accordance with the Copyright, Designs and
Patents Act 1988.

First published in hardback in Great Britain
in 2006 by Orion Books
an imprint of the Orion Publishing Group Ltd
Orion House, 5 Upper St Martin's Lane,
London WC2H 9EA

10 9 8 7 6 5 4 3 2 1

A CIP catalogue record for this book is available
from the British Library.

ISBN-13: 978 0 75287 486 9
ISBN-10: 0 75287 486 1

Printed in Great Britain by
Clays Ltd, St Ives plc

The Orion Publishing Group's policy is to use papers that
are natural, renewable and recyclable and made from wood
grown in sustainable forests. The logging and manufacturing
processes are expected to conform to the environmental
regulations of the country of origin.

Every effort has been made to fulfil requirements with
regard to reproducing copyright material. The author and
publisher will be glad to rectify any omissions at the
earliest opportunity.

www.orionbooks.co.uk

To my two wonderful children, Rebeca and Joni; to Lowri, who was there for me through the good times and the difficult ones, and to my folks who supported me from the start.

Acknowledgements

It wasn't an easy decision for me to agree to this look back at my life. I had to be certain I had a worthwhile story to tell about the modern footballer and was able to relate the considerable highs and lows that have been part of my experience. It wasn't always a comfortable feeling as I drew back the curtain, but it was essential to tell the truth, however revealing the memory.

There are many people I want to acknowledge who have in some way influenced my life either privately or professionally. First mention must go to my close friends Shane Fox, Karl Fitzgerald and Paul Glover. Several other friends are mentioned in the pages that follow, and if I don't include them here I assure them no offence is intended. I'm sure they all know how much I value their friendship. These are the people who have stood shoulder to shoulder with me when others were happy to walk away.

I also acknowledge the love of my family. They have always been there for me – my folks, my older brother James, my sisters Hayley and Victoria – all of whom I hope have enjoyed my success as a footballer. And I acknowledge Lowri, my partner in the good years.

My thanks to all the football men who have been so much a part of my life: David Pleat, George Graham, Harry Redknapp,

Mark Hughes, Gordon Strachan and Martin O'Neill. And to all the player mates who were part of the great adventure, still on-going, but particular acknowledgement to all my friends at Celtic who helped win us so much.

There would have been no meaningful start to this project without the research of Daniel King, and I thank him for that. My thanks also to Alex Montgomery, an exiled Glaswegian who listened to my story in some of the great city's best restaurants (we have a common interest in food as well as football) and put it together in the right way.

To the Orion team led by Ian Marshall and his assistant Lorraine Baxter, copy-editor Philip Parr, and Jonathan Barnett, David Manasseh and Johnny Whitmore of the Stellar Group, thanks for your advice and patience over the years, and to Patrick Deane who has always been there for me.

Read on – and be kind: 'When you walk a mile in another man's shoes, only then can you understand why he acts the way he does.'

John Hartson

Contents

Foreword by Gordon Strachan   xi

1 Resurrection   1

2 A Ball at my Feet   27

3 The Good, the Bad and the Plain Ugly   39

4 In with the Big Boys   52

5 Wembley – A Dream Cup Run   70

6 Arsenal – You Can't be Serious   85

7 My Highbury Hell   104

8 Arsène and Out   113

9 Claret and the Boys in Blue   129

10 Crazy Days   151

11 Wales – My Wales   166

12 One of the Bhoys   189

13 Glory and Despair   202

14 Losing the Plot with Martin   218

15 Divorce – A Fateful Decision   238

16 The New Boss – Rising from the Ashes   248

17 Reflections   267

Career Statistics   280

Index   283

Foreword
by Gordon Strachan

There are few things you can be certain of as a manager – John Hartson scoring goals for you is one of them. The story goes that if I had signed him earlier than we did at Coventry when I was manager he would have produced the goals that would have kept us in the Premiership. It's perfectly true, if I had been able to complete the transfer quicker there is no doubt we would have escaped relegation. But, and I say this with respect and on reflection to Coventry and their fans, I'm glad we didn't or our professional lives would have turned out differently. Would he have gone on to join Celtic? Would I have taken over as manager from Martin O'Neill? I took a little longer than him to join Celtic, but it eventually worked in my favour and I am certain John can only feel the same after such a brilliantly successful career with the great club.

I didn't know what the future would produce for me at Celtic Park, only that John would continue to score goals and that his presence would be a force for good in the dressing room: knowing that was a comfort. I have played alongside some of the best players this country and many others countries have produced. I have managed quite a few along the way too – John Hartson is among the very, very best, not only as a marvellously talented footballer but as a wonderful character – straightforward, honest, extremely likeable.

As a footballer, John's remarkable talent was recognised as special when he was a youngster. It was in him to be a top professional. His goalscoring record was exceptional then and has been since, year after year – at Luton, Arsenal, West Ham, Wimbledon, Celtic and Wales. You can't hide at clubs as important as those or for your country. Perhaps there have been those who somehow managed to undervalue him, but that would be their mistake, because John is a presence the rest of the squad want in the team.

For a big man his touch is fantastic; he knows where to go and he can score any type of goal. One game at Old Trafford remains vivid in my memory. It was with Coventry and we were beaten, but John was immense. He battered their centre halves and at the end Roy Keane put it neatly and correctly in context when he said, 'John was unplayable.' I have heard opposition managers say the same on many occasions.

John is a big man physically and there is this perception of him being a monster when in reality he is a big cuddly type. His size can be both an advantage and a disadvantage, as he has found to his cost. Referees aren't always as protective towards him as they should be. They take his size for granted. They will watch him being hammered by defenders, a regular occurrence, and do nothing about it.

Their thinking seems to be: 'He's a big guy so he should be able to take it.' If he has the audacity to complain about it then he is reproached. That is unfair.

I admire what John has achieved, I admire his exceptional ability, I admire his courage.

I have never heard one person he has come into contact with, be he a player, manager, coach or club official, say a bad word about John. Fans, players, managers – they all want him in their team. There is no higher accolade in our business. When I was asked if I would wish to contribute this foreword I didn't hesitate to say yes. I am delighted and privileged to do so as it gives me the opportunity to thank John for what he has produced for my teams and what he has given football.

chapter 1

Resurrection

There have been incidents in my life I deeply regret and which have earned me notoriety. The physical side of football I have learned to cope with, revel in: I can take the punishment which comes with the job and will defend myself if I have to. But there are other episodes, some publicised, some not, which chill me on recollection and have at the very least been a source of acute embarrassment to me and those closest to me. What I want to make clear from the outset is that my past actions, the ones that unsettle me, cannot be related in any way to my upbringing in Swansea, which was gloriously happy in a family who have never been less than loving towards each other.

Of all the situations I have had to confront, the only ones I have been unable to control are those involving medical opinion. With the rest I have been able to explain my reasoning and, if necessary, make an apology or be apologised to. When medical opinion is involved there is no appeal. The doctors may be right or they may be wrong, but they cannot be argued with. That's how it was for me between 2000 and 2001, when a series of scans – four, to be exact – apparently showed up a weakness in my knee which drove me close to despair. It took me to the very edge. I can't think of any other player who has had four separate deals, each worth up to £6 million, collapse under him on the strength of four failed medical tests. It is some sort of record, one I don't like being associated with, and even now, five years later, it makes me cringe at the thought.

I suffered, although I went on to win three Scottish Premier League Championships, two Scottish FA Cups and one Scottish League Cup. In the process I have scored enough goals to keep people off my back and played for Wales forty more times before retiring with fifty-one caps; all after being rejected by those clubs who were willing to pay big money for me and then said 'no' on medical advice.

This is my side of the story – the full, unexpurgated story; as my friends in the press would say, 'The Truth' – how it developed and how at one time I felt the career I had worked hard to improve since I was a toddler in Wales was in danger of imploding. That is not an exaggeration, so I think it right to start these recollections of my professional career at the point when it was in danger of disappearing from the radar screen altogether. It has been cathartic to recall the bad as well as the good times. Overall, I have been able to exorcise any demons in the system – and there *have* been other problems, most normal, a few abnormal, along the way – but the crisis was initially created by those transfer rejections.

The trend was reversed in my favour thanks exclusively to one man: not Martin O'Neill, as most people would expect, as he gave me the opportunity to be a champion, but Gordon Strachan. Gordon picked me up when I needed to have support and a sign of belief from someone with his pedigree in the game. He was the one who took a gamble on me and on my ability to continue performing at the highest level. This was when he was manager of Coventry City, so it was some time before we were to link up again at Celtic.

My future as a professional footballer had been seriously threatened by the failed medical tests, which were conducted as conditions of transfers planned by four clubs – first Tottenham, then Charlton, Glasgow Rangers and finally Coventry City – all of whom had agreed the fee with Wimbledon. The money involved, apart from the transfer fee itself, offered me huge pay hikes, virtually doubling my Wimbledon salary. It would have been top money for the day. Fabulous money! So good I couldn't afford to turn it down.

To my disbelief, all four clubs, and that initially includes Gordon's, told me they were sorry but, unfortunately, they couldn't go against medical opinion. I was deemed unable to satisfy insurance cover, labelled basically unfit to play at the very moment when I thought – I *knew* – I was at my strongest, at my physical best. It was a condemnation and I was the condemned man. The word 'surreal' has been used over the years to explain the extraordinary circumstances as the transfers were halted at the very last minute, but, believe me, that in no way does justice to the depression which threatened to overwhelm me. There was a feeling of helplessness, then anger and a genuine and justifiable fear that my career was out of my control, that something was so chronically wrong with my knees that I would break down completely at some time in the near future. As it turned out, that was nonsense, but I could not see into the future, so you can imagine my position. Imagine how it would affect you.

To fail one scan could be dismissed as unlucky. To fail four is as bad as it gets, and certainly pushed me as close as I have ever come to despair, at the age of just twenty-five, with a young family to support. The best years of my career should have been ahead of me, but the doctors were telling me that it was virtually over. It was all so shocking to me psychologically, but that was the reality of my position. However, I didn't accept the findings; and thanks to Gordon, who decided to ignore the medical advice, I was able to move on and fulfil a lot of what I wanted to.

It all began with Wimbledon deciding to sell me. It was good money all round, particularly for the South London club and its chairman–owner Sam Hammam. I had been happy at the club, and my family were happy, but Wimbledon were regrouping for expected life well away from the top league: they sold a raft of players, which left me isolated. It just wasn't the same for me: players I knew and respected were no longer in the dressing room, and I began to feel a little like the odd man out, although that is no criticism of the guys who were there when I eventually left. I was a major financial asset to the club, so in that climate it was inevitable that I would move, whether I wanted to or not. By the time the offers came in I was ready for the off, ready to try something new with a club ambitious enough or big enough to inspire me.

That apart, when Tottenham come calling you tend to say, 'Yes, please, where do I sign?' The first notification that they were interested came from my agent and friend Jonathan Barnett from the Stellar Group. He had been contacted by David Pleat, by then the director of football at White Hart Lane and my first manager when we were both at Luton. He made it clear that George Graham, Spurs' manager and my old boss at Arsenal, wanted to sign me. That could be a bit tricky as a former Gunner, but what a move for me! As it was told to me, it was simply a question of going for it, so I did. There was no problem about money, which was sorted out between Jonathan and David in the lounge of our family home at Brookmans Park in Hertfordshire.

It is always exciting when a club contacts you, and if it is a club with the tradition and status of Tottenham that is even more satisfying. When the manager knows what you can do and has already paid big money for you in the past, then you feel comfortable, good about yourself. The only downside seemed to be the North London aggro possibilities. I had made friends at Arsenal both within the club and among fans. But how can you turn down such an offer? If I had to win over the Tottenham supporters then I was confident I could do that. And at that stage I had no reason to believe it was anything other than a done deal.

I was told the terms of the contract after they had been agreed between David and Jonathan: £25,000 a week over four years. Unbelievable! There was only one reaction – let's get on with it. The rest really should have been a formality. I had absolutely no fitness problems when I arrived at White Hart Lane: I felt great, and I certainly had no worries about my knee. I met the doctors, I shook a few hands and then I was driven to a hospital with one of the specialists. David and Jonathan stayed at the ground. My knees were scanned, as were my hips and seemingly everything else. By the evening, I was relaxing in the comfort of my own home with Jonathan.

Then David Pleat phoned and asked to meet us in a nearby hotel: the Swallow at Waltham Abbey in Essex. We drove out there, and once we'd sat down David put his hand on my leg and said, 'I'm really sorry, John, but we've had a chat and the doctors feel that your medical condition, your knee, is a problem. It's a lot of money for a public limited company with that clouding it. We can't pursue the contract.' He was straight to the point. Was he embarrassed and disappointed? I don't know. I can't remember much more of what he did or said or what his demeanour was. Spurs had sent their doctor along with David to explain the medical situation. I think he said, although again this is a blur, that it would not affect my career, it would in no way finish me, that I just had to work my muscles, but that they still could not recommend the transfer.

As for me, well, it's difficult to put into words how I felt:

disappointed, certainly, but not as much as you might imagine, considering what had just slipped through my fingers – a great club and financial security. At that point I was not despairing, although despair was an emotion I would experience not so far down the line. No, I was simply thinking, Well, I'm training tomorrow and that's what matters. I focused on the concerns I'd had about signing for Tottenham, given my Arsenal connection. Maybe I was just looking for any positive aspect of the rejection, because obviously, if the doctors had given me the thumbs-up, I would have signed, gladly.

'No problem,' I said. 'Thanks for your time.' I shook David's hand and said goodbye.

Jonathan was upset, as you would expect any agent to be. He was undoubtedly concerned for me and my future. He spoke to the media about our surprise and disappointment, and came out with the statement that Mother Teresa wouldn't be good enough for Tottenham! That lightened the mood for a while. But there was no appeal: it was all decided. I woke up still a Wimbledon player to a mass of publicity: the back pages, the front pages, in the *Sun* and everywhere else – 'Hartson fails medical'. *Hell!*

What is it they say? When one door shuts in your face another opens! In no time at all that's what happened as I was playing cards in a pub in Watford with a good friend of mine, Mick Freeman. We were playing poker after a game of golf at my club, Brocket Hall in Hertfordshire, where I was a member. It's a fabulous course and I've retained my connection there. We used to play every Wednesday, and

after a round we'd go back to Mick's local, the Devonshire
Arms in Watford. I was looking at a promising hand when
my mobile phone went. I left the card school and moved
outside for a clearer signal. It was Alan Curbishley, the
long-time manager of Charlton Athletic. He got straight to
the point: 'John, we've put an offer in for you. Wimbledon
are prepared to sell you. Come and meet me tomorrow.' He
named a place at Theydon Bois in Essex I knew from travelling to the West Ham training ground. We were to meet
up at eight o'clock in the morning. The poker and beers were
off. Let business commence. I checked with Jonathan:
Charlton had offered £5.5 million; half a million less than
Spurs, but still big money. The line I was sold was that everything was official but secret. Although, for those who don't
know, very little that happens within a football club is secret,
and I'm talking particularly about proposed new signings.

I met Alan at a little restaurant he likes because of its privacy. At least we wouldn't be disturbed. He stressed that no
one must know of our meeting. We had some toast and a
cup of tea and were soon on our way to the hospital for a
medical. Once we got there, I had my knees scanned again;
the full medical, again. I had four or five hours of sitting
inside MRI machines; boring. What do you do in a claus-
trophobic tunnel? Some folks panic, but by now I was used
to it. I listened to the same music over and over again – a
song by Nancy somebody. I can't remember her name or the
record. I ran through the same CD ten times. The scan took
forty minutes for each leg, then twenty minutes for each
ankle. I was bored out of my mind. I've had loads of scans,

on my hips, my back, every part of my body. You go in feeling great and come out feeling rotten, with a bad back because you've been in one position for too long. Was it going to be worth it this time?

Later I met up with Alan Curbishley at Jonathan's office in Stanhope Place, London. I was told the deal was agreed, my money was agreed, everything was fine . . . pending the scan results. I let the two of them talk while I waited outside, having some craíc with a couple of lads and some of the girls in the office. It was half past five and I'd been on the go all day. The supposedly secret deal had already been in all the newspapers, as well as on all the radio and TV stations: 'Hartson for Charlton'. Then a phone call came through for Alan. He listened to what he was told by the person on the other end of the phone, then said: 'Sorry, can't do it. I'm afraid the transfer is off. It's the knee.' Just like that.

So another transfer fell through. Alan could not have been more pleasant or apologetic. I shook his hand and he told me: 'John, I wish you all the best and I am sorry this has happened. I would have loved to have you on board.' He is a gentleman, a real football man. I had spent a good day with him and got to know him well. But, gentlemanly or not, it hadn't worked out. And there was all that publicity. No complaints: it was true, and a major story, but somehow it made it worse to see it so widely publicised.

Two down, two to go: Rangers and Coventry. And it is the collapse of the transfer to Rangers which digs deepest and affects me the most.

What nobody seemed to notice when I was receiving the 'Dear John' messages was that, while Spurs and Charlton were rejecting me on medical grounds, I was playing for Wimbledon and scoring goals. But that didn't lessen my concerns or reduce the feeling of being publicly gutted. These weren't £100,000 transfers to the lower leagues that had been quashed but multi-million-pound deals to big clubs.

It was starting to get me down, and I could see that it was also starting to depress Jonathan, although he was always positive on my behalf. As you might expect, Wimbledon were now asking questions too, with manager Terry Burton contacting George Graham and Alan Curbishley in an attempt to find out exactly what was wrong. But they were as mystified as me. If I was knocking in the goals, if I wasn't being troubled by those 'weaknesses' in my knee, why the rejections?

Two months passed and Mark Hughes, who had just been appointed manager of Wales, called me into the squad for his first match in charge. I was buzzing, really up for it. Mark is a heroic figure, someone I love, and someone who likes me. I would go on to play forty games for Sparky. I was his number-one centre forward, I had great times under him and we shared the disappointment of just failing to qualify for the European Championships in Portugal in 2004. That first match for Mark was against Belarus. I was pencilled in to play and it was all going smoothly until he called me in on the Thursday before training at about nine o'clock and told me Rangers wanted to sign me. Don't get me wrong, that was good news. 'Look, their chief executive was on the phone late last night,' said Mark. 'They want to pay six million for you and they want you at Ibrox for a medical immediately.' Did I say good news? Mark had just told me Glasgow Rangers wanted to sign me. Hell, that was unbelievable! I phoned my dad and told him I'd have to leave the squad and head north. Mark issued a statement saying it was my career and they would miss me for this one, but they wished me all the best. The way he dealt with me was brilliant, and the other players were just as support-ive. The message was 'go for it'. They knew what it could mean to me to have the chance of joining a club with Rangers' standing in the European game. Glasgow's big two, a.k.a. the Old Firm, can have disappointing seasons like any other team, but they are never less than great to their vast supports.

I flew up from Cardiff with just my dad. We had booked a flight that Thursday afternoon, and if I needed any reminding of the sort of club I would be joining, it came at the press reception at the airport. There must have been two hundred people there: press, radio and TV. I was to be Rangers' record transfer and it was obvious the whole scene was going to be something else. I was greeted by the repre-sentatives who work with Rangers' owner David Murray.

Glasgow has a reputation in the south for being a great city, but a great city with attitude. I didn't know what to expect, but you had to be impressed by the attention to detail Rangers took on my arrival. My dad and I were driven to a fine hotel and restaurant in Glasgow's West End for dinner, where we met Jonathan Barnett, who had flown up from

London. The restaurant has a big reputation, and we ate very well: I was so hungry I had four portions just to fill me up. By the end of the meal I had started to relax a little, but the tension was still considerable, and I remained apprehensive about the medical that had been scheduled for the following morning.

I rose early; in fact I don't think I slept much at all. After breakfast, my dad, Jonathan and I were driven to Ibrox for a meeting with the chairman, David Murray, and whoever else he had decided was needed at the negotiations. But a few of the players met me first, which was nice and welcoming. They acted as if all would be well, and why shouldn't it have been? John Brown, the Rangers youth team boss, was also there. He had been a good player in his time, a strong, ginger-haired centre half. The German Jörg Albertz said hello, along with the Russian winger Andrei Kanchelskis. They knew I was signing that very day, so they walked me down the tunnel and on to the pitch. There are many great stadiums in the world, and I have played in a few of them, but Ibrox is up there with the very best. Looking up from the pitch it is enormous: you can only imagine what it is like with a capacity crowd baying for, or even against, you. Of course, I went on to have first-hand experience of the latter, but at that moment I was signing for Rangers – no doubt, no problems. As I looked around the pitch, and this is where the scene becomes bizarre, I saw the Dutchman Ronald de Boer holding up a Rangers scarf in front of about thirty photographers. Somebody nudged me and confirmed he had just officially joined the club.

Amazing: a Dutch legend is signed, and I'm going to be next! He paraded on the pitch and I thought, Hold on, Ronald, I'll be with you in five minutes, and we'll do it together. That's my mentality. After the disasters of the previous failed deals, this seemed like a little bit of heaven.

From the pitch I was taken upstairs to meet David Murray. I wouldn't say I was in a trance, but if they had asked me to float up to the chairman's office, I might have been able to oblige. The office was massive, with a huge marble and mahogany table with fifteen chairs round it – I counted them, so I must have been taking in what was going on. Mr Murray shook my hand. He is a powerful man with a deep voice. 'Imposing' is the best way to describe him; the type of man who demands your attention. Looking back, I think I was probably in awe of him, which was stupid, perhaps. Was it his personal presence or the atmosphere surrounding the deal in his office? Probably the latter, but there is definitely something about the man, too. Suddenly my mind began to imagine a terrible twist in the tale. Surely this couldn't fall through? No, no chance, not this time. I looked at my dad and Jonathan – my support team.

The terms were discussed and I was perfectly happy with them. I didn't query a thing. Remembering what had gone before, I just wanted to sign. It was a four-year deal on over £20,000 a week. It was not as much money as Tottenham had been prepared to pay, but everyone in that room knew Rangers had me in a no-win situation because of those mysteriously failed medicals. I didn't go into the meeting thinking, I want this and I want that. All I wanted was to pass the medical. My dad and Jonathan thought the same way. I might have been a thirty-goals-a-season striker, but realistically few clubs wanted to gamble on me because of what had been said about my knee. My consolation was that Rangers were determined to sign me.

In the late afternoon, the moment came when I had to visit a hospital for the tests arranged by Rangers, and I was now beginning to fear them, not because I felt I had a weakness, but because certain doctors kept telling me that I did. I was accompanied to the hospital by a big, tall Dutch doctor. Not exactly what you expect in Glasgow, but as the manager at the time, Dick Advocaat, was a Dutchman, I suppose it should not have been a shock. When managers move in these days they tend to bring all their own staff with them. But a Dutch doctor in Glasgow? I found that a bit over the top. On arriving at the hospital, my first surprise was that there were no pressmen to greet us. Glaswegian journalists are as well informed as any I have encountered in my career, but for once Rangers had made sure the location was kept secret. Then I had to endure just three or four hours of tests; not as long as expected, another surprise. On reflection, it was all a bit cursory.

After the medical we returned directly to Ibrox, where I was shown into Dick Advocaat's office. David Murray was nowhere to be seen. Strange, but we got on with it. Advocaat was sitting with his assistant and came straight out with the words I had dreaded, but this time had felt sure I wouldn't hear: 'I'm sorry. I can't do it.' I couldn't believe it. I was reeling, in shock. It was the lowest point in my professional life. I felt physically sick. My dad's a big man, but he was devastated for me.

After we were given that dreadful news, all I wanted to do was get the hell out of there, but initially it seemed that it was too late to organise a flight out of Glasgow. However, when the situation was explained to David Murray, he said he would loan us his private jet. On the way round the M8 to the airport, my dad turned to me and said, 'Don't worry, Son, you'll be back and you'll be back stronger after this.' After we had managed to avoid them earlier in the day, the media were waiting for us at the airport to record my misery. Once we had made our way through the pressmen, Dad and I flew from Glasgow to Cardiff in less than half an hour in our borrowed private jet.

But in spite of how fast we flew back, I had missed the chance of playing for my country, so I watched the game against Belarus at my folks' place. We won 2–1, which lifted me a little, but my mum and dad were devastated for me. And they were worried for my well-being. They knew my head was going and that I was starting to react badly when previously I had just taken the blows and got on with it. I was feeling so low now because I had left Glasgow thinking they had deliberately messed about with my career.

The disastrous events in Glasgow hit me hardest the next day while I was driving home, listening to the radio. A report came on about this guy Hartson failing the most stringent medical in Rangers' history. It went on and on about how complete the tests had been. When I heard that I wanted to wind down the window and throw up – what a load of rubbish! By now I had plenty of experience of pre-signing medicals, and the one for Rangers had been the simplest of the lot. A medic worked my hips and my legs, like they do. They then twisted each ankle and everything was fine, as good as new. Finally an MRI machine scanned both knees. That was it. And why shouldn't it be? I was playing for Wimbledon every week, doing everything right, scoring goals. The thumbs-down was pathetic, inexplicable. Rangers enticed me up there and made me believe that I would be signing for one of the biggest clubs in Britain. They waved a £3 million contract in front of my face, put me through a little medical, and then sent me packing back to Wales.

But what could I do? I had to keep going. I returned to Wimbledon and a few uneasy weeks passed. My family gradually brought me back to life, which was no easy task. I had mood swings, but the folks close to me, my family and friends, understood that I had been through hell caused by three professionally damning experiences and they helped me get over it.

Golf helped, too. And, strangely, I was again at Brocket Hall when I received another call that offered me a chance to move on. This time it was Gordon Strachan. I had never spoken to him before, but I'd always liked the way he came across on interviews on the box. I respected a lot of what he had to say on those occasions. He couldn't have been cheerier or more upbeat in that first conversation: 'Hello big man' was his opening salvo and then he went on to sympathise with what I had been through. He talked a lot of sense, explained that Tottenham and Rangers had been offering record money for me and could not afford to take a chance. Then he got down to the point of the call: Coventry City, then striving to survive in the Premiership, thought that I could provide the goals to keep them in the top flight. 'There's only one problem,' Gordon went on. 'My chairman says he won't pay big money for you, so will you come on loan?'

I thanked him but said there was no way I would sign for less than a proper contract. If he could not provide that, I'd be better off staying where I was. My argument was simple enough: sign on loan and you are on a hiding to nothing. If you do well, you keep them up and they don't need you any more. If you flop, you are back where you started. If they can pay the full fee at the end of a successful loan period, then surely they can afford it at the outset. Gordon said he could see my point and admitted he would demand exactly the same if he were in my position. Then he told me not to worry about it. I admired him even more for saying that to me. He signed off by explaining he would talk to his people and get back to me.

A week or so went by and then I got the word to drive up the M1 to meet Gordon and his Coventry chairman Brian Richardson at Highfield Road. I won't go through the full rigmarole of yet another medical test, but suffice to say that I failed again, number four. I have never been as close to packing it all in. I'd had enough. There is only so much you can take. If I had known or even suspected I had a physical problem, I would have accepted it. I wouldn't have put myself up for humiliating rejection time after time.

Meeting up with Gordon afterwards, I could tell that he was as sick as me. I was ranting again: 'Why do I need to go through this? I've got a beautiful daughter at home who needs me and who I need to see and hold.' I told Gordon that I was going back to London to be with my wife and child. I said I just wanted to shut the door and bury my head in a blanket. But surprisingly, after that outburst, things moved quickly, and for once in my favour.

Three days after leaving Coventry in the blackest of moods I took another phone call from Gordon. This time he confirmed he had spoken to my manager at Wimbledon Terry Burton and that they had agreed a fee of £4.5 million. I was offered a four-year contract at twenty grand a week. It seems Gordon had asked Terry all about me and my training so he could be clear in his own mind that there was nothing wrong with me. He explained that Terry had told him I did all the running required, all the ball striking, all the fitness work, that I played in all their games and that I hadn't missed a minute's training in the last six months. He finished by saying, 'So what's the problem?' Of course, I said there wasn't one and that I was fit and ready to play for him immediately. I don't know whether Gordon recognised the relief in my voice. I was ecstatic. He had just made the decision that changed my life.

I played twelve games at the end of that season for the Sky Blues and loved every minute of it. At twenty-six years of age, I was the fittest I've ever been. I scored six goals, including two against Manchester United at Old Trafford. Unfortunately, it wasn't enough to keep Coventry in the

Premiership, but I was back, my confidence restored and my form maintained. Gordon paid me the compliment of saying that if he had been able to sign me in January, when he wanted to, instead of in March, Coventry would have survived. The fact that we were relegated was a setback we both had to face. Perhaps we could have stayed up if I had been scoring for Coventry earlier in the season, as at the end we only went down by a couple of points. However, the damage had been done and it was to be the First Division (or the Championship as it is called now). Nevertheless, at least I was playing well and, even more importantly, I was happy.

There is no doubt that Gordon Strachan saved my career. It is all very well for me to say I never saw his decision as a gamble because I *knew* I was 100 per cent fit, or as near to that as any professional in his mid-twenties can be after years of wear and tear. But I can understand how an outsider would have thought he was being reckless, possibly idiotic, with Coventry's money. It takes character and self-belief to stand up against that. These are two of the essential qualities that made him a great player and now make him a hugely successful manager.

If Gordon saved my career, what happened next changed my life: Martin O'Neill moved to sign me for Celtic. I was back in Wales with some mates when I took a call from Jonathan. He told me Celtic wanted me, that he had spoken to Martin and it was 100 per cent. My first thought was *No way!* I couldn't face another media circus in Glasgow, more medical tests and another bloody doctor giving me the thumbs-down. As I said, in spite of the prospect of playing the next season out of the top flight, I was happy. And how could I go to Gordon and tell him I wanted out after his part in my revival and having just signed a four-year contract? But Jonathan was insistent. He said Celtic were going to sign me, and added that they had spoken to Coventry and were prepared to pay £6 million for me. He then explained that Coventry were reluctant to sell because Gordon wanted me to help them return to the Premiership, but suggested I should phone Gordon and explain that I wanted to sign for Celtic.

The more I thought about it, the more I was intrigued by the opportunity to play for the other half of Glasgow's big two, especially after what I had gone through at Ibrox. But when a man has saved your career what do you say? Eventually, two weeks before pre-season training was due to begin, I phoned Gordon, having rehearsed what I was going to say with Jonathan. My argument was a genuine one. I said that the club had sold Craig Bellamy and several other quality players. If Coventry had kept them, they'd have had a chance of promotion, but without them they did not. I then explained that I didn't feel I would be the same player in the First Division, and that Celtic, a great club, wanted me. Finally, I told Gordon that he could use the £6 million being offered for me to buy players who would give Coventry a real chance of returning to the Premiership. Gordon had things on his mind, but he was grateful I had phoned to talk things over and explain my position. He agreed I would score a lot of goals in Scotland but asked me for one favour – to meet him in person at a service station in the Midlands. It was the least I could do, so I drove up the motorway and pulled into the service station. There I met Gordon, we had a coffee and bit of food and sat talking for two hours.

He explained that he wanted to make me captain and to help him with training. He said it would be good for me, just as it had been for him when he had worked with Howard Wilkinson at Leeds United. He wanted me to lift the First Division Championship as his captain. He was compelling, but I had to stay strong. I had decided I wanted to play for Celtic, but I was in a serious predicament: it was a question of loyalty. I felt I was letting Gordon down, and that wasn't my style. We eventually ended what had become a frosty discussion, and I was gutted because I thought I had shown him disrespect. Again, that was unintentional and not my style. He was my manager, he was and is a good man, and he's honest.

Two days later he phoned me and asked me to meet him again, but this time with the chairman, Brian Richardson, at the Coventry City training ground. I had no idea what they might want to say. Gordon and Brian sat me down, officially offered me the captaincy, then said they would give me an extra hundred grand and another year on top of my existing contract if I stayed. Five years and financial security; that was the deal. It was certainly tempting. Lowri and I had been looking at a stunning house in Henley-in-Arden near Stratford. It was spectacular, in seven acres of land. I felt it was perfect for me and my family. Everything

I needed seemed to be in and around Coventry. The manager was on my side, the club treated me well. Talking it through, Lowri and I decided we'd buy the house, and that I'd sign the Coventry contract, make lots of money and be set up for life. However, Jonathan didn't agree, for one simple reason: I had to sign for Celtic, he said, for the sake of my career. I had to win titles. He eventually got through to me. If I played for a club like Celtic, under another winning manager in Martin O'Neill, I would lift championships and cups and play in Europe. That is what convinced me.

So once again I phoned Gordon. I thanked him for everything but said my mind was set and that I was going to sign for Celtic – it was something I needed to do. His attitude was as it always had been: sympathetic, helpful. He told me Martin O'Neill had gone on a cruise with his family so I should do pre-season with Coventry in Dublin, and that's what I did. And I worked my butt off. Carlton Palmer was on that trip. I love him, he's right up my street. He loves a beer, can't stop talking and is great fun to be with, though Gordon knew he was rebellious and didn't like me mixing with him too much. Carlton was a natural athlete – the sort who could knock back several pints and still run all day.

After training one morning, Gordon walked up to the back of the bus, handed me his phone and said there was someone who wanted to speak to me. 'Hi, John,' a voice said. 'This is Martin O'Neill. How are you doing, son?'

I replied, 'Hell, I'm excited. I've been training very hard. I feel fit.'

'Brilliant, brilliant, brilliant, well done, son.' He went on in his soft Northern Ireland accent, 'I understand you are in St Andrews next week, at the university with Gordon and the team ...' Gordon had arranged the trip for a bit of golf, a bit of work up at the university, and a bit of training on St Andrews beach. 'I'll come and meet you. I'll come and see you there, son, no problem.' Then he added, 'John, unless you've got a hole in your heart, I'm signing you.'

From that moment on, I knew I could trust him. He must have sensed I was reluctant about going through yet another medical, especially as I had so much going for me at Coventry. It was exactly what I wanted to hear from someone I respected from his CV alone, before I even knew how he worked. He was backing me. I have learned more about him over the years: he is the sort of manager who will listen to medical opinion but then go his own way. When Martin hung up, I asked the gaffer if I could use his phone to make some calls of my own. I phoned Lowri, I phoned my dad, I phoned everybody I could think of. I wanted to tell the world I was going to sign for Celtic.

When I arrived in Glasgow it was to a near-empty club: the lads were in Manchester taking part in a testimonial for Ryan Giggs. Instead of being met by Martin O'Neill, club doc Roddy Macdonald was there to sort out the medical. He could see I was nervous about it but he constantly put me at my ease. It was a stringent medical, twice as rigorous as the one I had had at Rangers. I had to wait for the scan results and went back to my hotel, but the vibes were good: I felt the doc was sensible and was on my side. That night I relaxed and watched what I firmly believed would be my new team impressively beating United at Old Trafford. Next morning I was given the news that I had passed the medical. The doc shook my hand and congratulated me. I thanked him and later in the day signed a four-year contract. I've since had my ups and downs with Doc Macdonald, mainly about my weight, but he was the man who used his expert knowledge to come to the conclusion that medically I was fit to play, and he has my eternal gratitude for that.

There are occasions when curiosity overtakes me and I would like to know the whole truth about the failed transfers. I would love to put to rest some of the rumours I have heard circulating on the grapevine for years. Informed people tell me Tottenham had legitimate concerns about my fitness. I am told there may have been an additional financial problem stopping me from joining Charlton. Coventry initially said 'no' but then took me on, so there is no great mystery there. However, the whole Rangers incident is intriguing. Two rumours are still doing the rounds. The first is that Dick Advocaat was determined to push through the deal to sign Ronald de Boer. However, it is said that Advocaat was told he could choose Ronald or me, but he could not have us both, so some excuse was needed for not signing me. The second rumour revolves around the fact that Rangers were ready to pay Chelsea some £13 million for Tore Andre Flo and that the deal had been lined up even as I was negotiating in Glasgow, so they didn't need two new strikers. I must stress that I am merely relating what I have heard here, and I am accusing no one of any wrongdoing.

There have been moments when I have felt bitterness at

what happened to me at Ibrox, but since signing for Coventry, and certainly since joining Celtic, any antagonism I harboured has paled into insignificance. I have achieved so much, and lived too well, in the years since Tottenham told me the results of that first medical to hold grudges. But to this day I could not even tell you which of my two knees is supposed to be the one with the 'trouble'. I have never had treatment on either right or left, not so much as a pack of ice on them, and I have never missed a day's training with any knee problem. I have played over 250 games since that Tottenham medical, which is a lot of matches for someone of my size and playing style. Over six years that averages to forty-plus games a season – on a supposedly bad knee! I have had two operations while I have been at Celtic, but both on my back, not on my knees. They kept me out for a spell, but otherwise I have done every kind of training that has been required of me, including gym work with leg weights.

My conclusion is that I don't think there ever was anything dodgy about my knees. If I hadn't enjoyed the huge success I've had at Celtic, I'd have been bitter about failing all of those medicals, no doubt about it. But I have had that success, so I am happy to see the collapse of all those earlier transfer deals as just plain bad luck. I have to admit I was an expensive signing and the clubs that were putting up the money had to be sure they were making a safe investment. The Tottenham deal was £6 million in fees and some £5 million in wages over four years. It was much the same for the others. I can see that if there was any doubt in their minds about my fitness they had to pull out. Fortunately, Gordon Strachan chose to ignore medical opinion, and then Celtic employed a doctor who came to the same conclusion that I had held all along: that there was nothing wrong with me. The truth is, if you scanned the knees of every professional footballer, then 90 per cent of them would show some flaw or another. That isn't my statistic – it comes from various doctors and surgeons I have spoken to over the years. It is the natural consequence of wear and tear in players who have been playing football with a competitive edge since the age of ten.

My folks always say that everything happens for a reason. If I had gone to Spurs, what would I have won? Maybe an FA Cup. If I had signed for Charlton, I would not have won anything, although I probably would have enjoyed life at the club. Coventry are still trying to regain their top-flight status and I wish them well. Rangers have won titles and cups, but not as many as Celtic. I have enjoyed scoring against the Ibrox club, not out of revenge, but because that is what I am paid to do. I never would have been able to do that if the scan organised by Rangers had given me the all-clear. In a strange, perverse way, failing that medical was the best thing that has ever happened to me.

chapter 2

A Ball at my Feet

Some lads grow up with a dog as their childhood companion; I grew up attached to a football. As far back as I can recollect I was within touching distance of a ball, ready to hold it, head it or kick it. My dad Cyril says it goes further back, to where my memory can't reach. He recognised me as a natural when I was barely a toddler – he had spotted the possibility at that early age that I could become proficient, maybe even a professional, in the sport he adored.

His judgement was spot on. He'd throw the ball and I would nod it back, but not like most kids would by just letting it bounce off their head. I would arch my neck in preparation to connect and return the ball from where it had come. Natural instinct showed me how I should deal with it. It was the same when it came to shooting and controlling the ball with my feet. You could say my style was sophisticated at an early age. It was uncanny really. I was obsessed with the ball and I grew increasingly obsessed with the game itself when I started going with my dad to watch him play for Afan Lido – a team from Port Talbot, near

Swansea. He did the rounds as a centre forward and moved back to centre half when he got older, but he carried on playing until he was forty-five in the Sunday League. He loved it and would still be playing now if someone hadn't told him he had to stop. He was well known in the Welsh Senior League, which has a high standard. So how good was my dad? Well, when I go back home and meet up with some of the lads in the pub, the older men will always say, 'Your dad was some player.' I must have inherited his football gene, and I am truly grateful to him for that.

However, I couldn't have had a less auspicious introduction to the beautiful game as a player. It was just so humiliating. I was only six years old, playing for Lonlas Boys' Club on a pitch at the bottom of a hill in a place called Skewen. It was a freezing-cold day and I was actually crying to be brought off. I couldn't move – I don't know whether I was frozen by the weather or by the fact that I was involved in a game with the Under-9s, lads much bigger and more physical than me. Maybe I was plain scared. Anyway, I stood rooted to one spot with my mam and dad on the touchline in their big coats and bobble hats. They were shouting, 'Go on, John, run around, get warm.' I heard them, and I knew it was good advice, but I just kept crying until I was led away at half time.

That was my first proper game as a kid, but I went on to have lots of good ones on that very pitch, which we nicknamed the 'Clinic'. Presumably because a clinic used to be on the spot where the pitch had been laid out. Now it has been turned into a scrambling track. Once we won 32–0, another time 15–0, and I scored six goals in one game, eight in another, and even twelve on one memorable occasion. As you might expect, as soon as I got over that first embarrassing appearance, I loved playing for Lonlas.

Football was clearly in my blood. Since the very first goal I scored for the team, not long after I had run crying from the pitch, I have loved every minute of a game that would eventually provide me with a great life as a pro. I helped Lonlas win trophies and they gave me the chance to express myself. There were good matches, bad matches and classic games, for that level, in which I made a habit of scoring last-minute winners. I got exactly the same thrill from doing that then as I did later when playing for Arsenal or Celtic. Winning a match with a late goal has always given me the same degree of satisfaction. That's how I remember those days – goalscorers never forget their goals, wherever and however they scored them. I always wanted to be a goalscorer, and thought it was the perfect role for me.

I was never put under any strong pressure to develop my game as a kid. My dad was there with me the whole time, and he could see I had good touch and a natural aptitude for football, but he kept me motivated not by force but simply by taking an interest in me. He wasn't a stage dad, although he would look after me, and there were times when he would pull me up, give me a talking to, tell me I had the wrong attitude. It didn't happen often, but he certainly wasn't shy about coming forward with advice if he felt I needed it.

My father – along with my mam, Diana – was the dominant figure in my young life, and he had a similar influence on my elder brother James, and my sisters Hayley and Victoria. Dad was in charge of the family. He was the man of the house, but never cruel or boorish. He was big – and I mean *big*, bigger than I am now – so when I was a youngster he seemed like a giant, the man I looked up to most. My mam was in charge of the house. Dad worked hard, brought in the money, and Mam fed us and clothed us with a lot of love and just as much humour. My dad would keep just a few quid for a couple of pints for himself and give my mum all the rest. He was old school. He was the bread winner, she cooked the food, and they went out together on a Saturday night as a couple for a game of bingo and a few drinks. Dad worked for a sign-erecting company – the 'For Sale' signs on houses and in gardens. He has his own business. Victoria's boyfriend Leigh worked with him for a spell, and he keeps telling me if he'd had this business going twenty years ago he'd be really well off by now.

We were a normal family living in a three-bedroom house on a council estate at Talycoppa in Swansea, not with a lot of cash but always enough. I can't think of a more loving or closely knit family. We've had some disagreements over the years, and I was at the centre of a few of them, but we've always survived them and now we are as close as ever. You read about so many people in the news who had bad upbringings of one sort or another but mine was idyllic, extremely happy in a very happy home. I am not saying it was easy for my folks, and looking back there must have been difficult times, but if there were they were always kept secret from us kids, so we never had anything to worry about. Isn't that the way it should be? My mam had three of us before she was twenty, so she must have had it pretty tough, but she rarely moaned and only ever if we caused trouble. When you know your folks are happy, that provides security. Many years later I was to have my own marriage difficulties, which eventually ended in divorce, and I know how much our problems affected both Lowri's family and mine. But we always ensured that our troubles never touched Joni and Rebeca, our two wonderful children.

At the start of my life it was three of us growing up together: James, Hayley and myself. Victoria was born seven years after me. In the boys' room we had bunk beds, with James on the bottom. There were little gaps in the wood and he used to lie on his back and kick up the mattress during the night just to wind me up. We used to fight like hell, but I wouldn't take him on now, he's so much bigger than me. Hayley and I went to the same school, a Welsh-speaking school, and I still speak Welsh fluently – it is, after all, the language of my country. (I was asked not so long ago to be a Welsh-speaking mentor to my countrywoman Charlotte Church, who may sing like an angel but didn't speak a word of our native tongue.) James went to a separate academy where the lessons were conducted in English. I don't know why my folks sent us to separate schools, but it meant Hayley and I became very close, and we still are. Being two years older than me, she always looked out for me in the early days. I suppose she felt she had to because I was a tiny child, very small for my age.

Looking back at my old school pictures, I was virtually the smallest in the class. I shot up only when I left school in my mid-teens; and I was twenty before my physique had fully developed. So whatever talent I possessed wasn't helped in the early days by a large, powerful physique. I wasn't one of those youngsters who mature earlier than everyone else to tower over their age group, enabling them to batter their way through matches for a while, but who then fail to survive when they are caught up by others who are more skilful and now capable of looking after themselves.

All of us kids would fight like cats and dogs at home, although it was never anything desperately bad. We used to tease my mam to distraction whenever we were in the house. We'd come home from school, all starving at the same time, and then there would be ructions for two hours during which she'd threaten us with Dad. I'm sure it's what happens in a million homes every day. The threat would be the old one of 'Just you wait till your father comes in – he'll sort you out'. And if we really angered Mam, he would do just that. We'd hear his van driving up outside and that was it, order would be restored. But it was all just playful fun, and Dad never came on overly hard. We weren't ordered to our bedrooms with a slamming of doors and kept in for the night. It was never like that.

I can't say it often enough: we were very happy as kids, although we were all very different. I'd spend a lot of time out and about, whereas my brother would always be inside studying. He wanted to be a vet and was very intelligent. He left school with lots of qualifications, but by then he had new ambitions and joined the police force. While he was studying I'd be on street corners and coming in late at night after hanging out at the youth club. I didn't create any serious trouble and the police never called at our door, but I detested school and homework. When people talk about school being the best days of your life I can only say it was nothing like that for me. Reading, writing, maths – I hated all of it. You need the right attitude to succeed in school and I didn't possess it. I had one thing on my mind, and that was to try to be a professional footballer. It was all I ever wanted to be; and it wasn't because of the money. That just wasn't an issue: I never thought about big houses and fancy cars. I just wanted to make the grade, and nothing was going to stand in my way.

My dad was very subtle in the way he coaxed me into developing my footballing skills. I said earlier it wasn't pressure, and it wasn't. He pushed me on because he knew how good I was, and how good I could become, so it would have been wrong for him to let me go my own way, which probably would have been out of football. If he thought I was losing concentration, he'd come at me, collar me and tell me I should be doing a bit of extra training. He never *made* me train as such, but I would go and train on my own and practise skills while my mates stood on street corners sipping cans of lager and having a few fags. These were the sacrifices I made as a youngster, and I think they helped me make an impact on the game while others who might have been blessed with more natural talent have not. Little things like my dad's perception and the knowledge he passed on to me made the difference. I can hear him cajoling me time and again with the phrase: 'You've got ability, you've got a chance, come on.' I had enough respect for him to do as he advised, but I think that respect works both ways. You have to have respect for what your dad's saying, but he has to respect you enough to let you go your own way sometimes, even if that might not be the best way.

There were unfortunate incidents like the time I wandered home having sneaked a cigarette, my first ever. To this day I've never bought a packet of cigarettes, but if I'm having a beer or two and a packet is being passed around then I might have one. I can't remember the circumstances, only the consequences of me smoking when I was a fourteen-year-old. Dad smelled me coming through the door and challenged me. He was on to it immediately and asked to smell my breath. Then he asked me to confirm that I had been smoking, which I did. There was no almighty row; he just said, 'What are you doing, Son? You're not one of them.' And I thought, What *am* I doing?

It's a difficult age, and I'll concede I went off the rails a bit, although others might say it was far more serious than that. When I was fifteen I decided I wasn't going to play football any more. Why? It was nothing more than selfishness and an opportunity to spite my parents. I don't know what sort of phase I was going through. I was gambling a lot on fruit machines and, to fund it, I was stealing money from my parents. I went in my mam's purse regularly, and I looked in my dad's wallet, too. I was stealing for a habit I had developed, an addiction which stayed with me for quite a time and caused me and my family real grief. My gambling exploits were publicised later during my career, but I have never revealed my deep shame at some of the tricks I became involved in when I was a teenager in Swansea. No one outside of my immediate family was really involved: the only people who suffered were my parents and myself, through embarrassment, mainly, and a lack of trust. Sometimes I'd go into the bookies' and lay money on horses and dogs, but I've never known enough about them: I don't read form, I just look for a name or a number. I'd occasionally even go to the local casino, looking for a big hit.

I worked in Baron's nightclub in Swansea, collecting glasses three nights a week, from the age of thirteen to fifteen. It was hardly glamorous, but I'd earn eleven pounds a night and on a Friday I'd get my wages. I had a guaranteed pay packet of thirty-three quid (plus tips) coming to me every week, and once I'd collected it me and my then brother-in-law Carl Fitzgerald (still a great friend of mine) would head over to the twenty-four-hour Riley's snooker club, where we'd play snooker and eat sausage rolls until five in the morning. But in addition to playing snooker, I'd be on the fruit machines, and there were countless times when I put every penny I had in them. They weren't like they are today: remember, this is seventeen or eighteen years ago. They offered £50 jackpots, whereas now you can win £500 for a £2 stake. In Riley's you got something like ten goes for ten pence, which sounds cheap, but I'd be on the machines for hours, and I'd finish up skint and miserable. I'd end up having to borrow money to pay the £2 subs that went towards the oranges and drinks at half time when you played football.

I am not sure why I became addicted to fruit machines, of all things. Maybe, having devoted so much time to football, it was a rebellious action. But that is no excuse for it. I certainly don't blame my parents, because they would have walked on broken glass to help me out. They knew I was playing the machines and my father told me often enough that if he caught me near the 'bandit' he would whack me round the head. He was prepared to do that even if it meant embarrassing me in front of all my friends. But he never did strike me in public; he was just trying to frighten me. I took this very real problem with me when I went to Luton, my first professional club. The desperate need to finance the habit brought me shame and embarrassment, and came close to finishing my career in football almost before it started.

I still love Swansea, and love to go back and meet up with the lads who were my raggedy mates all those years ago. I can understand people being less than gushing when they talk about the place, but they can't see past the working side of it. When you were brought up there, the attachment remains strong, and will last for ever, I suppose. And there is tremendous natural beauty in the surrounding areas: Mumbles Bay, the Gower Peninsula, Caswell Beach, all wonderful places to visit. These days I take my children there and show them the places I used to go with my folks when I was their age.

Several times I have wandered down to Mumbles Bay on

my own and reflected on what has happened to me in my life. I may have been playing for Luton at the time or Arsenal or West Ham or Celtic, and I'd thank the gods for allowing me to be a professional footballer. I would also think about old mates of mine, lads like Spencer Hoppe and Marcus Jones. We'd bunk off school, nick apples, knock on people's doors and run like hell. It must have been very annoying to our victims, but it was harmless enough. There were Nicky Jenkins and his brother Chris, Barry Howells, Michael Hill and Gareth Jones. It all comes back to me at the strangest times, but usually when I'm on my own and have time to consider my life. I particularly remember the moments when I was taught lessons.

As a fourteen-year-old I started work experience with Peter Gallagher, or Pinto as he was better known. He was a friend of my father and had a double-glazing business. The plan was for me to go out with him for a week or two and see how I would cope. The first morning I spent running back and forward from his van to hand him things he needed to do the job and take things back when he was finished with them. By lunchtime I was knackered. I never went back – it wasn't for me. When I meet up with him in the Halfway Inn, the pub now run by my mate Carl Fitzgerald, Pinto will always remind me of that day when I gave up trying to work. 'Just as well you have a talent for the round ball, John,' he says.

I think about my brother and sisters a lot. As I said, I was especially close to Hayley; Victoria was younger and so not a big part of my early life; and as for James, well, we weren't as close as we should have been, although I love and respect him and his family. As brothers we had different attitudes to life: I was a scatterbrain interested in sport and would see him only at mealtimes or when I came in late at night covered in mud after chasing around with my mates; he'd have his head in books. We were chalk and cheese, and I messed him about. We had bikes and while mine would be covered in muck, he was the type who looked after his, cleaning it regularly. I can see him now using a cloth to get the dirt from between the spokes. That was enough for me. If I was going out and had the opportunity, I'd take his clean bike and leave my dirty one with him. What got to me was that he was so clean cut. I wasn't kind to him, and if I had the chance to put one over him I'd take it. I once spotted him playing a fruit machine, which was very unusual for him. He lost his money and I said I was going to tell Mam about it. He pleaded with me not to and we came to an agreement: I wouldn't say a word if he paid me his pocket money. This was my own brother! How bad is that?

chapter 3

The Good, the Bad and the Plain Ugly

Nobody told me growing up would be easy. But what I didn't anticipate was how difficult I would make it for myself. It wasn't about my folks being awkward or pushy or expecting far too much of me; it wasn't that they neglected to warn me about what to avoid; it wasn't about my brother and sisters causing friction between us. Life was fine at home; everything was done to assist me. I just created problems for myself. I can't think what I was rebelling against, but maybe I felt I had to prove myself to my mates. Could it be that I felt different because of my promise as a footballer and had to show I was really one of them by gambling and boozing? (Although more gambling than boozing, I have to say.)

The only explanation I can offer is that I must have had a selfish belief egging me on, telling me I could do what I wanted whenever I wanted to do it. And I would have got away with even that but for my inability to walk past those fruit machines. It sounds ridiculous now – me as a fruit-machine fanatic. That's about as unglamorous as gambling can get. I wasn't exactly the gentle man of the turf studying form and joining the gracious and the good at Ascot. There wasn't even the fun of a night out at the dogs. No, it was the fruit machines of Swansea that did for me, and it grew from there. Those bandits led me on a path to near destruction, and only the good offices of a lot of understanding people, inside and outside football, eventually allowed me to find the strength of character needed to bring it under control.

When I was a teenager, gambling was just about the only blot on the horizon. I was working at my football, training as hard as I was able to, and being watched constantly by English league clubs. They saw me as a likely lad, one of the few that with the right discipline and good coaching could make the transition from youth football to the big league. And that, as it is for so many others, was my dream. I knew it was in me to make it to the top. My whole life was channelled towards attaining my aim of being a professional footballer. Schooling, as I said, held no interest for me, and if I wasn't going to make it as a professional then who knows what I would have turned to for a living. All I wanted was to join a league club and go on from there, maybe even to play for Wales. How proud would my family be if I did that?

I was developing into the type of player league clubs are always searching for: I scored goals consistently and these are the most precious commodities in football. I may only have been scoring for my boys' club or at local representative level, but goals have a value almost beyond price – whoever you play for. The chances are if you can score on the Clinic, you can drive them in at Elland Road or Highbury, too.

My local club Swansea were interested, but there was never any real chance of me signing for them. There are some good reasons for that. I needed to cut myself off from the familiarity of the life I was living. There were too many obstacles associated with staying at home, problems that would certainly surface sooner or later when I socialised at weekends. I needed to get away from that, and the choice was mine. It was just a question of selecting the club I thought would look after me as an apprentice, offer good facilities and the chance to work with people who valued me as more than a number, who saw something in me they could improve.

A lot of clubs talk good games when they are inviting you to join them. They get their chance usually with lads from the age of twelve by inviting them for a four- or five-day trial. My dad and I went to a few of those. They gather kids from all over the country, put them up in digs and supposedly spot the talented lad. These are snap decisions, and far from perfect. I can't think how many promising kids give up at that stage because of shyness or homesickness when a friendly arm round their shoulders could make all the difference. I was lucky: if my dad wasn't there with me, then there was always someone else to look after me.

My first digs were at Leeds United. I remember staying in a house run by a great character called Jack who had only half a thumb on one hand. I think he told us a different story each night about how he lost it. There were also stays at Manchester City, and Luton, of course. I used to go to some of these clubs with a lad called Dean Hill, who, like me, was from Swansea. We were the best two coming through when we played for the Winch-wen Boys' Club. He was a very good player, outstanding in fact, probably better than I was. Everybody was raving about him. At the age of twelve he was bigger, stronger, had more pace and scored more goals than me. But then he didn't develop physically and when he got to fifteen he was at a disadvantage. The chance just passed him by because of that, which was a shame. I still bump into him now and again when I go back to Swansea. I'm not really one for keeping in touch, but it is good to reminisce with Dean.

My school holidays when I was thirteen and fourteen were all taken up by trials, and I was always supported, not coerced into doing it, by my parents. I think it is wrong when parents rave over their lads who aren't even teenagers and say they are going to be this and going to achieve that. You simply can't tell at that age. When they are fifteen and up against seventeen-year-olds, then you'll have a better idea of a lad's real potential. If he shines against bigger, more competitive players, then you might have a player who'll make it big.

My trips to Luton were special. My dad would take me down to Swansea High Street Station as a fourteen-year-old and put me on the train with other youngsters. Mark Pembridge and Ceri Hughes were regulars, and Jason Rees would join the train further up the line. My dad was obviously concerned about my safety on these trips: I was still small for my age, so he would ask Mark to look after me. I was a nightmare on the train. I didn't want to sit talking with the others, as they were older, so I just used to wander up and down the carriages until we reached our destination. Years later we would meet up, with me now massive compared to them, and Mark would say he couldn't believe how my physique had changed so dramatically.

The first time I was invited to Luton I was just ten years old. We assembled at the team hotel, the Grange, and David Pleat asked me to sit beside him. He asked what I wanted to eat and I said beans on toast, and that's what I got. I remember being in awe of all the players when he took me to a pre-match meeting with the first-team squad. I never learned if he did that with all the youngsters or just with those he had been told had a future. David Pleat was my first manager, and you didn't speak to him unless you were spoken to.

I reckon it was always going to be Luton for me. The scout who picked me out as a kid was a great man called Cyril Beech. He was from the old school of scouts, those who devoted their lives to looking at youth football and picking out the boys their experience told them had a chance of making it with a club. David Pleat once told me that Cyril would send him twenty-page letters detailing the youngsters he watched, how good they were, everything about them. He had a van, and if the lads couldn't travel to Luton by train for the Sunday training sessions Cyril would drive them to Kenilworth Road and unload them. I suspect he had doubts about me making it as a pro, but he was the first to suggest I might have what it takes to go all the way, and as he recommended me to Luton I owe him so much. He was crucial to my progression.

When I was invited to train at Kenilworth Road, which I did regularly for years, they made me feel very welcome by always putting me in pleasant digs. And back then they had the plastic pitch, which I loved because it meant you could work out for hours without being chased. These days they have 'please keep off the grass' notices all over the place at grounds. We would kick a ball around the goals and I'd pretend I was Mick Harford, who was a legendary figure in my position as a front man for Luton. I'd look up to all the first-team players, hero-worship them, particularly those like Mick whom I wanted to emulate. These were great days, walking in the shadows of players like Mick, Steve Foster, the England centre half, and Brian Stein, who played for England just the once but was a wonderfully talented player. David Pleat was a real driving force, and he was assisted by Ray Harford, a great coach who died tragically young. Terry Westley, who eventually became Luton manager for a short spell and was in charge at Derby County when I was putting this book together, looked after the youths, and he was an enormous influence on all of us youngsters.

I fulfilled expectations at Luton, I have enough self-confidence to say that with conviction, and I was slamming in the goals for the youth team. At sixteen I was signed on to the Luton Youth Training Scheme, the YTS, which was a proud moment. But I knew it would mean nothing if I didn't work like hell, listen and learn. I was up for that, though.

What I couldn't come to terms with was gambling. By now it was a serious addiction, and like all addictions it had to be fed. When it's alcohol you drink like you have a death wish; when it's gambling you need more and more money. I was earning just twenty-six quid a week as an apprentice at Luton, which was never enough. So I stole to play the fruit machines. Just four months after signing apprentice forms, I went completely off the rails and nicked a bank card from the son of the couple I was lodging with, Steve and Joan Goodfellow. Their son, Scott, also happened to be in the Luton youth team with me. I withdrew £50 from a cashpoint with his card. It was the first and only time I have done anything like that, and revealing it here brings back the full horror of it. The amount of money was irrelevant, even though it was almost double what I was earning at the time, so it was a lot to me back then, and to the lad whose account I was raiding. What is important to me now is that I took it upon myself not only to take the card but to use it to lift someone else's money. All these years later, that still sits like a dark cloud on my horizon. It still causes me great pain to recall what I did, why I did it and what happened afterwards.

Of course, Steve and Joan found out. Then the club suspended me and sent me home to Swansea. My parents were stunned, as were the rest of my family. It looked like it was going to be the end of a career that had hardly started. At just sixteen years of age I felt like an outcast even back home. I had to get my head together, and maybe it needed someone like my best friend Paul Glover to point out what

I was throwing away. We were out walking one day while I was waiting to hear what Luton's verdict on me would be and he looked me straight in the eye and said, 'John, what do you want to do? Do you want to be like me? You've got a chance, you know. You want to go back and get your head down.' I remember the street we were on and the exact time, as if we were talking just yesterday. 'It's what you've got to do, John,' Paul added. 'You know that. Go and do it.' Somehow, his was the advice that seeped through.

I was always led to believe David Pleat's staff met to discuss my punishment, and whether I would be staying or shown the door permanently. I was told some were prepared to give me a second chance while others were not. But I have since learned that one man – David Pleat – decided my fate. Even now I can't find the words to describe how I felt after I had committed what was an abuse of friendship and hospitality. It was much worse than embarrassing. I expected to be sacked and I would have understood and accepted that. I had been desperate for cash, but that is no excuse for what I did.

At the time, I was very friendly with another Welsh lad, Kurt Nogan, whose brother Lee has been capped as a striker for Wales. Kurt had nothing to do with the cash-card incident, but I felt the club saw him as a bad influence on me. He also liked to gamble, and as he was older he'd sign me in to the local casino in Luton, where we'd usually lose all the money we had. Maybe he shouldn't have taken me there, but he never influenced me more than I wanted to be influenced.

When the full implications of what I had done became clear to me, I remember I kept asking myself the question: 'Why did I rob from a family who were putting food on the table for me?' Steve and Joan were much more understanding than I deserved. Our relationship was cold for a while, which was only to be expected. They did not insist that I should move out, but I felt I had to because the atmosphere was so bad. However, my folks have stayed with them since then. I have come across lots of genuine people like the Goodfellows over the years. When I think of folks like them it's easy for me to become emotional.

This is my public apology to confirm what was said to them in private. The incident never made the newspapers – I wasn't a name that merited a headline back then – and it has been kept within the club, thank the gods, until now. I could have kept it under wraps, but that would have been pointless and untruthful. This is my story, and unfortunately the cash-card incident is a part of it.

I can't be certain of why I wasn't shown the door at Luton and sent packing in disgrace. The cynics will say the club were thinking only of how much I might be worth in the years ahead, but I know for sure that some members of David Pleat's staff were opposed to me staying, no matter how much they might get for me in the future. David Pleat was brilliant with me, as was Jim Ryan, his number two. Ron Howard, the chief scout, was a gentleman. Terry Westley, the youth team coach, was a real tough guy, so I wouldn't be surprised if he initially thought I should be forced to leave. But the final decision was David Pleat's, and he came to the conclusion that I should be given a second chance.

Terry Westley went on to become a father figure to me. By now he was the one who was coaching me, not my dad, who was tied up with his business in Wales. I was a student at Luton Town and circumstances demanded that Terry would be more important than my father because he was with me every day, coaching me, passing on his knowledge. I'm certain my father won't mind me saying that. My folks kept in constant touch when I left home, and remained as supportive as ever, but mainly through BT rather than in person.

Terry was very hard on me. He didn't mess about, didn't ignore my failings or worry about my feelings. He did everything he could to improve my skills, and if I wasn't training properly or concentrating hard enough he told me straight. But I have to say he wasn't slow to praise me either if he thought I'd listened and taken in what he was trying to put across. And I soon showed progress: youth, reserves and first team were all achieved quite quickly. I loved it there and I know in my heart that Terry must have played a massive role in getting me into the first team by speaking to David Pleat. Not all my team-mates liked him, though. Vince Brittain was a close friend at Luton and he hated Terry with a passion. He felt he never got the break he needed, but the bottom line was he wasn't talented enough to be a professional footballer, although he was a great lad and I had a lot of time for him. And it wasn't Terry's job to be liked; it was his job to bring players on.

How did I develop my game? Constant work. I worked

on my heading, and studied Mick Harford to see how he timed his headers so perfectly. I worked at striking the ball and my finishing. It was work, but it was the most enjoyable work imaginable because I loved scoring goals. There is no more satisfying noise to a striker than the sound of the ball hitting the back of the net, even if it's just on the training pitch. Terry worked with me individually. It was like having a private tutor. He knew what I liked during training and what I couldn't hack (like running). To make it interesting, to make sure I didn't lose concentration, he would set up a goal area, just for me to hit the back of the net.

Along with the other apprentices at Luton back then, I trained bloody hard. The plastic pitch meant we could keep going until five in the evening, and we did, day after day: penalties, free kicks, crossing, heading, shooting. It was an invaluable experience, and I doubt I would have had as good an apprenticeship if I had been at a bigger club, where after-hours training is generally unheard of.

One of my greatest assets as a sixteen-year-old was my aggression. I think you would rate it as committed – not dirty, not violent, but effective. Defenders knew they were in for a tough time when they were up against me. David Pleat would quite often use the youth team to front the seniors on a Friday. He would set us up like the opposition – just for half an hour – to try to get his team shape, throw in a few set-pieces and fine-tune the players' positions for the next day. I used to go in there and batter Trevor Peake and big John Drayer and then think I should be in the first team the next day, not playing against Bristol City youths. I always thought I was ready, even though the Luton strikers at the time were formidable, and soon included Kerry Dixon, who competed for a place with Mick and Brian. I saw every game, even these training matches, as a chance to show what I could do. I'd go out to win headers and kick the central defenders. The gaffer must have thought I was a lunatic, but the physical side of the game appealed to me: the fifty–fifties, the tackling. I don't do much of that these days, but when I was younger it was a joy to me. Crunching tackles, no problem. That's one of the things about Mick Harford that really appealed to me. He was aggressive but not violent: he didn't go in and smash people off the ball. He was what you'd call an aggressive header: when he went up to connect he would see only the ball. I loved big Mick and the way he'd make his presence felt and snarl at the defenders; it would get my tail up.

Steve Claridge was another larger-than-life character I met and looked up to as a youngster. He was an athlete, a player of considerable ability and a possessor of a personality I wanted to be around as often as I could. He gambled, which was an attraction, and I used to talk to him when our paths crossed in the local bookie's. He was scruffy, that is an abiding memory, with his jersey outside his shorts, one sock up, one down. He only stayed with Luton for a short spell, but he made an impression on me. I don't believe he received the credit his talent should have earned him. But Steve was highly rated inside the game as a professional's professional: that would have been good enough for him.

David Pleat needed players of experience to help his

youngsters during their introduction to the senior team. Some have remained good friends. Chris Kamara is one of them. Players like Steve and Chris were looked on as god-like figures to apprentices and reserves who were striving to become as good and hopefully take over from them. The moment I came into contact with Chris I knew we would understand each other. He was a senior pro and I admired his athleticism and his style as an extremely hard-tackling midfield player. He was one of those players you listen to rather than talk at when you are a kid in the game; a top professional who knows all the tricks and kindly passes them on. It doesn't surprise me that he had the character and intelligence to remain within the game when his play-ing career finished. It is not a coincidence that both he and Steve have coached and managed, and become involved now in media work. I still regularly talk with Chris and appear from time to time on *Goals on Sunday*, one of his programmes at Sky Sports.

After Luton had given me that second chance I was more determined than ever to prove I deserved the faith they had in me. I knew I was on trial, and in a way what happened has acted as a warning I have used to steady myself, to bring myself back from the brink of further indiscretion, when, on occasion, basic instincts have threatened to overtake me. It hasn't always worked, although I have never again been so stupid or so crass as to use someone else's money to fund my gambling. That was a serious lesson learned.

chapter 4

In with the Big Boys

Luton Town FC guided me through what was a sometimes troubled journey into maturity. I was going to say it's where I became a man, but that would be impertinent and should be for others to judge. But it was certainly where I learned my trade and where I became a professional footballer. The club helped mould a marketable centre forward from a raw Welsh lad, albeit one with considerable ambition and determination. They gave me a first-team debut at eighteen. I cannot be certain what my future would have been had I joined one of the Premiership's major clubs as an apprentice, but at a guess I don't believe I would have been given such an early chance to break into the senior side. I might have had to wait until I was twenty-eight. (As anyone who knows me will tell you, I don't really believe that. While I don't think I have a huge ego, I certainly have enough self-belief to see me through most situations I meet out there on the pitch.) Luton is where I scored my first league goals and where I introduced English football to the aggressive style that was to become recognised as a major part of my game.

It is also where I received my first red cards.

It may not be the most fashionable town in the country, but I have nothing but very fond memories of Luton, the manager who backed me, the staff who coached me, the players I worked alongside and learned from, and the fans who support the club. Luton gave me the chance to mix with some quality professionals. These days the team is a Championship side that has emerged from the doldrums and is now forging its way back to some respectability. Back in the early nineties they were a bright little force who always tried to play good football in an attempt to reap some reward for all the planning and work that went into the club. Our reward came in an FA Cup run that took us all the way to a semi-final at Wembley. Can you imagine what that meant to young players like myself: Wembley – the FA Cup – unbelievable.

Luton were never going to challenge Liverpool – the team I supported from my earliest years – or Chelsea, Arsenal or Manchester United, but under David Pleat's management they had signed some terrific older players and mixed them with up-and-comers who were willing to express themselves on the field. But successful runs come and go for the likes of Luton, and ours was never going to last. Clubs like Luton flutter, make an impression, then wilt. Nevertheless, when I was there you knew it was a club run on proper lines, a club that would always give youngsters their chance, even if sometimes it was only because there was no alternative. They brought me on, honed me and taught me values, some of which took longer to sink in than others. Put simply,

Luton's heart was in the right place. They wanted to be successful and they wanted the same for their players. The ability players possess is a gift of the gods, but even the best have to be taught how to maximise it, and that means having good teachers. You could say I had a crash course compressed into no more than two years before making my full debut with the senior team in 1993.

It had been a natural progression for me: I had been going well in the youth team and the reserves; the goals were flying in. I was doing what they expected of me and my immediate bosses had only good things to report about me. Well, almost. I had stretched their patience with the cash-card incident, and tried to redeem myself by working hard at improvement. While I wasn't a model of sobriety – I was still gambling, and I enjoyed a beer, although that never got out of hand – I reckon I deserved what I achieved. If I had been told when I was sixteen and three-quarters, after I had happily left school behind, that I would make my pro debut in a year and a half, I would never have believed it possible. But my scoring rate accelerated my progress: I scored forty times as a YTS boy at the age of sixteen. In my second year, aged seventeen, I signed professional forms. The reserves were the stepping stone to the full squad – youths, reserves, first team, that's the sequence.

What must be realised is that no matter how much promise you show at youth and reserve level, the judgement on whether you are going to succeed or fail is made when you are in there with the big boys, with them and against them. It is common enough for exceptionally talented young players to fall at the very first hurdle once they join the first team. It can be as cruel as that: he might just not have the pace, or the courage, or the energy, or the confidence. And you are only going to find that out when you play him. It means a lot of pressure is exerted on the player, but if he is confident about his own ability, at ease with himself, then it shouldn't be too much of a problem, or at least not a long-term one, even if you have a stinker on the big day.

I came on as a sub against Cambridge United at Kenilworth Road for the second leg of a League Cup match on 24 August 1993. It was my first appearance for the senior team and we lost 1–0. Four days later, I made my full debut in the starting eleven against Nottingham Forest in the league. That's the one that matters to me, and to David Pleat, who didn't seem to take the League Cup at all seriously. Cup runs can be money-spinners and we were going to have one of those later in the season, but I don't believe the League Cup was of any concern to anyone at Luton at the time. The manager selected me for the squad purely to give me a little taster of life prior to an important match with the senior players. I don't think he even planned to send me on, and he certainly didn't make a big deal of it, so neither did I. Having been told I was going to be on the bench, I turned up not expecting any more than that. My chance came when Martin Williams had to come off because of an injury.

I am not being flippant when I say the Cambridge match was no big deal. Luton's preparations were designed to ease the young players into the first team, teaching them lessons along the way as painlessly as possible rather than just throwing them in. And I was a quick learner. I don't know how many youngsters fitted into that approach, but I can't say it was anything other than helpful for me. They tell me I was sensitive, and I was (I still am). They say I was naïve and I reckon I must have been. But against that I must have had the mental and physical strength needed to stick it out and make it work.

David Pleat was equally nonchalant about my full debut against Forest in the league on 28 August. The players had known me as one of their own coming through the ranks, so we weren't exactly strangers, and the gaffer and Terry Westley had prepared me for the opportunity when it came. I have never been troubled by nerves. My stomach churns like everyone else's, but it has never been with fear or concern that I would not be good enough or that I would be unable to deal with the situation and deliver on whatever expectations the club had of me. Any butterflies I have are a signal that I am keyed up and ready to go. It has been a recurring feeling before every competitive game with all of my clubs since then. So I wasn't intimidated by the occasion, despite its significance. I just couldn't wait to get out there and show them what I was capable of. (David Pleat has labelled me 'uninhibited' more than once.) It didn't matter to me that it was Frank Clark's team I would be up against. And at the time it was a very good team, peppered with quality, maybe not as much as the side that had won two European Cups a decade or so before, but still with enough good players to make them dangerous opponents. In the back four they had Stuart Pearce, Vance Warner,

Steve Chettle and Des Lyttle; further upfield they had excellent players in Steve Stone, Neil Webb and Kingsley Black. With quality like that, they were the best possible challenge to gauge my chances of future success.

Mark Crossley was in goal for them. He and I eventually became team-mates in the Welsh national side and we developed a friendship which over the years has meant a great deal to me. We call him Big Norm because of his resemblance to the former Manchester United player Norman Whiteside. I have never been good at keeping in touch, but our friendship gelled and I have seen a lot of Mark and his family over the years. But on that day in August 1993 he was the enemy, the man I was determined to score against. And I managed to do just that. In fact I got the ball past him twice, although one was ruled offside, and eventually we lost 2–1. Nevertheless, it had been a great day for me. You talk about dreams coming true – well, that's the best way I can think of describing how it worked out for me. I scored first to give us the lead, but unfortunately Forest were too strong and, as is so often the case, it was the player up against his old club, former Luton player Kingsley Black, who scored the equaliser before Ian Woan got the winner. It was kind of galling, but not even a defeat can diminish the importance of my full senior debut or the feeling of total satisfaction which enveloped me when it was all over. All these years later I have never lost that sense of fulfilment that comes from scoring, even though it can be tarnished when you are on the losing side.

That one game told me a lot about myself. It told me that

I could play and score against top opposition, so the future was as bright as I wished to make it. The goal I scored was a header from a cross. Some would call it typical of the type I would score throughout my career. I can remember it was a boiling summer's day, anything but perfect for me and my dislike of playing when the temperature soared, and I can remember everything about the goal aside from who put in the cross. I suppose a sports psychologist would explain that as an example of the goalscorer's selfishness. I saw the cross as it came to me, having already sensed the correct position to be in for contact, then I jumped, connected, and directed the ball past Big Norm. At that moment everything in my life seemed perfect. There had been a few experiences that had made me doubt if I would ever make it to the very top, but once that goal went in I realised my future was in my own hands, under my control, and that if I continued to work at improving my game there was no reason why I couldn't climb towards the summit of professional football.

I hadn't been given much time before the Forest game to dwell on it, which was another strategy that David Pleat used to ease youngsters into the first team. Nobody had told me I was definitely going to be playing, although I had a good idea that things were moving in my favour. The first-team players kept saying, 'You'll be in, John,' or 'Looks like you're set for the next match, John.' But it is one thing for a squad player to say that and quite another to hear it from the manager. David just gave me enough time to warn my folks that I was in and they immediately made arrangements to travel up from Wales. They were sitting in the stand to watch my entry and were more excited about it than me.

I enjoyed every second of it, even though we lost. It is said that football people hurtle through life without giving themselves time to smell the roses on the way, but I have always tried to do that and I certainly smelled them that day as a big but trim eighteen-year-old. Forest were still getting used to life without Brian Clough, who was a legend because of his remarkable success in winning domestic and European titles with a club that had a great tradition but limited resources compared to the likes of Manchester United and Arsenal. Of course, I knew what he had achieved, but I wasn't greatly interested in him until I moved to Celtic many years later and listened to two of his former players, my bosses Martin O'Neill and John Robertson, tell stories about how he treated his players and moulded them into a team of winners. Robbo in particular was always going on about his old mentor. It was only then that I realised how special the man had been. When I became involved in Cham-pions League football with Celtic, Robbo would say, 'Any club can win the European Cup once, but only the very best, with the very best players and the very best planning through their manager and coaching staff, can win it twice in succession.' That was exactly what Clough achieved with little, unfashionable Nottingham Forest.

David Pleat did congratulate me, but managers are never best pleased after a defeat, and if this was a memorable occasion for me it was a loss of three points for Luton Town, and that was what mattered most to David and his staff. With me, it was more personal, as I had decided that football was to be my life and now I felt I was closer than ever to achieving that goal.

It is so important for a youngster to select the right club at the beginning of his career. I'm not saying they should always avoid Arsenal or Chelsea or Manchester United, but I do think it's wrong to ignore less glamorous clubs. I have never regretted my decision to stick with Luton and be properly schooled by men like David Pleat, Terry Westley, Wayne Turner, John Faulkner and Jim Ryan.

John Faulkner was in charge of the youth team when I was coming through. He was a terrific coach, sympathetic without being weak, and I owe him a lot. Jim Ryan was another excellent coach who moved on to join Manchester United's youth academy. He would always go out of his way to come and say hello, and he has done so on numerous occasions over the years, when I was with Arsenal, Wimbledon, West Ham and Coventry. I played in the same youth team as his son Neil. The reserve team manager during my spell was Wayne Turner, another coach who helped me on my way. These guys don't have the reputation, or the backing, of an Arsène Wenger or a José Mourinho, but they are the difference between success and failure to a lot of youngsters breaking into the ranks.

They all took an interest in me and my contemporaries because young players were the lifeblood of the club. If they needed new faces, it was extremely unlikely that they could just write out a cheque and buy some. The big-money clubs can do that without speaking to their bank manager, but the

Lutons of English football have to find them, nurture them, play them and then, if they have the potential, sell them on. That somehow produces a camaraderie which is quite special. To this day I still keep in touch with a number of the lads who were in the youth team with me; seven of them attended my wedding. We had come through so much together. Some succeeded better than others, but they were all good and understanding people, and that's surely what matters most. It was also important that Luton never made me feel like a star of the future. I was a promising pro, nothing more, staying in digs and earning bugger all compared to what a young player in a similar position today would be picking up.

I made forty-two appearances in total for Luton – thirty-four in the league, five in the FA Cup, one in the League Cup and two in a so-called 'minor competition', the Anglo-Italian Cup, although I can't remember a thing about those two. I scored six league goals and one in the FA Cup. Throughout my time there I remained in digs. What I was earning then, £350 a week, was fine, no complaints, but I certainly was in no position to go and buy myself even a modest flat or a terraced house. It was more than any of my contemporaries were earning, but I'd always be the one who was broke at the end of the week. My team-mates saved while I gambled. Money has never been the most important thing in my life because gamblers don't think that way. What I was earning then simply came in handy. It was a means to an end.

I was bowled over with the 1993–94 season. Everything

fell my way; it was exciting and new and I was newsworthy, maybe not every day but certainly every now and again. There was a novelty about it all which appealed to me and I wanted to experience more of it. Being in the first team was all that mattered to me, that and training, listening to what people were saying and trying to put it into practice. Thankfully, I had recovered from the cash-card incident: I had buckled down and I was committed to going as far as I could, as far as my ability would take me. I didn't want to end up being in a position where it could be levelled at me that I should have done this or should not have done that. I took the business of establishing myself in the game very seriously indeed, even though I still couldn't go through a day without having a bet . . . if I could find the cash.

At the start of the 1993–94 season, no one ever told me I was going to be a regular in the line-up. Kerry Dixon and Scott Oakes were the established players up front, but Kerry couldn't go on for ever, though he was still great at holding the ball up, while Scott was very popular with the fans. Others were vying for the positions up front, such as Ian Benjamin, who was soon sold to Brentford, and next season David Pleat signed the fast, tricky striker Dwight Marshall from Plymouth.

All the threads seemed to be coming together not only with Luton but for Wales in that first season. In addition to becoming a regular first-team player I established myself in my country's national squad. It's impossible to overstate the excitement and importance of playing for your country and I love the warmth it has always given me. My first representative match was an Under-21 international against Cyprus in October 1993, hardly the most difficult opponents, but we hit them for six goals and I scored twice. That gave me a lot of pride. Anyone who knows me will say I'm patriotic, but I find those who seek to isolate themselves through their nationalism difficult to understand. They don't seem to realise that there are places outside of Wales that are worth exploring. They think there is no place like Wales, but I know differently. I may well eventually decide to live in Wales again, but over the years I have been in a position to spread my wings and have learned that there are other things out there to look at and enjoy.

I learned a lot of other things, too. I may not have moved with the pace of a sprinter, but I could think quickly enough. But every now and again I was caught out, and never more so than during a match at Stoke, when we were informed there would be a pitch invasion, which was apparently a tradition at the end of every season there. We were told that the referee would warn us a couple of minutes before the final whistle and that we should start moving towards the tunnel, but I was too engrossed in the game to hear his warning. When the game ended I was caught on the wrong side of the pitch and was swamped. It was worrying, but it wasn't the first or the last time I ignored the orders of a match official.

I have a reputation for being a hard man, a reputation that began at Luton, yet I was sent off only once in my two seasons of first-team appearances for David Pleat. I admit I used my physique and I was involved in some explicit confrontations, but most of them were enjoyable, and I would guess the defenders felt the same way. That's why we were there facing each other. What you didn't want was to receive or make a tackle or challenge that crippled you or your opponent. Often you knew it was going to hurt, but that wasn't a problem so long as you survived to play in the next match. There was one particularly memorable battle between Crystal Palace's Welsh central defenders Chris Coleman and Eric Young and myself. We are good friends, and Chris is even a Swansea boy, but between spitting blood and wiping it away from my eyes we kicked lumps out of each other. In the end, Palace won 1-0, with Chris scoring, so I suppose he would say he came out on top that day.

An end-of-season clash against West Brom, whom I was to sign for in 2006, was particularly tense, nasty and chaotic. Two players were sent off and three hospitalised. It was unusually violent because it was all about survival. We were both in danger of relegation from the First Division, and when a season reaches that sort of do-or-die climax it tends to produce the best and the worst in sporting conflict. There were just two more matches remaining in our fixture list after we played West Brom on 3 May 1994, and we felt we had to beat them. We were 1–0 down, then 1–1, then 2–1 down, then 2–2, and finally we found the goal that ensured our survival. Paul Telfer (who ended up with me at Celtic after we had also been together at Coventry) was in our team, and our keeper was Jurgen Sommer (who was injured during the game). The midfield included Ceri Hughes and up front it was Scott Oakes and me. Matches like these don't generally make the headlines, but the experience of playing in them is invaluable. It teaches you about commitment and about winning, not at all costs, but very nearly. The will to win, the determination to score goals, is just as high in the so-called 'lower-league' clubs and their players as it is at the very top of the Premiership. We had more glamorous games during that season, for instance during our FA Cup run, but none was as important to Luton Town as that battle against West Brom.

My first red card as a professional was due to misbehaviour and a lack of discipline, and it came just after the West Brom game. I was dismissed against Bolton on 5 May 1994 for elbowing big Alan Stubbs when we both went up for a corner. That was one incident that did generate headlines, and I was singled out as a rough-and-tough, up-and-at-'em centre forward. I will accept that I am aggressive, and I am proud of the fact that I will challenge hard and defend my ground, but I am not a dirty player. What I did that day was wrong, out of order, and I take full responsibility. It happened early on, in the first half, early enough to handicap my team. We went on to lose the match, and though no one can be certain that my dismissal cost us the points, I have to accept that it contributed to our defeat. Why did I do it? It was a reflex, but I dare say it was still painful for Alan Stubbs to take. The cross came over, I threw my elbow, it caught him, and he went down holding his face. The referee pointed to the tunnel immediately. I didn't offer any argument and the Bolton players didn't say a word. I had made a serious error of judgement and that angered me. As I walked off,

Bruce Rioch, Bolton's manager, and his assistant Colin Todd were waiting in ambush. This was the same Bruce Rioch whose house I had visited as a guest of his son Gregor, who had been in the Luton youth team with me. I didn't expect any sympathy from him, but I could have done without the verbals from Rioch and Todd. I suppose they thought it was justified in the circumstances, but it's not what you expect from managers and their staff. I replied with the traditional 'Go and fuck yourself'. It wasn't a dignified exit from the match.

No player wants to be sent off. You are the first to be dressed, you sit there waiting for the rest of the team to come in, you mope about and you are embarrassed when you apologise for letting down your team-mates, your manager and yourself. You tell everybody you will be smarter next time as if you are sure there will never be another red card.

At half time I was with David Pleat when we met Joe Jordan, who was manager of Stoke City at the time. David put his arm around Joe's shoulder, introduced us, and asked him if he would sit beside me and have a word with me. I think what David was really saying was: 'Joe, will you tell him how to be a good centre forward and not get sent off for elbowing?' Joe certainly knew how to handle himself against defenders after taking years of abuse from them. As we sat watching what was left of the game, we didn't mention elbows, red cards or anything else along those lines. I was just pleased to be sitting beside such a legendary player. (Only later did I remember that it was Joe who had cost Wales their place in the 1982 World Cup finals, when, by all accounts, he handled the ball for the goal which put us out.)

That ordering off may have cost me a real chance of signing for Liverpool. It would have been the ultimate transfer for me: Swansea was my hometown club, but the Reds had always been the team I followed and who inspired me. The players of that era, Ian Rush, Kenny Dalglish and the rest, were my idols. To follow in their footsteps would have been marvellous. I didn't realise it at the time, but many years later I was talking to Roy Evans, who was the manager of Liverpool back then, and he told me that he had sent his scout Ron Yeats to check me out that day. There had been rumours saying Liverpool and a number of other clubs were interested in me for some time. It was intriguing and good for my morale: players usually dismiss such stories as newspaper hype, but I always enjoyed it when my name was linked with bigger clubs. There is no doubt Liverpool rated me, and although Roy never said it in so many words, I think I lost out when I stuck my elbow into Alan Stubbs' face. I have no idea what was contained in Ron Yeats' scouting report, but it couldn't have been up to much: I didn't have time to make any impact on the game other than with my elbow, and it was all over for me within twenty minutes.

If the newspapers were getting it right, then Queens Park Rangers were also bidding for me. And the manager of Southampton at the time, Alan Ball, has recently confirmed to me that he was interested, too. I knew nothing of that at the time, though. Managers tend to get annoyed when players' names are mentioned during transfer conjecture, but I've never understood that attitude. I've never been able to work out why they make it sound like a capital crime. How can a player be anything other than boosted by knowing other clubs and other managers think they are good enough to buy? It would be a very strange player who was unsettled by transfer talk before an important match. There is a good chance it would give them a renewed incentive. And if one of the managers who want to sign you happens to be Alan Ball, who played such a magnificent part in making England World Cup winners in 1966, then you can be nothing but honoured by the attention. When I met Alan in Marbella not so long ago, he made it clear he would have loved to sign me, but Luton were having none of it. I thanked him for thinking about me.

An agent wasn't considered an accessory a young footballer at Luton Town needed, but I certainly could have used one with so many clubs watching me. A good agent, and they should be close enough to be regarded as a friend, would have made contact with the interested parties and told them exactly what my intentions were at the time. I would have explained that I was happy at Luton, though naturally I would not be averse to the idea of moving on and progressing my career while increasing my weekly salary by a factor of ten at the same time. An agent might advise you to say 'no', he might twist your arm to try to make you say 'yes', or it could be such an obviously great move that you both say 'yes' immediately. But mostly they provide someone to discuss your options with, and they can be there for you when important decisions have to be made.

The 1993–94 season was eventful off the field. There was

the unforgettable moment when I turned on the television at my digs to learn from Teletext that I had been named in an England Under-21 squad by the then manager Dave Sexton. My first reaction was to laugh. Then I wondered how they could possibly make such a mistake. I'd already been selected and played for Wales Under-21s, when I'd scored twice against Cyprus. So how come nobody at the Football Association had researched my nationality? I wouldn't presume to blame a football man with the status of Dave Sexton for the mistake, but he was the one who took the stick from the media afterwards. I guess their checking system just wasn't as good as it should have been. It was all pretty amusing, but I also recognised it as a huge compliment. For any player to be called up by England is an honour, even if they are Welsh. I considered it further proof that my career was moving in the right direction, and I enjoyed every minute of the few I had as an honorary Englishman.

chapter 5

Wembley – A Dream Cup Run

The FA Cup can be your best friend, and in my first season in professional football it was for me. Luton's cup run kick-started my career, pushed me towards the fast lane, and gave me a series of memories that will last a lifetime.

It can be the thinnest of lines between success and failure, between staying where you are and moving upwards and onwards. That was made clear to me on a dramatic night in Newcastle when I thought the wonderfully talented Peter Beardsley had buried our hopes of an FA Cup victory that would have been one of the more remarkable giant-killings in a competition littered with the corpses of the great and the good of English football. But we survived and went on to what is known as a 'glory run', and in the process I scored a special goal that confirmed I had cleared stage one of my apprenticeship. I often wonder where life would have taken me had Newcastle gone on that night and sneaked a winner, as they were fully expected to do. We would have been nothing more than brave little losers.

When you play outside the top league and you are young

and the future is bright, the FA Cup is the competition that offers you the best chance of being tested against the very best. But it can also expose your weaknesses: if you find it intimidating to walk on the same turf as the elite then you have little or no chance of succeeding. You might as well pack it in before you waste any more of your time. You have to be in the mood to take on all comers, and that was exactly the mood I was in as Luton prepared for 1993–94's FA Cup.

In recent years what was once universally acknowledged as the greatest domestic club competition in the world seems to have diminished in the eyes of some of the big clubs. And their attitude has rubbed off on the punters, the men in the street, the fathers and sons, wives and daughters who are the lifeblood of the game. I find it hard to believe that the fans don't still enjoy the David and Goliath confrontations so many unfashionable clubs have relished over the years. So why do so many people now knock the FA Cup? The experts tell us it is no longer the attraction it once was, although you could argue that's just a rumour put about by major clubs who want to have as many free days as possible between their Champions League and Premiership commitments. Shame on them.

Those of us at Luton in 1994 certainly didn't see it as an annoying sideline when the third-round draw was being made. Like everyone else from the lower leagues, we were dreaming of lining up against Man United, Arsenal, Liverpool or Newcastle. Obviously, you want to progress as far as possible in the competition, but you also want the chance of coming face to face with players you may only have seen on television, even if that makes an early exit more likely. We didn't get the glory of Premiership opponents or the relative comfort of facing a non-league side. Instead, we were drawn against Southend, who had the potential to be our worst nightmare. We were in the same league, but their form since the start of the season had been better than ours.

It was hardly the glamorous tie we had been hoping – or in my case praying – for. Off the field I am reticent in new company, a little shy, and certainly not the pushy character that some people expect. But on the field I have always felt I am in my element, and I dearly want to confront the very best the game can offer. That was especially the case in my first season, when I needed the chance to prove that I had what it took to be a top-flight striker. Yes, I was up against highly experienced, quality footballers on a fairly regular basis in the Championship – Forest's defenders being the most obvious examples. They would be a different prospect to Southend, for sure.

As it happens, David Pleat made me a substitute. He obviously saw the dangers Southend could pose to us, and on that occasion he wasn't prepared to gamble on me from the off. He gave the job to Kerry Dixon, who partnered Scott Oakes in the Kenilworth Road tie. The game was as tough as David had anticipated, and although I came on for Kerry, it was Paul Telfer who scored the only goal of a tie I remember as being hectic and raw, typical of its type. The relief throughout the club at making it into the fourth round was considerable, and there was real satisfaction to be taken from that result: it was good for morale and it left us with the possibility of a major draw in the next round, which, apart from the experience it would give the young players, would earn the club a lot of money.

This time the draw was a cracker: we came out of the hat with Newcastle United. The only downer was that we had to play at St James' Park, but even that had a plus side, as there would be a 30,000-plus crowd, rather than the 7,000 we could expect at Kenilworth Road. That meant more money for both teams. At the time Newcastle were managed by Kevin Keegan, and they were very exciting to watch, playing in his distinctive, attacking style. As well as Beardsley, they had another great goalscorer in Andy Cole, who was on fire that season, and quality defenders and midfielders like Steve Howey and Barry Venison. You could say they were close to their peak, and they were backed every week by one of the most passionate crowds in the country. For our match, 32,216 packed into a stadium that Geordies treat more like a place of worship than a sports arena.

The pundits reckoned we didn't have a hope of achieving a result. The best chance we were given was that we might force a draw and squeeze through after the replay, but the odds were long on even that happening. During the build-up to the game I saw things differently, but who was going to listen to me? What the hell did the big kid know?

Once the match got under way, the fact that we were underdogs may have worked in our favour because I think it reduced the collective nervousness of our team. If people don't expect you to win, then you don't worry about losing.

To everyone's surprise, we took the lead through Tony Thorpe. He belted a thirty-yard screamer past the United keeper, Mike Hooper. That set us up for one of these extraordinary victories that are traditional features of the FA Cup. And that's how it looked to us at half time – let's just say we were optimistic. The boss told us to keep playing as we were, to keep focused, to maintain our concentration. There was no 'We've got it in the bag' crap.

After the interval we were more confident, and Newcastle seemed less, not more, likely to produce an equaliser. But the tie had one more goal in it, and it came from the penalty spot courtesy of the boot of Peter Beardsley. There were two major disappointments when Beardsley drove his spot-kick past our German keeper, Jurgen Sommer. First, we had drawn a game which our self-belief was telling us we should have won. Second, and this was even more disappointing, we didn't win outright on the day because Beardsley earned the penalty with what I thought looked like a dive. The anger would have been even greater if it had been a winner rather than an equaliser, but it subsided fairly quickly because we knew we had to prepare for the replay. Now Peter will always be high on my list of players I admire and loved to watch. I respect him as one of the best forwards England has produced over the last few decades, a super performer who not only played a great game on a ridiculously regular basis but by all accounts was also a great lad off the field, quiet and unassuming. I always enjoyed watching him on the box and reading about him in the papers.

The ease with which some players go to ground is hardly

considered a major crime these days, although it is still bloody irritating when it goes against you. It is one of those illegalities that have become part of the game, and increasingly so in Britain because of the foreigners who now ply their trade here and seem to view it as something of an artform. Players usually escape punishment for diving because of weak refereeing. The laws are there to make those who dive pay for their 'crimes', but believe me, when I'm long gone players will still be taking advantage of officials who either can't see the offences being committed or don't want to punish the offenders. You can call it cheating, but it often pays dividends. For the record, I have never dived – it's just not my style.

For some reason, Newcastle were even firmer favourites to beat us in the replay two weeks later. Now I am something of an expert on bookies' odds, but I can't understand why they were quite so strongly in favour of Keegan's lot. This was a classic FA Cup tie: mighty Newcastle, with a number of outstanding players, against gutsy Championship opposition on their own small ground and, in all probability, on a dark, miserable winter's night. The bookies should have seen that it could go either way. The hype that followed Newcastle down from the North-East acted as an extra incentive to us, I am sure of that. We had our own good players, although some were untried at this level, and we were committed, ambitious. A number of us also wanted to make a special mark on the game to prove we were progressing. That made us dangerous opponents. But once again we entered the game as outsiders in everybody's minds but our own. Our attitude was 'Let's go and get 'em'. We were determined to stick two fingers up at the so-called 'experts', especially as the TV cameras would be at the ground: Sky had the good sense to take a chance on us, seeing the potential in the tie for a shock and therefore great television. Someone had made the mistake of asking Brian Kilcline to be a pundit for the match. He had signed for Newcastle the year before, but he was unavailable for the tie, which was why he could try his hand as a summariser. In that role he ridiculed us before the match, claiming the game would be a formality and that it was a question of how many goals Newcastle would score. He underestimated us. We had the utmost respect for Newcastle, who have struggled to win the trophies their army of loyal supporters surely deserves. But it didn't turn out the way Brian had hoped.

It was bad for Newcastle, perfect for Luton, and on a personal level . . . well, it was my night. I knew a good performance could fast-track my career. There are turning points one way or the other in every professional footballer's life: one day you can score an exceptional goal and be on your way; then a week later you might break your leg. My breakthrough moment was against Newcastle. Thanks to the television cameras, a lot of folks throughout the country latched on to who I was for the first time. I went from 'unknown' to 'highly promising' because of my performance and the goal I scored in that match: it was the first in a 2–0 victory. Trevor Peake sent a pass down the right and I ran on to it. Mike Hooper came out to cover but I went round him and guided the ball into the net. It was spectacular and well executed. I felt unstoppable, and that goal set us up for a victory that upset almost every bookie's odds. I was too busy celebrating at the end to see how the Newcastle players reacted to a defeat that must have made them feel sick, but I do know that Kevin Keegan was, to quote the boss, a 'gracious loser'.

What a difference one good, well-taken goal makes. After that they were all tracking me – Liverpool, Southampton and QPR for sure, but also Arsenal and others. My life had found a new perspective.

I was happy at Luton. By this stage I was in love with my future wife Lowri, who had come to stay with me even though I was still living in digs. I didn't see my gambling as a problem, and I enjoyed nights out with the lads. I was more recognisable after the goal, although in Luton I was still able to have a life of my own, which gave me freedom, but which also led to some embarrassing incidents. As the press were not that interested in me yet, I felt I could behave just like everyone else when I was out on the town. There were occasions when Lowri would leave for a few days, and on one of them two of my Swansea mates, Jason Wright and Kevin Davis, came up for some fun. And we had some! We got absolutely bollocksed, and at about three in the morning we found the minibus that was to take us back to my place. But on the way we stopped beside a field and stole a sheep that was minding her own business, threw her in the back of the van and then drove on home for a sleep. There was understandable pandemonium in the morning. I had a hangover and had completely forgotten about the sheep, which was roaming around the back garden in a state of some distress – almost as much distress as the house-owner. We bundled her back into the van and dropped her off in the first field we found with any sheep in it. Somehow we got away with it.

Cardiff City were to be our next opponents in the FA Cup. They were in the division below us and were struggling. For a boy from Swansea it couldn't be much better. There is serious rivalry between the two cities. Actually it's worse than that when it comes to football: they detest each other. The pressure would be on me, but I was looking forward to it. I had a strong belief that there was no way we could lose: I would go there, be pelted with stuff from the terraces, spat at, verbally abused for ninety minutes – and win. The ideal outcome. The Cardiff fans didn't disappoint with their welcome. They gave me stick from the moment we arrived at Ninian Park and I stepped off the coach – booing me, trying to unsettle me. They were calling me a Jack Bastard (that's what they call us Swansea lads). All the abuse was aimed at me and I loved it. I felt even better when Scott Oakes scored our first goal. When that went in I couldn't resist turning to the Cardiff fans and showing my pleasure. I gave them a clenched fist that you can see quite clearly on the video of the match.

Our second goal was controversial and so made the hostile atmosphere inside the ground even worse. Ceri Hughes was coming back from an offside position when David Preece ran on to the ball. This was just after the offside rule had been changed to include the 'not interfering with play' part, and many people, both players and officials, were confused by it. Anyway, David ran through, scored, and the ref said the goal should stand. Bedlam! There was a danger that the situation could spiral completely out of control. Luckily, David Pleat spotted the warning signs and hauled me off before I became a focus for the crowd's anger. For once, as it was for my own protection, I was happy to be substituted. If he had left me out there I have no idea what might have happened. There could well have been a pitch invasion and it probably would have headed straight for me. I ended up with a police escort from the changing rooms on to the bus. We were stoned and spat at by rogue City fans, but were still delighted to leave with a win.

Cardiff City have a group of fans who have had a bad reputation for years . . . and it's well deserved! I think it might be a collective inferiority complex. They aren't as successful as Manchester United, Arsenal, Liverpool or Chelsea, and they feel they should be. Perhaps the troublemakers think that the only way they will ever make an impact on the footballing world is through violence, and I suppose in that they have been successful. Ninian Park has never been a place for those of a weak disposition. If you play there, you can't let them think they are getting to you. If you rationalise it, reduce it to basics, accept they are doing it to intimidate you and throw you off your game, then you can deal with it. It can be difficult and even frightening when players start to imagine what might happen. I simply try to take that sort of reaction as a compliment. If they are so determined to have a go at me then they must think I can do their team damage. To be fair, I should say that Swansea have a group of fans who can be every bit as volatile and troublesome as the lads from Cardiff, especially when the two clubs meet. The police are always kept busy at those games. Back then, I couldn't imagine that any rivalry in football could be as intense as that between Cardiff and Swansea. But, of course, I hadn't taken part in an Old Firm game at that stage.

For Luton, the FA Cup had developed into a wondrous experience – even for the older players who had walked round the block a few times. As yet we were in no position to talk publicly about FA Cup runs and gloriously sunny May days at Wembley, but the thought had already germinated in my fertile mind. The further you go, the closer it comes, but there was still a lot to be done. West Ham were our quarter-final opponents. They were in the Premiership and respectably placed mid-table. They were safe from relegation but had no chance of winning the title, so the FA Cup would have meant everything to them that season. There was the added bonus that if they won it they would be in Europe next season. They were a good side rather than a spectacular one – Frank Lampard, Rio Ferdinand and Joe Cole had yet to progress through the ranks. After a 0–0 draw at Upton Park, we beat them 3–2 in the replay when Scott Oakes got all three goals and earned us our place in the semis as well as the match ball.

Our next opponents were Chelsea, and it was decided that the match would be played at Wembley. So whatever happened we were going to play in the great stadium, with the chance of going back there a month later. But the boss wasn't happy about the choice of venue, and nor were the senior players, who afterwards were convinced we would have won if the semi had been played at Villa Park or Hillsborough. The national stadium might have given the game added cachet, but David Pleat said he'd have preferred the game to be played at another venue, or even on Chelsea's home turf, rather than at Wembley. Naturally, I didn't agree with that: the thought of playing at Wembley was a marvellous prospect. I had never been to the great old stadium before, so this was special for me and for a few others. It was also a semi-final – one step away from an FA Cup final. What we had achieved was only just beginning to sink in. I was nineteen years old and buzzing.

We had Eric Hall to sort out the players' pool. This was in the days when some extra cash was very welcome for any footballer plying his trade outside the Premiership, not just for me with my gambling habit. The senior players were earning enough to give them a reasonable standard of living, although it was nothing compared with what players in the Championship can make now. Eric Hall was *the* agent at the time. He talked quick, walked quick, smoked massive cigars and was always on the telly rabbiting on about this or that. I presume David Pleat brought him in, and Eric definitely livened things up. He got us wearing hats and T-shirts, the usual stuff really. But if he was the front man, Kerry Dixon and David Preece were pulling the strings. The young lads were thinking, If we're making £500 out of this, some of the senior pros will be making thousands. We were all given our semi-final ticket allocations, which were sold on at four or five times face value. I think we had six tickets each – not a lot, but it meant a bit of profit for us. I know some people will think that sort of behaviour is disgraceful, but it was almost a tradition in big FA Cup matches at the time and was seen as a perk for the players. I kept back two tickets for my mam and dad and sold the rest.

The promotional work was mainly done long in advance, so we were free to concentrate on the build-up to the match. It was such a pleasure to be involved in it. We stayed at Henlow Grange, the health farm, as we had done in previous rounds. Luxurious surroundings like Henlow are good for the soul as well as the body because they make you feel important. It was a novelty and a new experience for the likes of me, and I was determined to do what David Pleat had told us to do – enjoy it. I became very good friends with Steven Purdew, the owner of Henlow. He has quite a few other health farms, too, including Champney's and Forest Mere, but Henlow was ideal for us: the surroundings were superb and David's training was brilliant – so light, so enjoyable, no pressure. I've been told Brian Clough's training sessions were also like that: just playing with a football and enjoying yourself.

The day of the match was virtually tension free, too, with just the right amount of edge as far as I was concerned. I had been told I wasn't playing, and that the place was going to Kerry Dixon. I was disappointed, but not surprised. Wembley, 9 April 1994 was really the Kerry Dixon show. He had scored 190 goals for Chelsea and become a legend at Stamford Bridge, and this was him rounding off his career at the age of thirty-two. The vast majority of the crowd of 60,000 were supporting Chelsea, but they gave Kerry a great reception because he was still a god to them: they waved him on and waved him off at the end.

Our defeat wasn't a shock, but it was still a bitter disappointment. You can't help thinking what might have been. Tony Cascarino was immense for Chelsea. He absolutely battered our central defenders Trevor Peake and John Dreyer, and cleared the way for Gavin Peacock to score both of the goals that did for us. I was given the last fifteen minutes after a hassle over my shirt. I had left it in the dressing room, and when David told me I was going on I realised I didn't have it on under my tracksuit. The dressing room is a long way from the bench at Wembley, so I sprinted off, right round the perimeter track. I disappeared down the tunnel, got the attendants to open the dressing-room door, grabbed my shirt and sprinted back to the bench. I went on for Des Linton later than I would have preferred and I was unable to help turn things round. The game was virtually over by then. Chelsea went on to be hammered 4–0 in the final a month later against a Manchester United team inspired by the wonderfully talented Eric Cantona.

We couldn't have any complaints, although David has said it might have been a different result if he had played me from the start rather than Kerry. But that would have ignored the status of one of the game's great goalscorers, and would have taken away much of the occasion's spectacle. Personally, I think I should at least have come on earlier than I did, so I could have had a real chance to turn the tie around. I had played in most of our cup run, but I must admit Kerry had been brilliant against West Ham. Yes, you could argue David Pleat got it wrong, but you could also argue that we wouldn't have been in the semi-final but for Kerry's input.

Nevertheless, the semi was an unmatchable experience for someone of my age, and was far and away the biggest thing that had happened to me. In the fifteen minutes I had on the pitch, all I could do was show I wasn't overawed by the event, and I think I did that. Some feel that my little cameo earned me my transfer to Arsenal, but I never believed that. I was just a young boy eager to do well, and at the time there weren't many of us around. And the Gunners made their move for me some months later.

chapter 6

Arsenal – You Can't be Serious

David Pleat came over to me during training and asked to see me in his office. That was pretty unusual, so I bristled and immediately prepared for a row. I knew it must have been something extremely important. He only wanted five minutes with me, he said, so whatever he had to tell me was going to be short and, I guessed, not particularly sweet. When the boss wants to see you in private it's always best to be prepared for the worst, even though my recent behaviour had been bloody exemplary. I hadn't done anything outrageous, so I came to the obvious conclusion that I was about to be told that I had been dropped. I had cemented my place as the number-one striker, but I felt sure that the gaffer was going to bring Kerry Dixon back into the first team. What made this even more galling was that I had scored in my previous match. Typical: just when you believe everything is running smoothly something or somebody comes along and kicks you where it hurts. I built myself up to face him and to tell him I wasn't prepared to accept it. I was sure he would shoot me down, show me the door, but that was a risk I was prepared to take. No matter how difficult the situation became on that Thursday morning of 12 January 1995, my intention was to confront the manager who had given me my big break and make it clear that I was as upset as it was possible to be.

But, as it turned out, none of that was necessary. I knocked on David Pleat's door like the schoolboy called in front of the headmaster. He asked me to come in and close the door behind me. 'Look, John,' he began, 'go home, put on a suit and have a shave. We're going to meet George Graham.' That was it: no more instructions, no more explanation. I was stunned. I didn't have an agent at the time, and I had started only thirty-odd league games out of fifty-four since my debut in 1993 – often coming off the bench to replace one of our more established strikers. I can't remember if I said anything in reply, but I suspect not. I rushed out of the office and straight into my little Ford Escort, which had cost my dad four hundred quid and which he had driven up from Swansea for me. The lads used to take the piss out of it because it had zebra seat-covers, making it look like a Luton minicab. I dashed back to my digs and as I didn't have a decent shirt I ran to my landlord Tony's wardrobe and grabbed a white one, then I found the only tie I possessed, which I had received as a Christmas present. It had a Disney motif on it. I didn't have a suit, so I put on a pair of smart trousers and a thick brown jacket. You can imagine what I looked like – a bloody mess. When I got back to Kenilworth Road it was about 3.30 p.m., so time was moving on. David Pleat then drove me to Highbury, just the two of us, in his big, fancy Mercedes. I was still in a daze. I couldn't believe I was sitting next to the boss on the way to meet George Graham, and presumably on the way to signing for Arsenal. Of course, I knew all about Arsenal. Who didn't? They were one of English football's traditional powerhouses, but I'd never been to Highbury before and, just like my first game at Wembley, it was all exciting new territory for me.

During the drive, David Pleat's car phone rang about every thirty seconds as different journalists called to ask about the deal. Clearly, the word was out. This went on all the way to the stadium, with David mumbling answers into the phone. He didn't say a lot to me: he just asked me if I was relaxed. Relaxed! I had never experienced anything quite like what I was going through. It was a mixture of anticipation and excitement, so there was no way I would describe myself as relaxed, but nor was I scared. It was an experience in my career I could not wait to confront. As ever, in spite of the constant enquiries from the press, David *was* relaxed. He always has a cheeky little smile on his face, and I can never envisage him losing his temper and flying into a rage like some other managers do. Not once during the journey did he say I would definitely be signing for Arsenal, but as we reached Highbury I was sure that I would be. All I could think of were the possibilities for my career, and with it my life, if this went through.

I desperately wanted to ring my father, but I didn't have a mobile phone and I couldn't pluck up the courage to ask the boss if I could borrow his. This was going to be as big a shock for my family, my friends and my Luton team-mates as it was for me.

We arrived at Highbury and were escorted in by a couple of security men. It was all very hush-hush, which made it even more exciting for me as we were ushered through the marble halls to where George Graham met us. 'Hello, son,' he said and shook my hand. He had a strong Scottish accent, and this must sound rather bizarre now, but I didn't know any Scots back then. He was probably the first one I had ever met, but he came across as someone I reckoned I could work with. That is not always the case, but this time it was. Once the pleasantries were over, the two managers disappeared for ten minutes. When George Graham came back, he immediately offered me a four-year contract worth £3,250 a week. As I said earlier, I was earning £350 a week at Luton. The contract also guaranteed me a £1,000-a-week rise every year. George was extremely impressive, friendly and businesslike. He said that if I signed I would make my debut the following Saturday, as Alan Smith, his first-choice striker along with Ian Wright, had been injured in training that morning. 'If we can push this through,' he said, 'you'll be in against Everton alongside Ian.' And he added what he must have felt was an incentive, 'And it will be in front of a full house.'

My reply was immediate: 'Give me the papers – where do I sign?' I hadn't been told what the fee was; it was irrelevant to me, academic, a matter between the clubs. I wanted to sign for Arsenal and as quickly as possible. The official signing of the forms took place the next day. I haven't thought about it until now, but I suppose what I must have signed in George Graham's office was a declaration of intent on my part, a sort of pre-contract. I could not help thinking that what was happening was totally unbelievable. I was just a kid and I could not get my head round the speed of the transfer and the immensity of it. I mean, Luton to Arsenal completed in a couple of hours and all the time wearing a Mickey Mouse tie!

Unlike the failed transfers that were still far in the future, I didn't have a medical for this move. I doubt Arsenal even gave it a second thought. I was a nineteen-year-old who had never been injured and had never missed a game. I hadn't even twisted an ankle. I was a kid and I was super fit. The fee was a British record for a teenager: £2.5 million. I instantly became the most expensive and unarguably the worst-dressed young player in the British game. It would be another four years before the record was broken, when Leeds United paid Charlton £4 million for Lee Bowyer.

The whole day was hectic, but by late afternoon the crucial meeting was over. On the way back to Kenilworth Road, David Pleat again didn't say much to me – as on the journey to Highbury he was on the phone for most of the time. I was buzzing. I couldn't wait to tell everyone I had just signed for Arsenal and was going to be a squad member at one of the world's greatest clubs. I eventually got through to my folks from my digs, and they were as shocked as I had been by the news. Shocked, but delighted. Then I spent the rest of the night phoning everyone I knew. My landlady, Trish – who tragically died of breast cancer not long after I left – was a great friend to me during my time at Luton. Even today I often think of her and her children. I miss her warmth and her trust. As I ran up her phone bill that night, true to form, she was as happy for me as I was for myself.

On the day of the Arsenal deal Lowri was in Wales, staying with her family. By that stage we had been courting for a few months, and the plan was for her to come up with her folks and watch my debut. My own mam and dad were determined to be there, too. Dad actually travelled up the very next day, and he was beside me when I officially signed for the Gunners in the Luton Post House Hotel beside the M1 motorway. It would be inconceivable these days for any player, even a teenager, to conduct a transfer of this magnitude without using an agent. I am sure that having one would have made a difference to the contract I received, but I was delighted with it. My dad even managed to negotiate a signing-on fee for me – an additional £50,000. This was on top of the £150,000 that had originally been offered, to be paid over the four years of the contract. George Graham didn't quibble but immediately agreed: 'No problem,' he said. Dad and I have often wondered what would have happened if he had asked for £200,000! But that was it, negotiations over, and I signed.

In my digs at this time I had the *Sun* delivered every morning. (I also got the *Racing Post* every day. Yes, I was still betting, although it was limited to what I was earning.) That Friday morning the *Sun* had carried the headline

'Graham gets his man'. It was the first big headline I had ever received. I've had quite a few more since then, and not all of them enjoyable, but that first one was. It convinced me I was in the big time, and I was on cloud nine.

A convoy was heading up from Wales. Dad was already with me, of course, but Mam was on the way, and Lowri and her folks, Anne and Aaron, were coming too. I had to settle down, control my excitement and prepare to meet them. I had already met my new team-mates that morning, before I had even officially signed for the club. Most of them were international footballers and all of them were household names. When I walked into our changing room at Arsenal's training ground they were all there. If you were going to be intimidated, that's when it would have happened, but they couldn't have been more welcoming or helpful. I was introduced to Tony Adams, Paul Merson, Wrighty, Kevin Campbell, Alan Smith, Nigel Winterburn, Lee Dixon, John Jensen, Stefan Schwarz, David Hillier, Ian Selley, Ray Parlour, Steve Bould and David Seaman. So many big names, all seasoned pros, and there I was, a kid just signed from Luton. Everything was brand new to me. Wrighty was messing about and just the sort of man I thought he would be. It would be wrong to say I was in a trance when I met him and the others, but I'd been in a whirlwind for the previous twenty-four hours. When something as big as this happens, you tend to get swept along, but there was always going to be a moment of truth, and that would come when I had to start the process of convincing the North Bank supporters and the rest of Arsenal's fans that I was worth the money. That applied equally, or more so, with respect to my new team-mates.

The form at Arsenal before matches is to assemble at the South Herts Golf Club for a pre-match meal, and that's where I met up with them again on the Saturday morning. George Graham read out the team to face Everton, and, as promised, my name was there alongside Ian Wright's. It was all very matter of fact, although hardly so for me. I'll never forget the date: 14 January 1995.

I felt shy, which was hardly surprising, considering the situation, but Andy Linighan sat next to me and helped me settle down. He would have been through this moment himself: the slight feeling of self-doubt, the hope that you didn't let anyone down. He understood the internal turmoil that had to be controlled. Martin Keown, who was to become a legendary figure at Arsenal, helped me relax, too, and that started a friendship that was to stretch through the years.

From the golf club, we drove our own cars to Highbury. Knowing this in advance, I had decided to ditch my Escort and sped down to the ground in a borrowed RS turbo. The convoy was made up of Mercedes, BMWs, 4x4s and other top-of-the-range jobs. I'm no snob, but I think my Escort would have looked slightly out of place, and aside from anything else I wouldn't have been able to keep up with the rest of them and probably would have ended up getting lost.

Everybody at Arsenal, George, his staff and the players, made me feel welcome. I soaked up the atmosphere and I was glad that my stomach was churning. That meant I had my edge and I was in good condition. I knew what was expected of me and I enjoyed the match, although we only drew 1–1, and it was Wrighty who scored our goal. George even showed his confidence in me by playing me for the full ninety minutes. The game itself was good enough, although Everton's Duncan Ferguson, the big Scottish striker, was sent off. The fact that I didn't score was a slight disappointment but hardly a disaster, and I felt the crowd were sympathetic to me.

This was halfway through what had been a disappointing season domestically for Arsenal, and the next week things got even worse. On the Wednesday after the Everton match we were knocked out of the FA Cup by Millwall in a replay. That was a downer, but we went to Highfield Road on the Saturday and I scored my first goal for the club in a 0–1 win over Coventry. I was ecstatic. Three days later I scored again in a 1–1 draw against Southampton. Two goals in three games: it was a good, promising beginning. Scoring so quickly gave me some room to breathe. I had fitted in immediately, the goals proved that, and they would have impressed my new team-mates. That eased some of the pressure the media were applying because of the amount of money George Graham had paid for me. And there is nothing the supporters like better than a goalscorer. If they had doubts about the kid from Luton, then they had already seen enough to believe that I might be an asset to them.

However, it turned a little sour for me when we travelled up to Hillsborough for a Premiership match against Sheffield

Wednesday, my fourth match. We lost 3–1, a poor reward for the effort we had put in, but to make it an even more depressing night in Yorkshire, Tony Adams and myself were both red-carded. I was dismissed for what was described as a 'scything tackle' on the Romanian Dan Petrescu. Tony's crime was to elbow Mark Bright. The good impression I had created with my goals in the previous two games was scarred by the dismissal. It also alerted the FA to the possibility that I could be one to watch. I went on to collect a series of yellow cards during my two years with Arsenal but, contrary to what many people might think, I received only one more red in my time there.

The important thing was that my mood didn't change. I was enjoying my football, I liked the training and I didn't feel overawed in this company. I was particularly happy with George Graham's style of management, and I was working with good guys, like the coach Stewart Houston, in training. Unfortunately, though, George Graham didn't survive for more than a handful of matches after signing me. He was dismissed after being found guilty of accepting payments from the Norwegian agent Rune Hauge. I know nothing of that scandal, only that George was great to me. He was particularly skilled when working with the forwards, which was hardly surprising as he had been one himself. He would coach Alan Smith and Ian Wright on a regular basis, and helped me when I joined them. I have been lucky with my managers. They have all taken time to work with me, specifically on the centre-forward role. Like George, John Toshack and Mark Hughes had both been strikers of high repute before managing Wales, so there was an affinity between them and me. They never expected me to do anything I couldn't do. It almost sounds too simple, but they made sure I concentrated on what I was best at, so they would tell me I had to win headers, hold the ball up and get into the box. It was of no concern to them that I didn't run up and down the channels. They hadn't done that when they had played either, and they knew that, being a big man, it wasn't part of my natural game. But if I didn't supply the goods in the areas that *were* part of my game, they would slaughter me.

Around the time I signed, there was a great deal going on with Arsenal players both on and off the pitch. On the playing side, one of my earliest games for the club was in the European Super Cup, when we played AC Milan home and away. It was a goalless draw at Highbury and we lost the return 2–0 in the San Siro. The first leg was more memorable as Paul Merson's comeback after his drink and drugs rehabilitation. Addiction, mainly to alcohol, was a problem for one or two of the players. It was an accepted part of the game, not only at Arsenal but throughout the professional ranks. Most players drank regularly, and some caught the bug like a virus that could destroy them. I wasn't immune, and enjoyed my beer. I loved the craíc in pubs, and quite a few of my new colleagues did, too. The cavalier attitude to hard drinking among footballers would eventually disappear, but it was still charging full pelt when I was at Arsenal. It was something Mers and the skipper, Tony Adams, had to confront in the full gaze of publicity, but many learned a valuable lesson from them in how to keep their drinking within more reasonable limits.

Of course, I had my own addiction to deal with – gambling – but Mers had the full set: drink, drugs and gambling. I got to know him well, and I can talk about his problems openly here because he has always been willing to discuss and confront these addictions. He has battled to beat the illness (and that's what it is) which has caused him so much grief. We used to see a lot of each other and became great mates. I'd go to his house to watch late-night fights. At the time the heavyweight division was brilliant – Mike Tyson and Evander Holyfield were slugging it out for the right to be called undisputed champion. I've so much admiration for boxers and the sport had been part of my sporting life when I was a kid in Wales. Mers and his wife at the time used to invite me and Lowri round and we'd have a Chinese meal delivered. This was in a period when Mers was as clean as a whistle after he'd gone through rehab, so there would be no alcohol, but we still had a great time. Steve Bould and Nigel Winterburn were also regulars on these nights. It was a terrific group which recognised Paul's strength of character and the efforts he had made to shake addiction out of his life. We knew how difficult it had been for him.

I was caught up in my own 'drug scandal' not long after joining Arsenal. I have never been into drugs or part of the drug scene, but I was inquisitive, like most young men are, and I dabbled in it. Perhaps a more accurate way of describing my involvement is to say that I was drawn into it. It had all started some time before, when I was still at Luton, during a holiday in Ibiza with a mate. We were on a two-week break, and I was game for most things – a few beers, girls and, as it turned out, the amphetamine better known as 'speed'. To start with, girls had been uppermost in my mind. We had a bet about how many we could have sex with while we were away. I hit the deck running with three (or was it four?) in the first few days. In one club I spotted a sensational-looking girl in a shimmering white dress. My friend, like every other bloke in the club, was eyeing her too, and he said, 'Pull that, John, and you win the bet.' Well, I did. She was French, and in spite of the language barrier we got on well and she invited me back to her place. She said she had transport, but that turned out to be a Vespa scooter. We'd both had a few to drink, and I was hanging on to her round the middle as the pillion passenger, zipping through what passed for roads on the island. Unfortunately, she wobbled on one bend and the bike skidded. The poor girl could do nothing about it and neither could I as I scraped my side on a rough surface for quite a distance. When I finally came to an agonising stop I was soaked in blood, although thankfully the girl was OK. We eventually arrived back at her little flat, and she spent the night cleaning my wounds, which were so bad that I couldn't go to the beach for the rest of the holiday and returned to Luton covered in scars. And, since you're wondering, no, we didn't!

That gives a flavour of the type of holiday I was having. Could it get worse? Well, yes, with my introduction to speed. I wouldn't even have thought about taking it had we not met a couple of lads. They were into the drug and offered it to me. I took just two or three pills. What did they do? Not a lot, to tell you the truth: they gave me enough energy to stay up through the night and remain alert. It was fun at the time, and although I can say now that it was stupid, I always knew that I wasn't going to be involved with it on a long-term basis, so it was harmless enough. Although some will say that my gambling proves I have an addictive personality, it was never like that for me with drugs. After I left Ibiza and our two 'friends', I never considered using speed or anything similar as an alternative to drink. In fact, I had forgotten all about it until months later, by which time I was at Arsenal, and I took a call from my newly acquired agent, Steve Davies. He told me a national Sunday newspaper was running a story in the morning saying I had been on a drug kick in Ibiza. The lads had seen it as a nice little earner and had sold the story to the highest bidder.

Just as I had with the cash-card incident, I simply had to hold my hands up. The story was true, although nowhere near as lurid as the newspaper made it appear. I had to face up to the consequences because I could not deny that I had taken the stimulant, and I should have known better than to expect loyalty from casual acquaintances who are in the habit of offering around drugs. The phone call from my agent was a serious moment for me. Only those who have been caught in something that is going to make headlines the next day can understand the fear and anticipation it creates. After I put the phone down I could have curled up in a corner at the thought of the repercussions. I feared Arsenal would give me hell, and ran through all of the possible punishments they might inflict on me because of the adverse publicity I had brought on a great club.

But Arsenal were fantastic – they just ignored it. Their attitude would probably have been different if they thought I was addicted, but it was obvious from my fitness level that I was clean. Nevertheless, the whole experience was shocking to me. I couldn't understand how people I had befriended, albeit briefly, could then betray me for money. They had hooked me when I was a Luton player, unknown and therefore not big enough to interest a national newspaper. The opportunity came when I moved to Arsenal – and they took it as soon as they could. I dearly hope that whatever they made didn't do them any good, but I was definitely taught a few lessons, the most important being to be more wary of people. That's difficult for me, though, because I like people and tend to give them the benefit of the doubt. I am not looking for sympathy by relating this incident, just pointing out the dangers of entrapment that are everywhere for young, high-profile sportsmen. For any normal lad of my age in that era, what happened in Ibiza would have been filed under 'experience' and never mentioned again, but because of who I was, an expensive player at one of the country's top football clubs, it turned into a national story and a major embarrassment.

Tony Adams is a shining example of a player who triumphed over addiction. I wasn't wide-eyed and naïve, but I knew I was in the company of immensely talented individuals, many of them world-class players, and they contributed to my education in so many ways. Tony is an exceptional man. He was by far the best captain I've played under because he was a leader among men. His speeches to the players before a game were so inspiring that the hair would stand up on the back of your neck. He was very emotional, very powerful. 'This is our turf,' he would say. 'It's our patch. *No one* comes here and wins. This is Highbury. This is Arsenal.' He'd bang the door as he said it, and I could see then why George Graham had so much respect for him.

I was young, but I knew even then that he was exactly how a captain should be. At the time he was in his late twenties – a seasoned pro – and the England skipper. He had such authority. There were loads of big names in that dressing room, but when Tony spoke they'd all listen. There was another side to him, though: this was when he could not control his drinking. He and Ray Parlour would come in for training obviously already having had a few. It didn't matter to me. I just thought that's what they do. Sometimes they would be lethargic for the first twenty minutes of training or so, but then, in the distance, you would see George Graham in his dark blue coat entering the training ground, and by the time he reached us we would all be in top gear. I think that's why George let Tony get away with it. He knew he was a one-off, and when it mattered, on match days, he was there, fully committed as a highly respected leader. He knew exactly what he'd get from him as a captain. Tony certainly got away with more than other players, but I think that all managers do that with exceptional footballers. They have to compromise.

I'm afraid I was the player who put Tony out of the game

for a long time after a training accident. I know I have a reputation for being very physical in training, but this was a seemingly innocuous, simple block tackle, with the two of us going for the ball. We collided and his knee just went. Of course, I felt awful about it. I apologised, but the damage was done and he was out for months. It was the type of tackle that happens all the time in training, but I must have connected when his knee was at an odd angle or something and it popped. If any good came out of it, it was that Tony was as fit as he had ever been when he returned.

The loss of George Graham was a considerable blow to the vast majority of the players. There was real sadness that he had been forced out after he had done so much for the club and the team. He had taken them on to a new level, and that earned him the admiration of many, not just within Highbury but throughout football. I didn't know the ins and outs of the decision to sack him, and I still don't. I had a decent relationship with George, and I have always wished that it could have lasted longer than just a few weeks. He had a nice, easy way with him, and that is something I've always appreciated in my managers. Stewart Houston was given the role as caretaker boss while the board considered who they would approach as George's permanent replacement. I worked well with Stewart, another Scot, who had played at the highest level, including at Manchester United, in a distinguished career. He spent a lot of time with the players, but he had taken over at a difficult time, and it was a question of him doing the best he could until the new man arrived. As I mentioned, the club had been struggling before

I arrived, and our domestic results remained disappointing until the end of the season. We would win a couple and then lose a couple – we just could not put a decent run together in the Premiership. We knew that more was expected of an Arsenal team that had enjoyed so much success under George. It certainly wasn't Stewart Houston's fault – the man has nothing to reproach himself for because it had been exactly the same before he stepped into the job.

But in spite of our poor domestic performance, it was a thrilling period of my life because we reached the European Cup-Winners' Cup final in Paris on 10 May. It is one of the quirks of football that you can have a lukewarm domestic season yet still reach the summit in European competition. The lads had disposed of the Cypriot side Omonia of Nicosia quite comfortably over two legs and then seen off the Danish club Brondby, although that had been a lot tighter, with Arsenal going through on the strength of a 2–1 victory in Denmark. Both of those games were played before my arrival. Once I was in the team, we had really difficult ties to face against the French club Auxerre and Sampdoria from Italy's Serie A. But we found our form in those matches to reach the final against the Spanish club Real Zaragoza.

It provided a meaningful end to what had been a disappointing season in so many ways – disappointing, that is, for everybody but myself. As we approached the final I was still on a high. I was enjoying being an Arsenal player, the status, the sense of pride in playing for such a big club and feeling that I actually belonged there. The warmth of the welcome had begun with George Graham and had continued for the three months that Stewart Houston was in charge. He spent a lot of time working with me on various aspects of my game – heading, shooting, positioning – and assessing how my strengths could be utilised to best effect by the team. I knew he rated me, so it was no surprise when he selected me in his starting line-up for the final. So much had happened to me in a short space of time, but to play in a European final made my step up from relative obscurity to the big time seem complete.

Arsenal players want for nothing in terms of preparation. Everything is laid on for you, which is one reason why you feel a strong responsibility to produce 100 per cent in return. Real Zaragoza were a good team, but we felt a result was achievable, especially after I scored to equalise. However, it went against us when Nayim, the Moroccan who had once played for Spurs, hit a lob from the halfway line with David Seaman achingly far from his goal-line. The big man tried desperately to recover, but the ball sailed past him. It was the sort of goal you hate to concede but would have loved to score yourself. Sadly, some would say embarrassingly, it cost us the cup.

The season was over and we would soon know who our new manager would be. At that point, we were all looking optimistically towards the future, but that feeling would be short-lived for me.

chapter 7

My Highbury Hell

It's easy to understand why Arsenal appointed Bruce Rioch as George Graham's successor. A few of us players, perhaps all of us, would have been happy for Stewart Houston to continue in the job, but Rioch had an excellent reputation. His CV was impressive, both as a World Cup player for Scotland and as a manager. He hadn't taken the easy road to the top either, but had started with Torquay and worked his way up via Middlesbrough, Millwall and Bolton. Now he was at Arsenal.

He was a good, steady operator, not scared to take on difficult jobs and generally doing them well. But if you had analysed his career up to the point when he joined Arsenal, there was a hint that he might struggle to deal with some of the strong-willed players at Highbury, such as Ian Wright, to name but one. With hindsight, I think Rioch can best be described as a man whose nature would not allow him to turn the other cheek.

Of course, I had had a minor run-in with him when I was sent off against his Bolton side, but I certainly was not worried about my future when he was appointed manager at Highbury. As I said earlier, I already knew the man and his family well. I had been a friend and team-mate of his son Greg in our Luton Town youth days, and I had been warmly welcomed into their home. There I had listened and watched as Bruce had played videos of matches and pointed things out to myself and Greg that a man of his experience would want to pass on. Aside from that little bust-up on the touch-line at Bolton, I had been shown nothing but kindness and friendship by the Riochs. Before Bruce's arrival, I had settled into life at Highbury. I was giving it my all, I was fit and I was focused on a new season. The new manager couldn't expect any more of me. I was enjoying my life and my football. But not for much longer.

Bruce Rioch joined the club on 8 June 1995, and for the fourteen months he was in charge I had the most unhappy spell of my footballing career. I grew to hate him in a way that takes even me by surprise when I think back to that time. He demoted me to the reserves, which I could just about cope with, but at the time I most needed him to explain why he had selected other players or made a succession of decisions which seemed to work against me, I didn't get the support I needed. Because of that, my resentment welled up inside me.

The reason I was dropped was that he signed Dennis Bergkamp from Italy, which has since been proved to be a brilliant buy, but obviously it meant I was now behind both Dennis and Wrighty in the pecking order. At just twenty, that was a reasonable position to be in – third-choice striker at one of the biggest clubs in England – but I didn't see it quite like that. Maybe I should have been more patient, but it was partly my driving ambition that had got me to Arsenal in the first place, and I felt Rioch should have had the experience to recognise that. I needed a manager who wanted me to be as successful as I myself wanted to be. I needed him to tell me that I was good, that although he was leaving me out of the team for the moment, I would be given a chance to prove myself. I needed communication with my manager and I didn't receive enough of it and I cursed him for it.

Of course, being Dennis Bergkamp's understudy is hardly a slight. He was world-class then and has remained so over the last decade. But he wasn't the reason for my discontent: that was caused entirely by Rioch's seeming indifference towards me. At a guess, I would say he thought I wasn't good enough for Arsenal, although I felt his attitude towards me sometimes seemed more personal than that. He came across to me as full of charm one minute, unapproachable the next. There is nothing new in that sort of behaviour from managers, but merely knowing that someone might behave strangely does not make it any easier to take when you are on the receiving end.

The question became how to resolve the problem. That season, I didn't appear in a game until we played Manchester United at Highbury on 4 November, when I came on as sub. It had been a long wait through pre-season training, into August and through most of autumn. I didn't score against United but we won 1–0 and I felt the victory might help my cause. Unfortunately, it was two weeks before the next match, against Tottenham at White Hart Lane, so I didn't know if I would have another chance afterwards. In the event, I was to keep my place for the next six league games.

Almost the only instruction I received from Rioch was that I had to be weighed twice a week. I talked to some team-mates about the situation and some would say it wasn't personal, that Rioch wasn't having a go at me. I thought otherwise. Because of my feelings, I hated going in for training at our London Colney training ground, and that has never been my style. I felt his concerns about my weight began to damage my confidence. The end result was that I was kept out of the first team for much of the season, making only nineteen league appearances in 1995–96, and played a hell of a lot of reserves football.

I know I played my part in the deterioration of our relationship. We all make mistakes, and I made a major one when I slaughtered Rioch and his managerial skills in a newspaper article. I felt I was driven to it through desperation, but in the years since I have realised how badly I was advised by my then agent, Steve Davies, to go on the record about what I was feeling. He should have told me to buckle down and keep on learning from Dennis and Wrighty, and to make the most of a very privileged lifestyle. Instead, he made a phone call to the *Daily Mirror* reporter Tony Stenson. I spoke to Tony and the article appeared the very next day. It was a moan from start to finish – it was all factually correct, but it should never have been said. My only defence is that when you are used to life progressing at a certain pace, it is difficult to cope when that progress slows down or even goes into reverse. When you feel you have lost touch with your manager and are completely outside his vision, it makes you resentful and reckless about what you say and do. You feel there is nothing to lose when your livelihood and reputation are at stake.

Rioch's reaction after the article was published was as furious as you'd expect. Here are some of the choicest quotes from my piece: 'I've been treated like a dog. I have tried to put my views to the manager but he won't listen. I don't know what is going on' . . . 'I know this could cost me my place but it is time I said what I feel. I am not a big I-am, nor a big I-do. But I know I deserve better than the way I am being treated right now' . . . 'There was a stage when I felt my career was slipping away. Now I am falling so fast and I haven't even got a parachute' . . . 'I am going through hell here' . . . 'Imagine my feelings week after week when I sit on the subs' bench with the fans calling my name and I never get a chance. It is desperately upsetting.'

As you can see, it was a serious blast. Basically I was complaining about not playing often enough, but when I look back now I can see how self-destructive I was being. I was young and frustrated and thought I knew best, whereas Bruce Rioch was a seasoned manager who had played at the highest level for his country. Arsenal had bought a great player in Dennis Bergkamp and also had the England centre forward Ian Wright. I was the next man in line. Most people would realise that's not at all bad, but unfortunately my instinct deserted me when I needed it on this occasion.

There is no right time to be highly critical of your manager in a national newspaper. This one appeared with the predictable provocative headlines before a League Cup semi-final second-leg match against Aston Villa in February 1996. We had drawn the first leg 2–2 at Highbury, which was a big disappointment in itself. Dennis had scored both of our goals and Dwight Yorke had scored theirs. Unsurprisingly, I was left out of the team for the match at Villa Park. There was no reason given by Rioch, but if you step out of line by trying to nail the manager you hardly expect a warm welcome. In fact at that stage, I hadn't played a league game since Christmas, so I was unlikely to earn a recall. Even more than that, I seemed to be blaming a great club for my misery. Rioch would scarcely have been the only person at Highbury incandescent with rage at what had been printed. To cap a dreadful week, we drew the match 0–0 and went out on away goals.

After the game I was sitting in the team coach on the way home, and that's when Rioch decided to respond. His attack was face to face and fully deserved. 'See you,' he screamed, 'you're a disgrace.' He went on in that vein until I eventually rose out of my seat. At the time I was thinking, I've fucking had enough of you, Rioch. I was determined to stand up for myself. I knew I was probably already heading out of Arsenal, so with nothing to lose I let him have it. There was a lot of shouting from both of us, and it needed Tony Adams, who had been sitting alongside me, finally to calm it all down. But even when we had both regained our composure you could cut the atmosphere with a knife.

The outcome was interesting. Rioch ordered another player, Steve Morrow, and myself in for special training at 11 a.m. the next morning, having given the others a day off. I have no idea why Steve was involved, but Rioch ran us for an hour. He ran us until my legs gave in. To be fair to him, however, two days later I was picked, and scored a goal, and went on to get three goals in three games. Perhaps we understood each other better after our confrontation.

Inevitably, others had their run-ins with Rioch. Wrighty also seemed less than comfortable around his new manager. They had their moments of high tension, including a horrendous set-to at half time in a third-round FA Cup tie against Sheffield United at Highbury. It was a poor performance, as I am certain the fans who watched it would tell you. We were a goal down at the interval, and Rioch was shouting about the great players this club had once possessed. It was the way it was said that Wrighty took exception to. He tore off his jersey, threw it right at Rioch and stormed into the showers. Stewart Houston had to go and talk quietly to Ian. He told him he had to play, that Arsenal needed him, that he was the best chance we had of reaching the next round. Ian finally relented, picked up his jersey, went out and scored the equaliser that earned us a replay at Bramall Lane.

Stoking up the team if they have been lacklustre is normal, recognised and understood. But what he said here seemed to upset some players and I don't think it was the right way to get the best out of the team. You could argue the bust-up got us through the match, but we lost the replay to a goal from United's Australian striker Carl Veart anyway.

The vibes just weren't right in the dressing room and that affected performances and results. On a more personal level, I had looked forward to my first full season, but it turned out to be disappointing for me. I made only fifteen starts and scored just four goals, way below what I and the club had anticipated as a return for the money Arsenal had paid for me. Against that, when I did play I stayed out of trouble, with not a single red card and only two yellows against my name.

Fortunately, considering all that was going on at the club, my social life was happy; in fact, it had never been happier. By now Lowri and I had our own home, we had a great circle of friends and we led the life we wanted to lead, which was spending a lot of time with each other quietly. We'd go to the pub if it fitted in with Arsenal's match schedule, but more often than not we were happy doing not very much. And for the first time in my life I was banking money.

Then things seemed likely to improve professionally, too, when I heard of Bruce Rioch's dismissal. I felt it would give me a chance to start again. When any manager leaves a club, some of the players in the squad are certain to say 'thanks'. It doesn't matter how good or bad the manager has been, there will always be those who will want him out of their life and that applied to Rioch. Despite the success any manager has had, there will be players offering up prayers of thanks at his departure, while some of their team-mates will be telling the media how devastated they are.

I can now recognise, even more fully than perhaps I did at the time, how wrong my attitude towards Bruce Rioch must have appeared to him. But when you are young, head-strong and erratic, you make errors of judgement. The fact that he had me back in his side so quickly shows he was not a man to hold a grudge. At that time, all I could see was that my career was being blocked by not being a regular in the first team. The fact that Arsenal also had Ian Wright and Dennis Bergkamp did not matter to me, because as a professional footballer it is instilled in you to fight for every scrap, and to oppose those who you feel are holding you back.

With Rioch's departure, Stewart Houston again took over as caretaker manager until the permanent replacement was installed, and, having been in the doldrums for a year, I was suddenly back in favour. I could only hope that the new manager would share Stewart's faith in me.

chapter 8

Arsène and Out

Arsène Wenger is known as the 'Professor', but when he joined Arsenal he was 'that French so and so'. We'd heard of him, but at that point he had limited appeal within the game here. Of course, he's a cult figure at Highbury now.

Wenger and Sir Alex Ferguson are accepted as the best manager-coaches of the modern era. If it were a race, I suppose Sir Alex would be the leader because of the number of titles he has won, but Wenger led the revolution that has transformed English football at the top level by introducing ultra-modern methods of training and preparation. However, the day he joined us, we didn't realise how exceptionally smart he was. He had been successful in France with Monaco, with whom he won the French Championship, and where his methods were endorsed by Glenn Hoddle, who was the first to spread the word in England. His next move was to take over at Grampus Eight in Japan, which looked like a backwards step – and indeed the only explanation for it is that I guess it made him financially secure for life.

I was delighted to see a different face, no matter whose it was. We knew that whoever came in would have to be very good to re-establish Arsenal as a championship-winning team. Manchester United were running away with the Premiership year after year, with a wonderful mix of great young players and experienced older ones. Eric Cantona epitomised what they were all about – a team with poise, a team that felt it had to entertain, as if it were part of some unwritten constitution at Old Trafford. They had David Beckham, Paul Scholes, my mate Ryan Giggs from the Welsh national side, the Neville brothers and Nicky Butt as hugely talented youngsters. Good fortune had favoured Fergie in finding so many stars at the same time, but it was his uncanny intuition that won him Cantona from Leeds United.

Arsène Wenger did not have the luxury of so many gifted youngsters coming through the ranks and had to get by with an older squad. They weren't on their knees, but a defence of David Seaman, Lee Dixon, Steve Bould then Martin Keown, Tony Adams and Nigel Winterburn could not be expected to last for ever. Nevertheless, it was a considerable legacy left by George Graham, and undisturbed by Bruce Rioch, and one that allowed the new boss to negotiate some tricky obstacles.

Wenger's first tasks were to prolong the careers of the older players and find exciting new ones to create attacking opportunities from midfield: he would soon welcome Emmanuel Petit, Patrick Vieira, Freddie Ljungberg and Robert Pires – the list goes on and on. Add the grace of Thierry Henry and you are in business. His philosophy was simple: employ the

Aged seven, here I am proudly wearing my Swansea shirt, and cuddling my baby sister Victoria.

A win double. I pick up the Most Improved Player trophy – and it's no heartache that the prize-giver is Bonnie Tyler, one of Wales's most popular singers.

In action for Luton during the FA Cup semi-final of 1994. Our cup run that season was what brought me to the attention of many clubs. (*Colorsport*)

aring my dodgy tie (the only one I possessed at the time) and thick brown jacket, I sign
Arsenal in January 1995 – the most expensive teenage transfer at that time.
olorsport)

as thrown straight into action that weekend against Everton in a game we drew 1–1.
olorsport)

I score Arsenal's equaliser against Real Zaragoza in the European Cup-Winners' Cup fin
of 1995, but sadly we were to lose out to a freak goal from Nayim. (*Colorsport*)

What seemed like a rare shot of me in action during the 1995–96 season, against Spurs.
was a time when I was often left out and felt frustrated with the manager, Bruce Rioch.
(*Colorsport*)

New season, new manager.

(*Above*) I started the 1996–97 season with a goal against West Ham, and found a new lease of life under the enlightened management of Arsène Wenger (*right*), who brought with him new ideas on stretching, fitness and diet that would help prolong many a career. (*Colorsport*)

My home debut for West Ham was a fantastic 4–3 victory over Spurs. Here I do battle with Sol Campbell. (*Colorsport*)

e of my goals in our 3–1 victory over Coventry that helped keep the Hammers away
m relegation. (*Colorsport*)

reputation was not helped by some disciplinary problems on the field, as here when I
ared up to Manchester United's Roy Keane (*above, left*), but particularly because of the
orious kick at Eyal Berkovic (*above, right*) in training. As this picture shows, it wasn't
vays like that. (*Colorsport*)

Tussling with former team-mate Rio Ferdinand (*left*) soon after I joined Wimbledon in a record £7.5 million transfer. (*Colorsport*)

With failed fitness tests behind me, Gordon Strachan (*top, right*) took the risk on signing me for Coventry in the hope I could help his team stay up. I didn't manage that, but I still had some successes, such as when I scored twice against Manchester United – this is my first goal (*above*). (*Empics/Getty Images*) best to produce the best. Not for the new Arsenal the direct style that can win games but which makes football torture to watch. He wanted his side to win with flair. That was never going to be an overnight job, but it would be worth the wait. And it suited me because, big as I was, I always liked to play with the ball at my feet.

I can remember virtually nothing about the mechanics of Wenger's arrival: there wasn't a big roll of drums or an official introduction to the squad. It was all very low key. There was a picture in the morning papers of Ian Wright and Wenger, as if Wrighty was the players' representative, welcoming the new manager to Highbury, but I have since heard that he just happened to be at the ground when Wenger walked through the door.

It always takes time for players to trust a new boss, but with Wenger being French and with his methods being so untested in England, on this occasion it was bound to take even longer than usual. So much has been said about Arsène Wenger's methods over the years that they have become almost legendary. There were press rumours circulating early on that we were being fed drugs to increase our stamina, which would allow us to train longer, but this was because none of the players either confirmed or denied the stories about the food supplements and vitamins we were getting at the time. We all felt that it was pointless even to deign such ridiculous stories with a comment.

A typical day's training would start at 9.45 a.m. Being late wasn't an option. We would have breakfast, which would consist of cereal, some fruit if we wanted it and a cup of tea. This would take place at the Sopwell House Hotel, which was our base before the super new complex was completed at London Colney. The Arsenal staff would then oversee our drinks, and obviously everything they gave us would already have been medically vetted and approved by Wenger. When you are a professional sportsman you have to trust the staff around you, and I don't think I was ever told what the supplements were, nor did I ever ask. We would then be taken by bus to the training ground. There we had a specific routine that lasted for one and a half hours. Everything was done by the clock. Under Graham and Rioch, a five-a-side match would go on until whoever was running the training session decided we'd done enough. There would be no precise time limit on it from the start. But Wenger had always planned exactly how many minutes we would spend on every part of every session.

The revolution started on the very first day. Some aspects of it were so alien that it took us a long time to realise their merits. Ultimately, though, the training was enlightening and very enjoyable. I cannot recall a single player who refused to accept the new methods that Wenger introduced to the club, because we could sense the professionalism of his preparation. I am not saying previous managers were unconcerned about the fitness of their squad, but Wenger put it all down on paper, so we could see the logic in the method he used. Nothing was too much trouble: heart monitoring and blood-pressure checks were regular occurrences, as were numerous other tests on our groins, hips and ankles, which were all scanned.

Everyone involved in the game, fellow players and journalists alike, was intrigued by what was going on at London Colney. As we maintained our silence, the rumours increased and became more bizarre: some even claimed we were having regular blood transfusions. We couldn't care less what lies they printed. Pretty much the only thing they didn't say was the truth: that Arsène Wenger used his vast knowledge and applied it with common sense. It could not have been any more straightforward or successful.

If the strikers wanted to do extra work, then Pat Rice would take us as a separate group. It was all fairly standard stuff, but with some twists and turns. On Tuesdays we concentrated on the physical side of the game, which meant a lot of running. After that it was back on the bus to Sopwell House in our wet kit and into the showers. We had all the facilities we needed – jacuzzi, massage and sauna – and we'd have lunch there, but it was always very dull – chicken, some peas, very few potatoes. There would also be extra dips with carrots and lots of fruit. It would not have been my choice – I just wanted steak and chips – but I soon became accustomed to bland food. I was usually on my way home by about 2 p.m.

The most obvious difference from our previous training experiences was the mandatory stretching after every session of training. Before Wenger's arrival, none of us really knew how important simple, disciplined stretching was to improve overall fitness and decrease the chance of injury. Under his instruction, we would all go to a room and stretch together. It is customary now, and was a normal part of training in most of the sophisticated footballing nations of Europe in the mid-nineties, but it was new to us. We'd sit in a circle around Wenger and he would work each of us, with a partner, from our toes right the way up. It would last fifteen minutes: calves, thighs, groin. You would stand and shake your hips, then do your elbows, back, neck and shoulders – every day, without fail. For the first few months it was a pain and I couldn't see the point: I'd be saying, 'Can't I just go home?' But then it became part of life and training. In the end players would never finish training without first having a stretch.

As a result, our fitness levels improved, most dramatically in the senior members of the squad. Partly because of these obvious benefits, any privately held negative opinions about Wenger's methods were gradually but relentlessly dispelled. The players came to realise the advantages of following the new boss's teachings to the letter. It became clear that if you did what he said – if you ate what you were told to eat, trained as he demanded you should train – then you would prolong your career. When you think about it, if you give a top footballer an extra year, it could be worth a million pounds or more to him. Someone like Tony Adams would have been earning in excess of £20,000 a week. All he had to do was apply discipline to what Wenger was saying and it could be worth £2–4 million.

With this new regime, after such an unsettling season the year before, life at the club now seemed almost perfect. And my home life was going well, too. I hadn't yet married Lowri, but we continued to be a happy couple who did everything together, and generally we spent our money wisely. However, my addiction to gambling hadn't been tackled as successfully as maybe Lowri and others close to me had hoped. I wasn't keeping anything from them; I just felt that what I did with my money was my business. And nobody was being deprived. The way I saw it, there are plenty of other ways to spend your money, and at least with gambling you have the chance to get back more than you put in. I was earning about £4,000 a week at the beginning of that 1996–97 season, still on the contract I had signed with George Graham. Lowri had given up her college course in Swansea to live with me. The extent of our socialising, apart from with my team-mates, was a little pub called the Black Boy at Bricket Wood, near our house, and we'd go down there for a drink every so often. Lowri loved the atmosphere that surrounded matches, the social whirl, and she'd be at every game.

Arsenal could not have made a better appointment than Arsène Wenger if they had contacted Central Casting with their requirements. There is a certain aloofness about him, much as there is about the club itself, but there is an inner strength there too, despite him appearing to be so quiet and unassuming. It was the ideal professional partnership: Wenger, a man with a scientific approach to preparation, in charge of the playing side of a club that takes the utmost care in ensuring that everything it does is correct. As an example, I will mention the planning that goes into Arsenal's Christmas parties. You might think that a party's just a party, but the way Arsenal organise their Christmas bashes tells you a lot about the club and the people behind it. The hotel chosen would invariably be one of London's best: I can remember the Park Lane Hotel as one venue. This wasn't the usual piss-up with the boys but strictly for couples in evening wear. There would be a car to take you there, and you would be greeted by a security man who would take your coat. Then you would be escorted downstairs, where you would be met by the chairman Peter Hill-Wood, the vice-chairman David Dein and the other directors. Then you would enter the banqueting room, and sit at your carefully assigned table. There would be speeches from Arsène Wenger, David Dein and Tony Adams, and certainly no jumping around, pissed up, on tables. This was Arsenal Football Club, after all. It would be professional, civilised, sumptuous and enjoyable. It made you feel proud that you were part of this institution. Arsenal always approach what is often a difficult, hairy-arsed business with style.

All those I had to deal with at the club were different class. I particularly liked Ken Friar, who guided me in so many ways when I first joined the club. He was one of those who taught me I had to adapt, and I followed his advice. The way of life I had signed on for soon became second nature. Lowri and I also made good friends with the Mersons, the Parlours and the Keowns.

For away games I roomed with Martin Keown, who is such a funny guy and not at all the serious bloke most people believe him to be. I cannot think of a better man to stand by my side. If you are going into a battle, there is no one quite like Martin. He is not a fighter, not an aggressive hard man, away from football; actually he is quite posh and very well spoken. But on the field you'd wonder if he would snap you in half to win a game or just to win the ball. All the top players possess that ruthlessness: Roy Keane had it, as did Alan Shearer and so has Patrick Vieira. Even the most creative players – such as Gazza, Wayne Rooney and Steven Gerrard – have that tough streak in their mental make-up. Pelé and Maradona desperately wanted to win and to do that they had to be ruthless, too. I am told Bobby Moore could be as physical as anyone. You could not mess around with any of those guys, which was one of the reasons why they were a cut above.

Martin was like that, and he was a brilliant room-mate. He would point me in the right direction both on and off the field. He asked how much money I was earning, and then made sure my pension was in order. I had been paying into one since the age of nineteen, but Martin took it upon himself to check that I was saving enough for the future. He saw that as his role, as my mentor, if you like. We were like chalk and cheese really, but he was determined to leave his mark on me, to send me down the right path. Perhaps he suspected that I needed help, particularly where money was concerned.

I had started gambling heavily again. And for the first time I was starting to run up debts because I now had accounts with several different bookmakers. At the end of my time with Arsenal I was earning big money– about £6,000 a week – which gave me the scope to lay bets while still paying the bills and without depriving Lowri of anything she wanted. When you are an addict you are always in denial about your particular addiction. If you are an overeater, you will always tell people that you are a stone lighter than you really are; if someone asks how many cigarettes you smoke in a day, you will say twenty when you actually get through forty. And if someone asks how much you are gambling and you are spending £10,000 every week, you will say £2,000. In fact, I didn't even admit to that. I had persuaded myself it was no one else's business, that I was the only one being asked to pay off the debts, so why should I burden anyone else with it? If pushed, I would admit that I was gambling, but no one had any idea how much.

I didn't always lose. There were some bloody good days amid the bad ones. The biggest win I had was on a single foreign football match. I was £30,000 down on an account with one particular bookie. I had £2,000 on the draw at 9/4; £2,000 on half-time and full-time scores being the same at 6/1; £2,000 on 0–0, which was 7/1; and £2,000 on no goal being scored at 9/2. The game finished 0–0 so I won on all of those bets. I cleared nearly £60,000 because of a boring (to everyone else) no-score draw! That went straight into my account so I was out of jail and paid off my debt. Then I banked £15,000 and left £15,000 resting in the bookie's account for the next time. Of course, that's big gambling, but I could see no point in betting £200. What was winning £500 to me when I was earning ten times that much every week? No, I wanted to win big, and to do that I had to lay out big money. There is no mystery as to why we gamble. It's enjoyable. It's thrilling. There are plenty of lows, but the highs are something else. You know you are not going to beat the book in the long run, but that doesn't stop you trying. And for too long I didn't stop. A crunch time had to be coming, and it wasn't far away.

I say my gambling denied my family nothing, although my father would argue with that. We don't see eye to eye when it comes to money. He would ask why I was buying a £500,000 house when I could live quite happily in a £100,000 home. Why pay a driver £300 to be picked up in a Bentley full of champagne to go to the races? Why not get the train – it will only cost £14 return? And why not drink lager rather than champagne? He's old school, but of course he has never earned the money I have. I tell him that when people have money, this is how they do things. Why stay in the Dorchester rather than a B and B? That's where he would stay. I say I do it because I can afford it. His reply is to warn me that I might not always have quite so much money, and then he'll twist the knife by saying that my mam has to work two weeks to earn £400. My dad is great at causing arguments. He can be very domineering, but I accept it because I think it is all part and parcel of the era he's from . . . and because I don't listen that much! Don't get me wrong – if he gives me good advice, I'll listen. But there are times when I think: hold on a minute, Dad, I've bought fifteen homes and you've never bought one. I left home at sixteen and have earned millions of pounds since then. You haven't. He has grafted throughout his life, and I've got great respect for him for doing that, but I will say to him, 'Don't tell me what I can and cannot buy.'

To this day he reckons he should have been my agent – just like that. I ask him how he would have done that – he's a sign-writer and he doesn't have any qualifications. He would also have to be part of the inside scene, and obviously he's not and never could be. There's no denying he would know how to talk to them, and they'd respect him, but it's just not his thing. Why didn't Ryan Giggs have an agent from his family? Why isn't Wayne Rooney's dad his agent? The deals are just too big, that's why. But sometimes he just won't accept that, so silly rows start in which he and my mam stick together. I love them both like nobody else, but we have these arguments because we are never going to agree about these things.

When you start bandying around figures about how much you gamble it is understandable that some people think it's crazy; but if the amounts seemed unbelievably big to them, they weren't to me. I was earning enough to cover my bets, I was paying the mortgage, there was food in the fridge and I had a few quid in the bank. I was still keeping up with my pension contributions. I drove a nice car, as did Lowri, and we had some great holidays. I gave my family money, and even gave some to Lowri's mum, too. I helped lots of people, nobody was going without, so I reckoned I wasn't gambling too much. At the same time, though, I could see it would only get worse unless I stopped completely. Lowri tried for years to put an end to it, but she failed and eventually gave up. Instead, she trusted that I wouldn't chance all I had on a horse or a dog or some obscure football match. If I fancied a night at a casino, she would come with me to keep an eye on me, and we would have just a few chips on the roulette.

But as I said, as I became better known at Arsenal, I knew it wasn't right for me to be seen jumping in and out of betting shops, so I opened accounts and arranged all of my serious betting over the phone. There is nothing unusual in that – thousands of punters have accounts – and for me and other people in football it is the only way to have some anonymity. An account ensures that the amounts you gamble remain confidential, between you and your bookie. But I took that confidentiality to a new level. It got to the stage that I would have a code if Lowri was sitting next to me when I made the call to place a bet. I'd say £100 and mean a grand. If I said £2,000, it meant £20,000. The biggest danger is betting to try and recoup your losses. If I'd just lost a grand, I would immediately bet £2,000 to try to recover. If that went down, too, I'd have £5,000 on the next race. In no time I would be down £8,000, and that's when I'd realise it was getting too much, but that didn't mean I stopped there. On a bad day I would just keep losing and might finish £20,000 down. Decent gamblers will tell you, 'Don't chase a lost bet.' If you do, your head's gone and you are sure to end up with nothing. It is best to walk away and come back the next day. A professional gambler will rarely bet, but when he does it will be £100,000 or more on a 'dead cert'. I'm not a professional gambler – I'm a shit punter who does not stake as much but will gamble on anything, including the proverbial two flies walking up a wall.

Obviously, football gave me the money to live the lifestyle

I had chosen for myself and Lowri – and the football was good. As I had hoped, once Arsène Wenger had taken over from Stewart Houston, I still made regular appearances. In twenty-six appearances I scored just four goals, which was a disappointing return, but I was getting myself noticed. However, I also began collecting yellow cards: from my second match of the season until the first week in February I was shown ten. And on 1 January 1997 I was sent off during our 2–0 win over Middlesbrough. It was stupid: I called the referee a 'shithouse', saying it loud enough that he would hear me, knowing full well what the consequences would be. I was frustrated by a bad decision and the red mist came down, but clearly I should have kept my opinions to myself.

My style of play had always been robust, but I must confess that eight bookings in eleven games is not a record I should be proud of. Nevertheless, maybe it indicated my commitment, and perhaps that was what attracted Harry Redknapp at West Ham. I was kept up to date with the situation by my agent, Steve Davies, when I was on the point of signing a new contract with Arsenal. Arsène Wenger could not have been kinder or more complimentary when he called me in for talks. He told me there was a contract for me if I wanted it, that he liked me, that he appreciated my style of play and that I had a future with him at the club. He advised me to stay so that I could work with Dennis Bergkamp and Ian Wright, and added that I could learn an awful lot from them. He concluded by saying that he hoped I wouldn't leave and join West Ham.

The Hammers were prepared to pay £3.3 million for me,

an offer that was now officially on the table. I had to make a decision, and Wenger had offered some compelling reasons for me to remain at Highbury. Arsenal is a great club, and it was already obvious that Wenger was going to be a highly successful manager. What is more, the contract he was offering was a good one. The only concern for me was that I would not play every week in the first team. I was still very much third choice behind Dennis and Wrighty. That worried me, because I was just starting to break into the Welsh national team on a regular basis. Ian Rush had called it a day and by then Mark Hughes was in the midfield for Wales, so I had a great chance to be playing alongside Dean Saunders up front. But I felt that I had to be playing week in, week out for my club side to be given that opportunity on a regular basis.

Harry Redknapp started to apply the pressure. He was on the phone telling Steve how great I would be for West Ham and how great they would be for me. 'We'll get the ball to him,' he would say. 'We have good players here: John Moncur, Julian Dicks, Ian Bishop, Stan Lazaridis and young lads like Rio Ferdinand coming through. I think he'll love it here. We are his type of club.' When we got round to talking directly, the clincher came at the end of Harry's little pitch when he said, 'You'll be number one, playing every week.' I decided there and then to leave Arsenal and went and told Arsène Wenger immediately. I thanked him and shook his hand. He reiterated that he didn't want me to go, but said if my mind was set, then Arsenal would respect my decision.

Harry had offered me a slightly better salary than I would

have got at Arsenal – £12,000 a week against £10,000 – but it wasn't about the money. I was just desperate to be a regular part of the Wales set-up. Remember how good our national team was then? We felt we could break through and qualify for the finals of a major tournament. Harry had offered me exactly what I wanted and needed: the opportunity to play in every game. My last appearance for Arsenal was against Leeds United in the FA Cup on 4 February 1997. We lost 1–0. I wish I could have left them with a goal after all they had done for me, but it wasn't to be.

chapter 9

Claret and the Boys in Blue

Harry Redknapp had spent a lot of time convincing my then agent, Steve Davies, that I should leave Arsenal and join him at West Ham, but the move was still a considerable gamble for Harry, as well as for me. We both had plenty to lose if I couldn't find the goals. If it blew up in Harry's face, it would probably finish him as the Hammers' manager. But Harry, like myself, is a gambler, and he was prepared to stake his future on a twenty-one-year-old who had cost his club £3.3 million. While he was chasing me, he was also chatting to Paul Kitson at Newcastle. We were the players he decided were capable of scoring enough goals to keep West Ham in the Premiership and salvage a season that was all about – what was the phrase they used? – restructuring. It was actually about survival. If they failed to remain in the top flight, the shit would hit the fan.

My valuation had increased by £800,000 from the £2.5 million Arsenal had paid for me two years earlier. It's always good to be wanted: good for morale as well as for the bank balance. And it was the beginning of the best of times, my best scoring season up to that point at the highest level. Unfortunately, there were also some incidents that ranged from the embarrassing to the humiliating to the self-destructive. But throughout them all, the goals continued to flow. When Harry signed me on Valentine's Day 1997, the understanding was that I would be the first name on the team sheet every week. Harry had offered me that incentive, and I doubt I would have signed without his assurances. I knew it was dependent on maintaining my form and fitness, but Harry delivered on his promise, while Paul Kitson and I delivered for Harry.

I made my debut at Derby twenty-four hours after signing. We lost 1–0, and then I had to wait nine days for my first match at Upton Park, which was an all-London clash against Tottenham. It turned out to be an extraordinary, high-scoring match. We came out on top 4–3 and I scored, the first of many goals over a twelve-month period. That goal was such a relief. Sometimes you can wait a depressingly long time to hit your first goal for a new club, but doing so in my second match when I had cost so much meant the pressure lifted from all of us. I played a total of eleven matches until the end of the season and scored five goals, including four in two matches – two in a 1–3 win at Coventry and two in a 5–1 home defeat of Sheffield Wednesday. Paul was doing just as well: he scored eight in fourteen matches. Harry's gamble in making the double signing had paid off. Our goals saved West Ham from relegation, but it was a damned close-run thing. We finished fourteenth, which you might think is quite safe from the drop zone, but we were on the same points as Blackburn and Everton, just one point ahead of Southampton and Coventry, who in turn were a single point ahead of Sunderland, who went down. That end-of-season table highlights how big a chance was taken by West Ham, Harry, Paul and me: one slip-up could have been disastrous. I still sweat when I think about what might have been.

Harry was brilliant. The first time I met him was at Waltham Abbey, with Peter Storrie, who was in charge of all the administration at West Ham. Harry called me Johnny from the word go and he has called me that ever since. We shook hands and within five minutes I wanted to sign for him. It was his enthusiasm which was so compelling. He was up for the challenge ahead and probably saw in me a player who would give his all at a time when the club was in deep water and sinking. He told me he was also bringing in Paul and had such self-belief that he convinced me if West Ham managed to survive in the Premiership then we would have a great season after that. It was some forecast: in 1997–98 I went on to score twenty-four goals and we just missed out on a European place.

Harry was special to me, and I'm happy to put that on record. We'd go to Walthamstow dogs together, just the two of us. He'd phone up and say simply, 'Johnny, Walthamstow, tonight,' and we'd be off for a great night out. We'd meet at a nearby hotel, then park and go in one car. It was pure enjoyment for two people, manager and player, who enjoyed that sort of evening. We'd have meal and a few bets. There was nothing outrageous about it, no huge money was involved, and we weren't bingeing because Harry's not a big drinker: he'd stick to a glass of wine and I only drank Diet Coke when I was with him. We got on famously. We were kindred spirits, we liked each other and we'd talk for hours about dogs, horses, families, just about everything under the sun, but mainly football. He'd phone me before a day off and say there was a good meeting at some racetrack or other and we would go and meet people there. It was all about respect, and I have retained a lot of that for Harry. I was also an asset to his club, so maybe he was looking after me. I got to know his son Jamie, who's another very likeable person. The whole West Ham period was a lovely part of my life with Lowri, and now I regret leaving them as soon as I did.

Harry was more of a man manager than Arsène Wenger, certainly during my time at West Ham. He knew all the players inside out, but would only get on the training pitch if he wanted to put a particular point across, add something to the session. Otherwise, he would let Frank Lampard Snr., Frank Burrows and Roger Cross get on with it. All four of them shared the same philosophy, so that was no problem. For Harry, it was all about having good players available. The training was interesting because he had an excellent squad to work with – John Moncur, Ian Bishop, Iain Dowie, Steve Lomas, Julian Dicks, Paul Kitson, Eyal Berkovic, Shaka Hislop. Not to mention that amazing group of hugely talented youngsters who have gone on to achieve such great things – Frank Lampard Jnr., Joe Cole, Rio Ferdinand and Michael Carrick. We were a class act. We made it to two quarter-finals, in the League Cup and FA Cup, and finished my first full season, 1997–98, eighth in the Premiership. We fancied ourselves against anybody under the floodlights at Upton Park – Manchester United, Liverpool, whoever. The crowds were just fantastic, real supporters of a club with a strong tradition in its community.

I have been very fortunate in my career because there have been relatively few periods when I have gone for a long time without scoring. Everyone hits the occasional barren spell, but I've always managed to snap out of mine fairly quickly. That's certainly how it was throughout my time at West Ham. The goals kept coming consistently, and I established myself in the Welsh national side on the back of my performances for the Hammers. I think I managed to prove that I had something to offer the Premiership, and I quickly came to the conclusion that I had made the right decision by leaving Arsenal. Regular first-team football had been crucial to my progress and I had it now. I was relaxed about my environment, confident about my ability, I was given the number 10 jersey, and I knew I was going to play every week. When pundits talk about goal runs, they should understand that they are impossible to achieve if the player is not given a regular starting place. That was all I wanted from Harry, he gave me it and I repaid his faith in me. I think I can be justly proud of my tally of twenty-four goals in 1997–98, and I just missed out on the Premiership Golden Boot award, which went to Michael Owen, who broke into the Liverpool side that season.

In addition to getting on famously with the manager, I hit

it off with many of my team-mates. I would meet Iain Dowie every morning and we would travel around the M25 together to the training ground. A great little group of us would have lunch every day – Kits, Iain, Steve Lomas, John Moncur and me. On Mondays, and sometimes Tuesdays, we would head to a pub called the Volunteer near Waltham Abbey for a few pints. We were sensible about it – never drinking from Wednesday to Saturday. Unfortunately, though, on other occasions I wasn't so sensible. Sometimes you learn important lessons in life far too late. For me, it was realising that laddish behaviour can land you in trouble. If you are member of the public, an indiscretion will usually lead to nothing more than a ticking off from the authorities, but if you are a professional footballer you can find your-self splashed all over the front pages of the tabloids. When that happens, it can set off a chain reaction, and before you know it you have a reputation as a troublemaker, a hard man and someone who is bad news for your family, your manager, your club and everybody else, except for the papers themselves, of course, who see you as a way to sell more copies.

It started for me at West Ham when I was staying at the Swallow in Waltham Abbey and my uncle Keith, my dad's youngest brother, paid me a visit. Now, he enjoyed a drink, so we had a few too many. Keith was always great company, with loads of stories about his travels around the world. Some people are natural storytellers, and he was one of them, always the centre of attention, no matter what company he was in. He was also intelligent, but common sense could desert him at crucial moments, and this night was one of those moments. It was a Wednesday evening, which is always a good night at the Epping Forest Country Club, where Keith was staying, so we went on to there in the early hours. We were tipsy, no doubt about that, and there were only a couple of other people in the lounge. There was no one at the bar, which was shut anyway, so Uncle Keith decided to go and pour himself a drink. He filled a glass with lager, and he might even have mixed himself a cocktail. We didn't mean to cause any trouble, and I remember saying to him, 'Keith, you can't do that, just sit down.'

While I was remonstrating with him, a barman appeared from nowhere and shouted, 'Oi! What are you doing?' He came over to Keith, who apologised and said, 'I just wanted a drink.'

The barman replied, 'We stopped serving an hour ago.' Keith seemed to pacify the barman, who left the lounge. By this time, everyone else had gone to bed. It was past 3 a.m. and quiet apart from us, but Keith was still full of running. Now he decided to crawl behind the bar, in the belief that nobody would see him. Unfortunately, he activated the alarm, which went off with a hell of a racket. The barman raced back in to confront him again. Clearly he'd had enough by this stage, so he phoned the police. I just sat there, hardly believing what was happening, and I can honestly say I hadn't once gone behind the bar or tried to nick any drinks. When the police arrived they placed us both in the back of their wagon, took us to the local station and locked us up for the night. Remember, I was meant to be training the next day. They didn't charge us; in fact, they hardly spoke to us throughout the whole time we were there. I was allowed one phone call, so I contacted my police officer brother the next day. James came down to arrange our release with a warning: 'John, don't be so stupid. You're playing for West Ham and you are in the limelight.' I could only thank him and off we went. Keith moved on and that was that . . . for him.

But it was far from over for me. The story ended up on the front page of the *Sun* three days later under the headline: 'West Ham star in late night row'. It was something over nothing but I'm not blaming anyone but myself. I know I shouldn't have been there. I know I should have gone to bed earlier than I did. And I certainly shouldn't have been on the piss until 3 a.m. when I was meant to be training the next day. I should have stopped Keith going behind the bar. It never should have turned into the mess it became, and I'm still upset by it. Harry Redknapp pulled me to one side and simply asked, 'John, what are you doing?' I told him the whole story and I wasn't even fined; there was no punishment. I guess Harry thought the embarrassment of what happened becoming public was all the punishment I needed. I still wonder who tipped off the *Sun*, the barman or the police.

It was all so irritating. I'd set myself up as a likely lad for the media to keep their eye on, and nobody does that better than the British press. It was imperative I had to watch out for myself in future. John Hartson of West Ham, formerly of Arsenal, once Britain's most expensive teenage footballer, was big news if he got into trouble. I could see that, even accept it. But I say again, it wasn't as if I'd mugged an old lady. It was just a bit of drunkenness with the lads, and if Joe Bloggs off the street had done it you wouldn't have heard a thing about it. I'm not trying to excuse myself, but sometimes it has to be acknowledged that I'm from a council estate, one of the boys, and I like much the same things that my mates do. I like having a pint with my mates every now and again. I'm interested in hearing the boys talk about their scaffolding or painting jobs – it's me, it's what I'm like.

It is easy to dismiss the country club incident as trivial, but it caused me a lot of grief both with my family and in my career. Some time later, a more serious accusation made it into the papers. By this stage Jonathan Barnett and David Manasseh had taken over as my agents. Now, as I said earlier, Jonathan is a great agent and a close friend, but he is always telling this story and he never gets it quite right. The story revolves around me allegedly headbutting a bar-man. Let's make one thing clear from the start: if I actually headbutted anyone, he'd still be in hospital and I'd be doing time.

The true story went like this: I was out with a crowd of lads in a bar in Southgate. I'd gone to the toilet and when I came back a barman had picked up my drink and was carry-ing it away. 'Where's my drink?' I asked. 'You can't do that. That's my drink.' He just said, 'We're closing.' It was eleven o'clock on the dot, so there was a bit of an argument. At one point he grabbed me and tried to throw me out. I grabbed him back, and as I did so his spectacles came off and caused a little – and I mean *little* – cut. No punches were thrown, no one was head-butted, the lads and I left, and that was the end of it.

But then the guy sold his story, claiming I had punched him and wouldn't leave the pub. Jonathan took a call asking him if I had been in the bar that night, so he phoned me and asked me the same question. In a stupid attempt to brush the whole thing under the carpet, I said, 'No, it wasn't me.'

'Is that right?' Jonathan asked, then added, 'It's strange. The guy who was in the bar was six foot, had ginger hair, was Welsh and had played for Arsenal. So were you in the bar?'

What could I say? 'Well, I might have been in for one,' I admitted.

The barman's version of events appeared in one of the Sunday papers that weekend, but the police never bothered to follow it up and I was never charged with assault, which obviously I would have been if his story had been true.

But I was in genuine trouble in another way: my gambling went completely out of control during my West Ham days. It was nothing to do with the betting fraternity at the club. It was all down to me and it could have ruined me. It became such a blight on my life I realised I had to try to do something about it. For a while I was betting more than my earnings, which built up a debt that came close to being catastrophic.

First I tried Gamblers Anonymous and went along to a meeting in Watford, more in hope than in confidence that they would miraculously cure me. I had to speak at the meeting so I just told the truth: that I was getting on my girl's nerves because of my addiction. Over the years, many people, especially good friends, have tried to stop me gambling. One of my mates, Paul, is a taxi-driver, so obviously he doesn't make as much money as me. That's a problem because it's difficult for him to understand the kind of amounts that are second nature to me. What I spend on shoes for my children might be a weekly wage to him. I don't mean to sound superior, and I'm really appreciative of all the friends who have taken the time to try to help me with my gambling, but harping on about how much I have spent is not the way to get through to me. The ones I listen to don't ask how much I'm gambling but simply say, 'John, you've got to stop.'

When I was deeply in debt, there was a story in the *News of the World* stating I owed £130,000 to bookies, which, bizarrely, worked out quite well for me, because they paid me a large sum to confirm it. Jonathan and David came to my house when they realised just how great my debts were and they were fuming. Things had got so bad that my credit cards had been blocked, so when they came over they brought my bank manager along with them. Jonathan spelled it out: 'I'm fed up with this. I'm not going to be your agent any more. I don't care about the money.' Then he added, just in case the message had not penetrated, 'I'm not short of a few quid and I certainly don't need your money. I love you as a person and as a friend, you're like a son to me, and I care too much about you to see you do this to yourself, so I'm off.' With that, he got up and walked out. I was devastated and felt I'd really let him down. Fortunately, though, he returned and helped me through it. Without him, I wouldn't have overcome the problem.

The debt was spread among five bookies, and Jonathan contacted them all by phone, explaining my situation and my wish to pay them back as much as I could. His negotiating skills solved the immediate problem of the incessant demands for money, and we came to a mutually agreed compromise. I didn't have the funds to clear everything I owed, but I passed on whatever I could afford to Jonathan and he paid the bookies. His argument was that it was the best I could do and the bookies said 'fair enough'. They were still getting a vast sum off me, but I commend them for making it easier than it might have been.

From the day the debt was cleared I agreed with Jonathan that I'd receive an allowance each week. My salary would go directly to Kevin Sawyer, my bank manager at Barclays, and he would then forward the allowance to me. He didn't return my credit card, and for a while I didn't even have a chequebook. I couldn't write a cheque! For a number of years after that I didn't gamble at all, not even a five-pence piece. As a result, I saved up lots of cash and got myself in order. I built up a property portfolio overseas and my pension, and Lowri and myself still lived wonderfully well. This was when we bought our family home, Brookmans Park, near Potters Bar. I also put money away for our children's future. Nowadays, I have the occasional flutter on a football game or a cricket match that catches my eye on the TV, but nothing like I used to. Sometimes I can go months without having a bet. If I go to the races, I will take £2,000 with me (my dad still says, 'You only need to take two *hundred*, John!'). If I win, I buy the champagne; if I lose, it won't change my life. And either way I will have had a great day out, enjoying the craíc with my friends.

The other type of gambling, the serious gambling, can take up so much of your concentration. There were times when Lowri wanted to go visiting or out for a meal and I refused because there was a football or snooker match on TV that I had bet on. I would sit there like a zombie, glued to the box, just because of the bet. That caused a lot of rows, but my family, as well as Jonathan and Kevin, helped me overcome my problem. I was lucky to have those people around me and I didn't want to lose them. The only solution was to treat me and my use of money as if I were a little boy, which is what they did when they worked out the allowance scheme. At the time I found that hard to take, but now I can see it was the only way forward.

There must be hundreds of thousands out there like me, always being tempted to have a bet. The ones that get to me are the gamblers who don't earn good money but stand in the bookies' all day and blow the little they've got. This isn't spare cash with them but the money the wife needs to feed the family. That, to me, is obscene. I'd like to grab guys who do that, take them outside and tell them to go home and look after their families. Men like that have wives who scrub floors for six quid an hour, yet they bet the house-keeping money on a horse or a dog.

Recently, like everyone else, I've read about the bets the Chelsea players are supposed to have had, and if true I think it's outrageous. I can hear the words 'pot' and 'kettle' being muttered, but they seem to be taking it much further than I ever did. To punt £250,000 in casinos is just flaunting it; it's madness. When I owed big money it had accumulated over a period of time; I never lost a fortune on one hand in a single night. Of course, it is up to players to do whatever they want with their money, and I am hardly the best person to lecture them on being financially sensible. There is definitely a valid argument that if you enjoy it, if you have the money and it is not harming your family life, then why not? Footballers don't have ordinary lifestyles, we have to live our lives in the public eye, and sometimes we need an escape. That might sound like a spoiled child's argument, but in many ways it's true. We are so institutionalised, going from home to training, back home, then to matches, that we need to find something to do that gives us some excitement and enjoyment – and for many that's gambling. And when you are earning the sort of money Wayne Rooney or the Chelsea players are pulling in, what a normal punter would consider to be an outrageously big bet is often easily covered by wages. Every now and again football gambling stories leak out to the press, as happened with Wayne in 2006, and invariably a big row follows. But if the stories were correct and he owed around £750,000, then that has to be put in the context of what he earns. As soon as the story became public, he was able to clear his debts. It was a warning, and hopefully he learned from it. I now look at gambling in the same way I view social drug-taking: it's pretty harmless, unless you do it to excess; then you could land yourself in serious trouble. But if any young, big-earning footballers are reading this, I would advise them to save most of their cash and get the maximum enjoyment out of the rest by spending it on something other than gambling.

Around the time I was finally getting my gambling under control, I was arrested in my home town, Swansea, and again drink was a contributory factor. There was a group of us, old mates, and all of us had had a few. At about 2 a.m. one of my friends decided to pick up one of these ornamental hanging baskets that the council puts out around the town. He threw it over to me, soil flying everywhere, and I kicked it. Everyone shouted, 'Goal, 1–0, Hartson.' We were just messing about; it was playful fun. Admittedly we shouldn't have done it, we were boisterous, drunk and a bit stupid, but it was hardly a major crime. From there we went to a restaurant called Steak by Night, and while we were sitting there the police came in. Three officers in riot gear grabbed me off my chair, cuffed me and threw me in the back of the van. One of my mates said to them, 'Look – just say it was me. You know he's John Hartson. You know it's going to be in the papers. We were having a bit of fun, no one was hurt, there were no fights, just say it was me.' One of the officers turned to him and said, 'No chance – it was on CCTV camera.'

Five of us were involved, but they came straight for me. I was locked up for the night, they took my fingerprints, and this time they charged me. I had to appear in court and turned up with my dad, smartly dressed. All the media were there – cameras, radio people, newspapermen, photographers. Remember, at the time I was the Wales centre forward. So I turned up in court with my lawyer and he told the court that it was just a bit of boisterous fun and it wasn't meant to cause anyone any problem. We even offered to pay a couple of thousand pounds for every hanging basket in Swansea to be replaced. That seemed like a worthwhile gesture, but the judge said 'no' and told me that I would be done for criminal damage. I received a sixty-pound fine. I know I was in the wrong and, hand on heart, I will never do it again. The police didn't have to make such a big deal out of it, though. If any good came out of it, it was that I realised I had to be more careful in future.

Although I was having a fine season for West Ham, I didn't seem able to shake off the trouble that stalked me. My brushes with the law and the press were regrettable, but they paled into insignificance compared to the moment when I kicked my Israeli team-mate Eyal Berkovic. In professional terms, that was the low point for me. When you are caught on camera kicking one of your team-mates in the head, it is seriously bad news for you and a great story for the media. And what happened that day between Eyal and me has had a considerable effect on my career and what people think of me. A lot of words were said at the time, though none by me, so this is the first time I have revealed my thoughts on the incident.

Eyal was one of the most unselfish players I have ever known. I would rate him alongside Chris Sutton, whom I would later partner at Celtic, in that respect. Eyal, for instance, could be in front of goal yet would still roll the ball to his striker and tell him to stick it in rather than score himself. I got on very well with him partly because he made a lot of the goals I scored for West Ham. And I loved playing with him because he was so easy to work with. On the morning of the incident Harry Redknapp had called a meeting of all the players to find out what had gone wrong in our previous poor performance in the League Cup, when we were beaten 2–0 by Northampton. That defeat was near the start of my second full season, on 15 September 1998. Losing to Northampton was a disgraceful result on the night and was bound to have repercussions, especially as we had finished in the top ten of the Premiership the season before. The most ridiculous aspect of it was that we had beaten Liverpool 2–1 at Upton Park just three days earlier. Maybe we were feeling just a bit too good about ourselves when we faced the lower-league side. But whether it was that or simply an off night, it was still unacceptable, and Harry wanted to know what had gone wrong and how the situation could be rectified. If there were players who had not given 100 per cent on the night, then he wanted their names, to have it out in the open, so there would be less chance of it happening again.

Everybody had their say, and it was a very stormy meeting. It might have been Harry's place to rant and rave, but he wanted us to face up to our mistakes and reveal our thoughts on where it had all gone wrong. My contribution was to say that I wouldn't play Eyal away from home in future. It was my honest opinion, and I will go so far as to say that it was the opinion of others, too, but it was me who said it. It was meant to be instructive, meant to be beneficial to the team, and that's how I thought it had been received. Perhaps I was naïve to think that it would be acknowledged by Eyal as positive and constructive criticism, because he immediately had a go back at me, saying that I didn't 'Fucking run for the ball away from home . . . or any other time.' It was that sort of meeting. There were a few more verbals, too, with Neil 'Razor' Ruddock having his say about the defensive work of the team. Eventually Harry called a halt and sent us out to train.

You don't usually remember training as well as you remember matches, but what happened next would be impossible to forget. John Moncur rolled the ball in my direction, but Eyal crept in and intercepted it. As he did so, I came in behind him and completely took his legs away. He started squealing on the floor and I went to help him up, trying to do the right thing. I apologised, but as I picked him up (and you can see this clearly on the video), he aimed a punch at me and caught me just below my stomach. I don't know what came over me, but I swung my left boot and kicked him under his jaw. I know it was wrong; I knew that as soon as I had done it. I also knew there would be big trouble in its wake, but normally when something like that happens in training it is kept in-house. Unfortunately, though, the gods were working against me, and it had been captured on film by cameras from Sky, which had been given permission to film the training session by Harry. The

TV people came over to us afterwards and told Harry and me, 'Don't worry, this won't come out, we'll forget about it, you'll never see it again.'

Eyal said nothing but went off in a huff, into the shower room. I caught up with him there later. He had a little blood on his lip, but that was all. I told him how sorry I was, we shook hands and he said, 'Don't worry, mate.'

The immediate outcome was that Harry fined me £10,000 on the spot; and to those who believe that clubs pay their players' fines, I can only confirm that's not the way Harry Redknapp works. I handed over a cheque for the full amount a couple of days later, and the cash went to a leukaemia charity. None of this became public, and I expected that the incident itself would remain inside the club, too, after what the people from Sky had said. But there was always a chance that someone would leak the story to try to make a few bob. I heard nothing more about it for at least a couple of weeks, but then all hell broke loose. It was someone in Sky who passed it on. I was so incensed that I refused to speak to the company for a year – I saw it as professional betrayal.

It was only when it became public that Eyal and myself began to have differences of opinion, shall we say. That was when the bad vibes really began between us. If it hadn't come out, I think our handshake would have ended it. In the aftermath of the story breaking in England, though, he went to Israel and said quite a lot in the papers out there. Many of his comments were directed at me, and I became very uncomfortable with the whole situation. Was he looking for a way out of West Ham? I don't know, but he soon left the club and moved to Celtic. Later that year I met him and his family in Disneyland, and he was fine, good as gold. We talked for a while, but not once did we mention what had happened between us.

When the video was broadcast in all its gory detail, the FA stepped in, suspended me for three matches and fined me £20,000. There are those who will say it served me right, and I wouldn't argue with them. I took my punishment, but I seemed to serve a sentence that was a lot longer than three matches. Some of the stuff I had to take from the press infringed on my family life. If my kick had been unacceptable, then so was the behaviour of the media. I will always regret what I did to Eyal, but the media attention was outrageous. In a way, the scale of the story proved that footballers' activities could be major news stories, rather than of interest just to a fanatical minority. I remember *News at Ten* warning viewers that if any children were watching they should perhaps be sent out of the room, because what was coming up next was so disturbing. They then showed a clip of the incident.

It was so bad that I had to get away from it all, and I ended up in France. I went to Cannes where I trained with a coach called Tibius Derae, who had been recommended to Harry by Ian Wright, and had worked with a number of Arsenal players because of his connection with Arsène Wenger. It turned out to be a brilliant week in fitness terms, but in every other way it failed to lift my spirits. I had to lock myself in my room for most of the time and eat whatever

Tibius told me to eat. Only one reporter managed to find me, and he came as a bit of a surprise to Tibius, who knew nothing about the kicking incident and had no idea that I was well enough known for a newspaper to send a reporter to the South of France to try to speak to me. Of course, I had nothing to say to him. During the week Lowri phoned regularly, and on one occasion she told me that a reporter from the *Daily Star* had turned up at the house and asked her what it was like to live with an animal. Her reply was that I was a darling at home who never lifted a finger against her. Obviously they were trying to portray me as something I wasn't, although I could see that I had opened the door for them.

It didn't help my reputation that I had quite a poor disciplinary record. In two years with the Hammers I amassed two red cards and ten yellows. That hardly amounts to a criminal record, but when you added it to the headline stories it was enough for people to want to have a go at me, ostracise me. I have to accept that the critics had something to go on, but after I kicked out at Eyal they seemed determined to label me a thug. Since joining West Ham there had been the incident with my uncle in the hotel, the arrest over the hanging basket in Swansea, and the gambling debt, all of which had made it into the papers. When I returned from Cannes and started training with the team again everything seemed normal at first, but the damage had been done. Soon, as I said, Eyal moved on and I was shunted on to Wimbledon. My last game for West Ham was against my hometown club, Swansea City, in the FA Cup. They beat us.

By that stage a section of the Hammers' fans had it in for me. I was getting booed throughout matches, which affected my confidence and my form. But it was the kicking incident that decided my fate. When you go from hero to villain it can destroy you as a player, and I didn't want to deal with that. At the time I thought it was best to leave, and I went to a club that appealed to me greatly.

chapter 10

Crazy Days

The news that West Ham were ready to sell me filtered through from Harry Redknapp via Jonathan Barnett. It didn't come as a surprise: I wasn't playing well and there was the row over Eyal. But perhaps what really swung it for the Hammers was that they were offered £7.5 million for a twenty-three-year-old they had bought for just £3.3 million a couple of years before. West Ham couldn't complain about what I had done for them: I had scored thirty-three goals, which had first helped save them from relegation and had then seen them finish well in the top half of the Premiership the season after.

The process of selling me became serious when I was playing golf on the Thursday after West Ham had been knocked out of the FA Cup by Swansea. I was depressed: that defeat somehow seemed to epitomise what was becoming a disappointing season after the highs of the previous one. Mick Harford, Andy King and Brian Stein were my golf partners and we were on the twelfth green when a little guy came out on a buggy and asked if John Hartson was in the group. What could have happened this time? He walked up to me and told me there was an important phone call that I should take. I returned to the clubhouse and it was Jonathan on the line. 'Get yourself home,' he said. 'Get changed. We are going to meet Sam Hammam in St John's Wood.' We then arranged to meet in a hotel on the way, where we discussed what was on offer before driving on to Sam's home.

The main meeting was between Sam, the Wimbledon manager Joe Kinnear, Jonathan and me. It was sociable and very pleasant. Sam was terrific, an amazing character, and it came across in that first meeting. I had met Joe in the past as he was very interested in greyhound racing. So the vibes from both men were good. I always feel it is important to be comfortable with the people who want to sign you, and I became increasingly relaxed the longer I sat talking to them. Sam talked without fudging when he said, 'We are prepared to pay an awful lot of money for you.' He wasn't kidding: no club of Wimbledon's size had ever splashed out anything like £7.5 million for a player. They had done brilliantly well since their amazing FA Cup victory in 1988 and had established themselves as a Premiership side with the lowest average crowds in the top league. But even so, and even allowing for the millions Premiership clubs receive from television money, for them to pay that sort of cash for me was highly complimentary. My salary would be over £20,000 a week, but it was the kudos that came from knowing a little club was prepared to pay so much for me that really impressed me. They had confidence in me, and I was happy to go along with it and join them.

Decades ago, footballers were virtual slaves to their clubs and had no control over their futures. When a club decided to sell, the player was sold, whether it was in his best interests or not. Those days are supposedly over, but in reality if a club wants you out, they have ways to make you leave and you might have to accept whatever offer is made for you no matter how unattractive it seems to be. Fortunately, though, having met Sam and Joe, I was quite looking forward to joining the Crazy Dons – or the not so Crazy Dons, as it turned out. I started to see the transfer as the change I needed and thought it would give me a chance to relaunch my career.

I arrived after the lunatic days of the Crazy Gang, which I suppose was a blessing. When I joined they were actually in the process of trying to rid themselves of that reputation. It had become a stigma, and one of the ways Sam decided to eradicate it was by buying quality players that he hoped would take them to another level. I always found Sam a good man to deal with, although I have heard stories of him going over the top at times, taking things too far. But I only saw the good, benevolent side. He took an interest in me, as well he might when you consider how much money he paid for me, but he was always there as a friend and adviser, the type who would take the time to ask how your family were doing. He and his wife even attended Rebeca's christening, and I can't think of many owners who would care enough to do that. For me, the only thing he ever did wrong was join the enemy some years later, when he became the owner of Cardiff City! When he was at Wimbledon he was very passionate. He would come into the dressing room before games and gee up the lads, which was hardly normal behaviour for a chairman–owner. He left the team talks and all team matters to Joe, but he did enough with us to ensure we knew who he was, what he wanted from us and what the club meant to him. I never saw him as an interfering chairman, although the managers who worked under him may have a different opinion on that score. He would often turn up and watch us train, but he wouldn't be directly involved. It was simply as if he was checking on his assets. When training finished he would come in and have some banter with us.

Joining a London club meant I didn't have to move, although it now took me an hour and twenty minutes each morning to reach the training ground, which was a hell of a drag, a drive I began to loathe. But on the plus side I felt Wimbledon might suit me, that they would play to my strengths, and that Joe was someone I could respect. We had spoken often enough in the past at various race tracks over a beer, so we weren't exactly new to each other. It was also important that Mick Harford was the coach. I knew what he wanted and he knew what he could expect from me. He was a very important factor in my decision to sign for the Dons.

I can't disguise the fact that Wimbledon was very different from anything I had experienced before. I had been used to big crowds, packed stadiums, a lot of atmosphere, whereas at Wimbledon you would be lucky to have 4,000 regulars. Teams like Manchester United, Chelsea, Arsenal, Tottenham,

West Ham and Liverpool would bring more fans than our home support and they made it feel more like an away match. All of this was very difficult for us players as well as for Sam, Joe and the rest of the staff. Sometimes in a crowd of 20,000 you would be lucky if 5,000 were Wimbledon fans, which made the whole situation a little unreal for me.

Joe Kinnear is very similar to Harry Redknapp in that he also has a great understanding of players. He can spot one in a lower league whose quality has slipped under the radar, sign him and turn him into a Premiership player. He would always look for the player who could win you a game, do the right thing, deliver the right pass, keep himself fit and be a good character. That's the type Harry goes for, too. It was very sad – although thankfully not tragic, because he eventually recovered well enough to return to management – when Joe suffered his heart attack and had to finish with Wimbledon just a couple of months after I joined the club.

With Joe gone, David Kemp and Mick Harford took charge for a while, but at the end of the 1998–99 season Sam Hammam sold the club to a Norwegian consortium, which brought in their countryman Egil Olsen as the new manager. Egil had been the national coach of Norway and a hero in his country for taking them to the World Cup finals in 1994 and 1998. He was a delightful person, very bright, but he lost the support of the dressing room. After a while the team was not going out there and scrapping, even for ourselves, let alone for the manager and the club. The simple fact is that we lost respect for him. Lots of the guys didn't understand his tactics, which focused far too much on the long ball. Maybe that was unsurprising as he had managed Norway with Tore Andre Flo as the big striker up front. Playing the long-ball game doesn't worry me particularly, because I have never minded competing for the ball that has been pumped into the box. And what's the point of going with a big striker and not supplying him? Wimbledon had three like that – Carl Cort, Marcus Gayle and myself – and we made it work for a while, but then it just went down, down, down. Even in the 1998–99 season we had ended by winning just one game in the last seventeen, so the following year was always going to be tough.

My anger and frustration surfaced after we had played at Bradford near the end of the 1999–2000 season. We lost 3–0 and I was sent off in my first game back since December. I should have kept my head down and got straight on the bus, but instead I ended up saying my piece on Sky. I should have remembered my embarrassment when I had used a press article to criticise Bruce Rioch in my Arsenal days, but that had obviously slipped my mind. Dave Bassett, a former Wimbledon manager, was a pundit on the box that day, and he gave me hell for criticising the manager the way I did. He was dead right, but Sky had managed to catch me on camera at a bad time and I just let it run away from me. They asked me what was wrong with the team (we were third from bottom at the time) and I should not have taken the bait. It was not my place to say anything. I should have said 'no comment' and walked away, especially as on the day I had let the club and the fans down more than anyone else by getting myself sent off, but instead I had the audacity to slag off Egil. Bassett said he didn't know what I was playing at, that we were fighting for our lives and that I should not be sticking the knife in.

It was a fateful day – 30 April 2000 – as much for the consequences of my sending off as for my comments afterwards. In the next game, against Aston Villa, I came off the bench and scored, which gave us a 2–2 draw and a lifeline. But when we went to Southampton for the next match, needing a win, I was suspended because of the red card at Bradford. We lost and were relegated. I can't help thinking that if I had been able to play, I might have made a difference. Egil was shown the door and Terry Burton took over, along with Stewart Robson.

I didn't agree with Stewart's approach. He had been promoted from the Under-19s and was all for the youngsters, which is fine, if they are of the highest quality. You often find this when people move up the managerial hierarchy after dealing with the kids. They want to promote the players they have been working with for a couple of years, the kids they are certain will make the grade. But in reality the ones who do find a regular place in the first team are like gold-dust. When most of the kids play with the big boys it is a bad experience for them because it's when they learn they are not good enough. There was one young lad in particular, Rob Gier, whom Stewart raved about at Wimbledon. No doubt he was a good young 'un, but the last time I checked he was playing for Rushden and Diamonds. He is doing fine, and I am sure he's enjoying his football, but there was something missing from his game which kept him from reaching the heights Stewart Robson thought he would achieve. Maybe it was bad luck or bad timing, but when a coach backs the wrong person they can harm two people, their favourite and the player he is keeping out of the team. It could have been me.

Wimbledon was another club that had a strong gambling fraternity, so the temptation was always there for me to revert to the bad old days. I didn't, but I did buy a few grey-hounds. I co-owned a couple of dogs with Joe Kinnear, and had another two with Alan Kimble. They had names like Code Harts and Code Kimble; one was called Left Peg. If you had a bet on any of these and lost, I apologise. Code Harts was the best of the bunch and had something like thirty or forty runs. Believe me, we had some good value out of him. He made us a few bob, but it wasn't about the money. Ownership was an interest which we even got the children involved in, although they looked at our 'investments' just as great big sleek pets. We'd go down to the Walthamstow track as a family for the midweek meetings, when it was much quieter, and after the meeting was over we'd take the kids round to the kennels. Lowri was insistent that when Code Harts retired we would keep him as a pet and I agreed. The plan came to fruition a while later when I was at Celtic, but it didn't work out quite as we had hoped. When the dog was due to be retired I phoned the trainer Gary Baggs and told him we would love to have him. We arranged for him to be transported up to Scotland, and Code Harts duly arrived at our home, where there was plenty of space for him to run around. That day Baggsy was on the phone: 'John, you've got to leave the muzzle on for the first month.' That got me thinking, and then I was thinking some more when the dog walked in the door: he was like a bloody horse – enormous. We hadn't realised he was so big, never having noticed his size in the racing environment. 'Lowri,' I said, 'he can't stay.' We had him for all of one night and he barked every minute he was in the house.

At Wimbledon the scene was starting to depress me. I was out of the top league and in and out of a relegated team. I was an ultra-high earner yet I felt worthless. I had to find a way out, but whenever a club came in for me those bloody medicals blocked the opportunity. I needed good, solid advice from people close to me who recognised how I was feeling. I received it from Jonathan Barnett, David Manasseh and my close friend Tom Walley.

Tom is an extraordinary man, someone who has been part of my life for many years. He has helped many footballers over the years, but none more than me. Alongside my dad and Terry Westley, my former coach at Luton, I would say Tom has been the most positive influence on my life. His knowledge of the game puts him in a class of his own. I have spoken to him on a daily basis for years, and we talk about everything from football to politics, but he is also the man I turn to every pre-season to improve my fitness before turning up for training with my club. He has put me through a fitness routine every year throughout my career. I first met him when I played for Luton's youth team and he was the manager of Millwall's Under-18 side. We came up against them in a Southern Junior cup final. Mark

Kennedy, who is now playing at Wolves, scored a hat trick and we lost 4-0, with Ben Thatcher marking me out of the game. My introduction to Tom that night was a straightforward 'Hello, well done, see ya' – that was it – but he soon became a considerable influence on my life as coach of the Wales Under-21s.

When I was at Arsenal, Bruce Rioch brought him to the club from Millwall, where they had worked together. That was when I really got into the habit of Tom's pre-season training and I have stuck with it ever since. The routine has been the same since those Arsenal days: end of season, holiday, training with Tom, pre-season training with club, new season. He will train me for two weeks in the back garden of his Watford home and I will stay in a nearby hotel. All the sessions are worked out beforehand: weights, stamina work, diet. Tom is a brilliant trainer. He knows exactly what I need and that ensures I turn up at my club in a much better condition than I would have been without him. His advice when I was at Wimbledon was exactly what I expected it to be: I was nothing if I wasn't fit, playing and scoring goals, so I should go and do it. I tried, but something had to give, and it was my resolve.

I entered a period when my life seemed more bizarre than anything Wimbledon's old Crazy Gang could have thought up. How many players have bought a hospitality box at their own club and entertained more guests than the directors at every home match? I did. It cost me £30,000 and it was worth every penny because it provided a welcome release at a time when I had all but given up on the playing side. I could not hold down a regular place in the team, I was unhappy and my confidence was decimated. I was just waiting for something to turn up, like a new club, but I had no idea how, where and when that would happen.

Although moving to Wimbledon had seemed like a good idea at the time, by now it was turning into a nightmare: small club, small gates and ever-smaller ambition. The tradition was there, but all the leading lights had left, and I wanted to follow them. I know that sounds a mite ungrateful to a club that had offered me a home after the trouble at West Ham, but it had got to the stage when I often asked myself why I had joined them. That's when I decided to buy the hospitality box at Selhurst Park, to give myself some fun and allow me to entertain my mates when I was out of the team. Terry Burton didn't use me as a sub because he and I both knew it is not a role I do well, so he either played me or left me to kick my heels. It was the same with Gordon Strachan at Celtic, who also preferred to leave me off the bench. When Terry told me I was out of the team, I would arrange for my mates to come to the hospitality box for a meal and a few drinks – sometimes more than a few. By this point in my Dons career I had all but given up and had decided to go on the piss. I would arrive at the ground, have a little bet on the match, and meet my mates, generally six or seven couples, sometimes including Jonathan and his wife. We would enjoy ourselves during the match, and once it was over I would go down to the players' bar for a few with the lads, then arrange for a driver to take us into town. If I wasn't playing, that was the routine at every home game for six or seven months. When I did play, Lowri would look after our friends during the match and I would meet up with them later. The club was terrific about it. And so they should have been. After all, they had boxes to sell and I had bought one; and it wasn't as if any other punters were queuing up to buy them.

The season we were relegated I made twenty appearances, scored nine goals, was ordered off twice and was cautioned three times. During the first half of the next season, 2000–01, I made twenty-three appearances and scored ten goals in the First Division. I can see now that I might have had a better career without the Wimbledon interlude, but I am prepared to state categorically that I have no regrets, and I have nothing but respect for what they achieved against the odds. It's just a shame that those days were coming to an end by the time I arrived, and the changes at boardroom and management level while I was there were always going to alter the set-up. I played some good football for them and maintained a decent scoring rate, even though I was in and out of the team, but so much happened during my time there that it took some of the fight out of me, some of the desire. Joe suffered his illness and left, Sam sold the club and left, we had Norwegian ownership and a Norwegian manager in Egil Olsen, who oversaw a run of poor results that led to relegation, and though we improved a little when Terry Burton took over things just weren't right at the club. Even back then it was easy to see that Wimbledon would be heading only one way.

October 1993, and I am gearing up for my Under-21 debut for Wales, against Cyprus. The serious face was replaced with a very happy one by the end as I scored twice in our comfortable victory.

In action against Italy in October 2002. Our 2–1 victory seemed to put us on track for qualifying for the European Championships in summer 2004. (*Colorsport*)

My penalty past Serbian goalkeeper Jevric drew us level in the last Euro qualifier in October 2003, but sadl our campaign ended in disappointment and controversy. (*Colorsport*)

Battling with Rio Ferdinand during our World Cup qualifier in Septem 2005. Later that autumn I announ my retirement from international football. (*Colorsport*)

score the first goal of the game in the SFA Cup final of 2002 against Old Firm rivals angers, but it wasn't enough to see us to a victory or the double.

he best goal of my career (so far): a thirty-yard drive against Liverpool at Anfield to help to the semi-finals of the 2003 UEFA Cup.

Henrik Larsson, my great strike partner for three seasons at Celtic, knows to get out of the way when I call for the ball.

Celebrating another trophy with Rebeca.

Alongside Martin O'Neill early in the 2004–0 season, when I scored twenty-three league goal but we were pipped to the title on the last day the campaign. (*Empics*)

shoot for goal against Hearts on 5 April 2006, with less than five minutes gone.
raig Gordon was beaten and we went on to win 1–0 and so secure the title. Cue the
lebrations!

Lowri and me on our wedding day.

My beautiful Nan.

The Hartson family en route to warmer weather: brother James, Dad carrying Joni, Hayley, Mum and Victoria. Rebeca's head almost makes it onto the picture but you can blame the camera-man for that. Guess who?

Rebeca, just one hour old, is cradled by my mum, while her doting father looks on.

Joni practising his football skills with my dad outside the family home in Swansea.

Christmas in Swansea for Joni and Rebeca. Like father like son for the shirt of choice!

My move to West Brom for the 2006–07 season could not have got off to a better start, a scored twice in our victory over Hull. (*Laurie Rampling*)

When I joined the club, Wimbledon were a mid-table Premiership team and had been in the top flight for fourteen years. A year and a half later they were relegated, which was a tragedy for a club that had come from nowhere and made a huge impact on English football with their success as well as their daftness and all the Crazy Gang antics. They had built a great reputation, and in Sam and Joe they had two exceptional characters in charge – one running the finances and the other managing the team. Even in the relegation season there were still a lot of good players there: Kenny Cunningham, Neil Sullivan, Ben Thatcher, Alan Kimble, Robbie Earle, Andy Roberts, Carl Cort, Marcus Gayle and myself. Unfortunately, though, when the club began to slide they sold just about everybody. It was a policy which might have brought in the pounds, but it was hugely detrimental to Wimbledon's long-term future.

I was doing little more than going through the motions. I would turn up at our training ground near Richmond Park, but I wasn't enjoying it any more. Terry was good to me, but I didn't know where I was going or what I would do. He knew my head wasn't right and that I was a better player than I was showing for Wimbledon, but really I was just a saleable commodity to them. Luckily, my agent Jonathan was there for support, and even more fortunately Gordon Strachan had the strength of character to ignore medical opinion and persuade his chairman to take me on. Wimbledon had found a buying club and that was it, I was on my way. I was being sent to Coventry.

They say that when an alcoholic's life collapses completely

and he ends up sleeping on park benches, it is either the beginning of his recovery process or the start of his slide into oblivion. I had been at my lowest point at Wimbledon, and I had to fight back or be forgotten – but at Coventry?

Gordon offered me the chance of recovery, but if I hadn't been absolutely certain about joining Wimbledon a couple of years earlier, I was quite sure I did not want to sign for the Sky Blues now. Why would I want to join a club who were second bottom of the Premiership? I had quickly learned a lot about Gordon Strachan, but I still didn't fancy them one bit. It was Jonathan who told me that it was my one way out of Wimbledon and if I did well it would not be long before I moved. This was one of those times when you think, What the hell's going on? I asked Jonathan to put himself in my position. He was advising me to sign for a club, to look happy and committed, all the time knowing I would be leaving them in the summer. I would be using them, and I didn't like that one bit. But Jonathan said I had to sign to get my career going and just do my best for six months, then hopefully I'd be with a new club. Of course, that's exactly how it worked out. It was ruthless of us, but I want to acknowledge again how important Coventry were for me, and how much regard I have for Gordon and chairman Brian Richardson, who took a chance on me.

While I was there I managed to regain my fitness and then take it to a whole new level. The training under Gordon was truly magical, albeit very demanding. By now I was twenty-five and able to cope with it. As I have already admitted, I hate running and that will never change, but I enjoyed the way Gordon set out training and created a competitiveness within the squad. I was always raring to go after travelling up the M1 every day as we were still living in Brookmans Park. In the twelve games I played I felt I made a good contribution with my six goals, but unfortunately it wasn't enough to keep us up.

I really took to the area, which is truly exceptional: Stratford, Leamington, there is nowhere finer. And when that was added to how much the club had gone out on a limb for me, I left with considerable regrets. But Celtic was to be my major step towards redemption. Little could I know that one day I would end up playing for Gordon Strachan again.

chapter 11

Wales – My Wales

There are few driving forces in your professional life that compare with representing your country. As a young sportsman it is your first target. When you reach the point when it becomes a reality, money couldn't buy the feeling of pride that surges through you. So it would always take something, or rather somebody, special not only to dent my enthusiasm but to come close to destroying the joy I had in playing for Wales. I might have had considerable reservations about Bruce Rioch at Arsenal, but I never dreamed I would come across an international manager who would drive me to distraction. That is until Bobby Gould was named manager of Wales in June 1995. The feeling lasted throughout all four years of his reign. But I'd had problems at international level even before then.

As I mentioned earlier, I made my Wales Under-21 debut against Cyprus as a youngster at Luton and my full debut in March 1995 when I was at Arsenal, but if my ambition was being fulfilled with those two appearances, it was also threatened by my impetuosity when Terry Yorath was in charge and his Under-21 manager was Brian Flynn. From the start I always took playing for my country extremely seriously when I was out there on the field, but just once I did not afford my selection the respect it was due off the park. That was when I was nineteen and reported late for an Under-21 squad gathering. All I had to do was turn up at the County Court Hotel in Newport at a time specified in a letter from the Welsh FA, but I was about five hours late, and that was inexcusable. Brian pulled me to one side and said with a lot of justifiable irritation, 'You're late and we are not happy about it.'

Terry was there, too, and I was told ominously that he wanted a word with me. At the time I had never met him, but soon he was right there in front of me in all his glory with that big red face. He stuck his finger in my chest and said without hesitation, 'Who the fuck do you think you are? You turn up late, yet you are playing for your country. I've got Rush, Hughes, Saunders, Horne, Ratcliffe, Southall – the best goalkeeper in the world – all here on time. Ian plays for Liverpool, Mark plays for Barcelona and you turn up late coming from fucking Swansea.' I had clearly insulted him. My attitude had offended him. He had decided I was taking the piss. I had viewed going back to Wales as a chance to see my mum and dad before sauntering in to meet up with the squad. It was unprofessional. I suppose it was a case of me saying, 'Don't you know who I am?' but Terry flayed me, and looking back I can see that it was a very important lesson to learn. I knew I had been in the wrong and I apologised. I never made the same mistake again and went on to play ten matches in six months for Brian's Under-21s.

With Bobby Gould it was a whole different story. It didn't take me long to realise he wasn't the right man for me in that job. It wasn't his fault, but I think his appointment dragged Welsh international football to its knees. Not only was he unable to improve our position, but we became far worse, a laughing stock of the world game. The original blunder of appointing him was made high up at the Welsh FA by those who for some reason decided we needed an English manager. That would have been fine if they had gone for someone with an international pedigree or a manager who had great knowledge at international level and would immediately be respected by the squad. Then the FA compounded their mistake by sticking with him when the results suggested he wasn't up to the task. They left all of us, players and fans, to suffer.

Of course, it was the players who were in the front line and had to cope with the flak that was flying around while Bobby was in charge. They were unproductive years, a waste of time, energy and ambition. Bobby wasn't a bad man, in fact he could be very good company, but I felt he was out of his depth and unsuited to international management. There will be those who regard that as an unnecessarily harsh assessment, but I am certain most who worked with and under him would agree with it. He had been remarkably successful with Wimbledon, in charge when they won the FA Cup in one of the great shocks in the competition's history when they rolled over Liverpool at Wembley in 1988. He had our respect for that. Unfortunately, though, he never gave any sign that he was going to come up with the same results for Wales. Being English may not have helped him, but initially he was welcomed, even though some considered him an outsider. I just don't believe he fully grasped what we were all about and how much playing for Wales meant to us, because he wasn't Welsh. He seemed to see us as little more than an extension of Wimbledon, an international Crazy Gang. But players of the class of Ian Rush, Mark Hughes and Ryan Giggs were never going to accept the sort of eccentric approach to preparation that had worked for him there.

You can cite any number of reasons for our poor results, but I believe a highly significant one was Bobby. No one expects Wales to win World Cups, but they do expect – and are entitled to expect – an honourable performance. Terry Yorath had steered us to within touching distance of qualifying for the World Cup finals in the United States in 1994. Thereafter, John Toshack (in the first of his spells in charge) took over for a brief spell before standing down for Mike Smith. Mike tried and failed to get us to Euro '96, but Wales remained a good side, with a high degree of confidence among the players that they had the quality to do well, even if the team had underperformed in the qualifiers.

Then it was Bobby's turn. I felt he made life virtually impossible for himself. Some might say that he simply couldn't handle big-name players, and at the time Wales had a number of them – Ian Rush, Mark Hughes, Ryan Giggs and Dean Saunders were four who could find a place in most teams. But he also didn't seem to know how to get the best out of the likes of Neville Southall, Gary Speed, Vinnie Jones, Chris Coleman, Eric Young, Andy Melville and Robbie Savage. I was in there as a young challenger full of running and equally full of confidence that I would score goals. I am not saying we were world beaters, but we had the ability to compete, and often we didn't even achieve that under Bobby. If he wasn't embroiled in a row with Nathan Blake (who refused to play under Gould after accusing him of 'racist' remarks), or falling out with Robbie Savage (when he insisted he apologised to an opponent for throwing a shirt in jest), or standing in the dressing room in stunned silence after being shouted down by Gary Speed, then he was challenging me to a fight. Put simply, the managerial style and tactics that had worked at Wimbledon did not – could not – work with Wales. His style was so different to what any of us had been used to, and whatever it was, it didn't connect with us. An international manager is really no different from a club boss – his success or failure depends on results – and under Bobby our results were horrendous. We tumbled down the world rankings and won only seven of the twenty-four games he was in charge. That sort of decline matters to players because we really care about playing for our country.

The first big problem I had with Bobby was that I felt he didn't pick me as often as he should have, making only eight starts during this period. Obviously, I am biased on this, but I do have my reasons. When he came into the job he had one goal: to ensure that we qualified for the 1998 World Cup finals in France. I started in just two of the eight qualifiers and Wales didn't make it. Saunders and Hughes were the first-choice strike pairing, with Rush having retired because he reckoned it was about time to do so after a fantastically successful career. Mark Hughes was still around, although he was thirty-three in November 1996 and prepared to slip back into midfield. That left an opening for one of me, Nathan Blake or Lee Nogan, and I felt there should have been a regular role for me in the team as I was scoring goals for both Arsenal and West Ham.

We still had a good squad, but we played poor football far too often. Our defence may not have been the best in the world, but we had big players in all positions, players with character, yet I think Bobby took us backwards not forwards.

It is almost embarrassing to recall some of the stories about him, when the players made him the butt of so many jokes, asides, whispers. Bobby took it all ridiculously well, sometimes even joining in, and while it's good for managers to have a relationship with their players, he should have recognised that his dignity was being challenged. Dean, one of the funniest guys around, would make fun of him on the bus in a jokey way, but Bobby would just sit in the front, knowing the lads were mocking him and not saying a thing.

Bobby's training regime was OK, but I found it increasingly difficult to be motivated, which is something that is very hard for me to admit. It's your country, and you want success more than anyone because you have been chosen to represent it, so anything less than 100 per cent should be unacceptable. Yet after a while, when it had sunk in that we were going nowhere as a team, it was hard to maintain our momentum.

One of the biggest rows, and without doubt the most unsavoury one in terms of national publicity, was the accusation from Nathan Blake that Bobby had made racist remarks to him during a training session. I don't think Nathan is oversensitive, and he has always been one of the boys who knows how to enjoy himself, so whatever was said must have been something serious. That said, though, I can't believe Bobby would consciously have a bad word to say about anybody because of his race, creed or colour. I can imagine it as one of these 'Wimbledon' moments – a smart-ass comment or a silly joke that in the circumstances was totally misplaced. I can't help thinking that the incident got blown out of all proportion. Blakey refused to play for Wales while Bobby remained in charge, and what had started as a training-ground rumpus turned into a national scandal. But while it went too far, it had all been started by a moment of insensitivity. I feel Blakey should have played much more often when he eventually returned to the international squad while Mark Hughes was in charge. He had so much to offer – he was big, strong, quick and could use both feet – but it didn't work out that way. In the end, he will be remembered as the player who scored the first goal for Wales in the Millennium Stadium – unfortunately, it was an own goal against Finland.

Under Bobby, travelling with Wales always became a jolly-up. I felt he didn't show me respect, but the feeling was pretty mutual. It was always going to be hard for Bobby Gould to tell Mark Hughes how to hold up the ball. Who could? If managers have been players of limited ability, as

Bobby had been, they often face an uphill struggle when they try to coach real talent, but some of them can still manage to get the best out of their teams, as the likes of Arsène Wenger and José Mourinho have shown. I am sure all the senior Welsh players went into the new set-up with an open mind, but the early impressions were rarely favourable.

There was one very embarrassing and disturbing incident involving Gould and myself at the end of a training session prior to the World Cup qualifier against Turkey in December 1996. By then he knew I didn't like the way he was going about his job, and I guess he had a similarly low opinion of me. It was one of those sham situations you have in life when you have no option but to plod along tolerating each other. Credit to him, though, this time he had the guts to try to find a solution; although it was another eccentric, Crazy Gang stunt. 'Hold it,' he shouted at me. 'Hold it.'

He had turned to face me, right in front of the other players. Then he said, 'Right, John, you and me, let's have a fight.' I didn't know what to say or where to look. I was only twenty-one at the time, and here I was being challenged to a fight by a middle-aged bloke, who also happened to be my boss.

Gary Speed shouted, 'Go on, Harts!' I laughed, but inside I was panicking, thinking, I can't do it – I can't fight the gaffer. But all the TV people had gone and taken their cameras with them, and there were no newspapermen left at the Newport training centre, so there would have been no witnesses. Apparently this was a technique Bobby used at Wimbledon.

However, on this occasion a circle of players had already formed and they were all up for it. There was no way out. We came together, me and my boss, and in truth I just grabbed hold of him for two minutes. I didn't throw a punch or aim a kick. It was a grapple, a bit of fun, I suppose, although for me it was very serious. I knew I was getting into a scrap against a man in his fifties, but I could tell he was still strong. Maybe he sensed it could have become too heated because he suddenly said, 'Right, that's enough.' He wasn't hurt, although there were some scratches on his face and his hair was all over the place, but it was all so undignified. It was probably his way of saying, 'You've had your revenge. Are you happy now?' but it was weird, bizarre. If it was meant to be a bonding exercise, it certainly didn't work with me. We went on to draw the game 0–0, and ended up above only San Marino in the group, which also comprised Belgium and Holland. That point against Turkey was the only one we gained in the qualifiers apart from against San Marino.

That confrontation was typical of Bobby. The best way to describe his approach would be 'laddish'. Once he organised a video session for us which was meant to provide some insight or other into our tactics, but, unbeknown to Bobby, the video had been switched by Neville Southall, who substituted a porno film. It's an old standby, I know, but I can think of some managers who wouldn't have seen the funny side. Bobby loved it, of course, and he got plus points with us for that. There were a lot of young players in that squad – Robbie Savage, Mark Crossley, Andy Johnson and myself among them. We were nervous, but that made us laugh, and in a silly way it made us feel part of the company. That was one thing Bobby was good at – making everyone feel involved.

On another occasion he paired us off, and I was put with Sparky Hughes. The full squad was present and we were facing each other on chairs. It was great to be given the opportunity to ask Mark some serious questions. What was the Nou Camp like? How was it to play in front of Bryan Robson? What's it like having Alex Ferguson as your manager? In return he asked me about life at Arsenal. As far as I remember, Ian Rush was paired up with Andy Johnson, and Neville Southall was with Mark Crossley – the two goalkeepers together. It's possible that Bobby did it because he thought there were some barriers between the senior players and the youngsters, because he believed we weren't close enough as a group. He asked us to discuss certain things, like who were the best players we had played alongside. It was an interesting topic, as many of the squad were legends and had played with the very best, and it was informative for someone of my age. Ian Rush named Kenny Dalglish as his main man. He talked about his perception, his great runs and how brilliantly he could hold up the ball.

I can remember this as if it were yesterday. Mark Hughes nominated Bryan Robson, who was his skipper at Manchester United and in a different class for England. Dean Saunders named Paul McGrath at Aston Villa as the best he had every played alongside. When Bobby asked me, I nominated Ian Wright. I said that Wrighty could do everything: head, volley with both feet, he was quick, he made great runs, he was tough when he needed to be, he was a talker and for me he was world class. (Wrighty was phenomenal, but I could equally have nominated several players who were in that room: Ryan Giggs, Ian Rush or Mark Hughes. They were all outstanding footballers (Ryan still is, of course) and brilliant exponents of the game. I have played in the same team as them and acknowledge their ability as awesome.) Bobby said, 'Excellent.'

It was then his turn to nominate the player he considered the best he has ever worked with. Remember there were some world-class footballers in the room, players who had become millionaires because of their talent. I can't recall who he named, but it definitely wasn't anybody in the room, and I felt strongly that it should have been. This is an example of Bobby Gould's attitude and an indication of why he was so hapless. Eventually Dean Saunders just said, 'Hey, what time's dinner?' and we all filed out.

Why did Bobby respond like that when he could have said, 'The best player I've worked with is sitting right here in this room – Ryan Giggs. At this moment, Ryan, you are the best player on the planet. You are the number one for me'? He could have named Ian Rush, with his three hundred goals for Liverpool. But instead he left himself wide open because of his ill-considered answer. It was absolutely typical of Bobby to do that when he had a perfect opportunity to praise a world-class Welshman to the Welsh national team. My other managers would never have made a mistake like that. Martin O'Neill would have used the opportunity to name someone like George Best or John Robertson, and then he would have explained to everyone why they were so good.

As you might already have gathered from the way he egged me on during my training-ground fight with Bobby, Gary Speed was not shy about speaking his mind. But his most serious run-in with the manager came in the dressing room after we had been beaten 4–0 by Tunisia in a humiliating summer friendly in June 1998. We had just beaten Malta 3–0, but our shocker against Tunisia rounded off a hat-trick of disastrous results: in November 1996 we lost 7–0 to Holland, and then in August 1997 we lost 6–4 to Turkey, both in World Cup qualifiers. During the build-up to the game against Holland, Bobby Gould had us in hysterics when he decided we should have a game of charades to relax. Because of his bushy eyebrows and mass of hair, when he stood up to begin his mime someone shouted K9, after the dog in *Doctor Who*. Suddenly everything had a canine theme: *Teen Wolf, 101 Dalmatians, American Werewolf in London*. Still the calls kept coming as the rest of us were crying with laughter, until he eventually realised why we were laughing and sat down.

You can imagine how low morale had got by that stage, after two years of poor results: to lose 4–0 against Tunisia seemed as low as we could go. That tour had gone ahead despite the fact that several key players were not available, and we had suffered as a result. Gary Speed had had enough, and launched into an attack on Gould, complaining about his tactics, training methods and all the rest; it was an emotional, passionate outburst.

Even in those circumstances I learned good things about many of the people around me. Barry Horne was a tremendous skipper and we all had respect for him. He would sort things out for us, smooth the way for golf days and the like. That sort of attitude is much more important than you'd imagine. There can be a lot of boredom when you are travelling as part of an international squad, so it definitely helps when someone arranges ways of countering it. But, if anything, it was too easy: you would enjoy turning up for trips because you would have a week in the sun. If we were playing in Italy, we would sunbathe on the beach until a couple of days before the game. In terms of taking Welsh football to where it should have been, it was a joke. We were treading water, waiting for the new manager to come in, which Mark Hughes did after we were defeated by Italy in a European Championship qualifier in June 1999. We lost 4–0, yet another drubbing. It was Bobby Gould's last game in charge and the end of a sad era.

One of the reasons why international football is usually so rewarding is the knowledge that everyone in your country is backing you. They want you to win; they want you to be successful. Being involved in international competition is the quickest way to raise the spirits, to make you feel good about both yourself and your country. I don't see it as straightforward nationalism, but pride in where you come from. Unfortunately, Wales last qualified for a World Cup finals in 1958, and we have never qualified for the European

Championship finals. But that doesn't mean we haven't been trying.

Too many people denigrate the value of international football. Many big clubs see it as an annoyance which interrupts their season and may cost them the use of their best players through injury. That, admittedly, could be the difference between success and failure in major domestic and European club competitions, but how often does such a situation actually occur? Very rarely.

There have been arguments for condensing the international season into just one month each summer, say in June. That would mean having to play all your World Cup or European Championship qualifiers in one hectic thirty-day campaign, and playing in the finals a year later. It could be done, but it seems to me that it would be putting the demands of the few ahead of the preferences of a far greater majority who enjoy playing and watching international football. I am one of those who believe in the value of international football for a number of reasons. As a Welshman, I identify with Wales; as a professional sportsman, I wanted to represent my country; and, as a spectator, I remember the thrill, the feeling of excitement and anticipation, that used to sweep over me when I watched those red shirts representing me in the days before I pulled on the jersey myself. Maybe coming from a minority in these islands gives me a greater sense of identity with my national team. It was always my ambition to follow in the footsteps of the players I idolised – like Ian Rush and Mark Hughes – and those I was told about, such as the great

John Charles. It was important in my community to know and admire these players for their ability, because their achievements reflected on us all. To emulate them was the great motivating factor in my life.

In contrast to Bobby Gould, Terry Yorath is a prime example of someone I could relate to, partly because he had played and managed at the highest level. I was in the senior squad under Terry and Mike Smith, and it was Mike who gave me my full debut against Bulgaria in Sofia at the age of nineteen. We lost 3–1, although I made our goal for Dean Saunders. Mike, like Terry, had a professional attitude which was acceptable to the players, and we always gave 100 per cent when we wore the red shirt for them. There are all sorts of reasons for our failure to qualify for the finals of the World Cup and the European Championships over the years, but lack of effort usually wasn't one of them.

Once Bobby had gone, we had some good years under Mark Hughes's management – memorable games that made us feel better about ourselves. We had so much to offer as an international team, so much to give to Wales, and we produced some excellent performances for Mark and for the country. In February 2002 we drew 1–1 with Argentina and a few months later beat Germany 1–0. Those were stirring results, and boosted our confidence, even if they were only friendlies, before the European Championship qualifying matches for the Portugal finals of 2004. We felt we were on the verge of something exciting, something to be proud of. Maybe we could achieve something that would be remembered and earn us the respect of our nation.

I think we were all in that mood as we went into our first qualifying tie in Finland on 7 September 2002, although we knew it was going to be difficult – the Finns are always fit and physical, a team capable of causing even the mightiest countries problems. We would be able to gauge our prospects from our performance, and more importantly the result, over there. We won 2–0 and I scored, so was doubly satisfied – for the team and for myself. Victory had been the target and we had achieved it with some style. When I am asked to name the most memorable match I have been involved in with Wales, I nominate that one against the Finns, because it gave us the flying start we needed. It might not have had the same cachet as getting a result against Germany or Argentina, but it confirmed to us how good we were and how much we could achieve in the coming campaign. We had a manager who knew what he was doing and players who could fulfil his demands.

After Finland we met Italy in the Millennium Stadium in Cardiff on 16 October, and beat them 2–1. Simon Davies and Craig Bellamy got our goals, but this was one of those occasions when I really didn't care that I hadn't scored. It was a night as emotional as any I have ever known. The singing, the delight of a Welsh crowd in full voice, is unique. There is nothing like it in the world of sport – it is sophisticated, uplifting and dripping with passion. We were to provide the fans with a few more occasions like that. Azerbaijan were next: 0–2 to Wales and this time I scored. We were rolling. The headlines were on our side. We were no longer

a joke, a team without hope, but one with a chance of qualifying for a major tournament for the first time since the
days of the great John Charles in 1958, when we lost to
Pelé's Brazil in the quarter-finals of the World Cup. The
whole country had been behind the national side back then,
and it was such an honour to be part of a winning team in
the modern era.

We went on to draw 2–2 in a friendly with Bosnia-
Herzegovina in February 2003, then hammered Azerbaijan
4–0 in Cardiff a month later to maintain a run of four wins
in four qualifiers. Fantastic. We could hardly *not* qualify
now. But sadly, unbelievably, cruelly, the optimism we had
created disappeared all too quickly. After winning twelve
points out of twelve to top Group 9, we finished with just
thirteen points. We lost some crucial games, 4–0 in the return
against Italy and home and away to Serbia-Montenegro,
and we drew with Finland at home. We were gutted. We
had seats booked at the top table, but we couldn't make the
date. Nevertheless, it remains a significant campaign for
me. Nobody could challenge our effort or our ability. It was
just our timing that was wrong. We were the best-supported
nation in Europe, regularly playing in front of bigger crowds
than England, Italy and Germany. Every game we played in
Cardiff was in front of a Millennium crowd of not less than
70,000. What support! England were playing to 45,000 in
the Stadium of Light; the Republic of Ireland had 30,000 or
so at Lansdowne Road; Scotland were performing in front
of paltry crowds at Hampden and Easter Road; Italy couldn't
muster a sellout at the San Siro. In the end we came second

in the group and played off with Russia. We drew in 0–0 Moscow, which was a marvellous performance, but then sickeningly lost 1–0 at home to the 'cheats from the east'.

The build-up to the play-off ties was extraordinary. There was a week of it. We played in Russia on the Saturday in the freezing cold and snow and it was all set up for us at the Millennium for the following Wednesday. We weren't complacent after the away result, there was no wild belief that we had already earned our place in the finals, Mark Hughes made sure of that, but we failed and I can't really offer a reason why. Mark said very little afterwards. What could he say? He just thanked us for our effort and that was it – all over. How do you cope as the manager, as a player, as a fan? It was devastating for all of us. I would say it was one of the biggest disappointments of my career, up there with missing a penalty in the FA Cup quarter-final against Arsenal, and missing one for Celtic (of which more later). It was a very sad and bitter changing room after the game. We had come as close as any Welsh team to qualifying for the European Championship finals and we had let it slip.

Compounding our disappointment was the fact that the Russians had included a player who should never have been allowed on the pitch. After the match we tried to get into the finals by the back door when it was revealed that Egor Titov, who came on as a sub in Cardiff, had earlier failed a drugs test. It was a scandal, and we felt that Russia should have been thrown out of the competition. No chance. UEFA's rules state that the team cannot be deemed responsible for the drug-taking of an individual. How can that be? Surely they are culpable if they play someone they know has taken drugs, and the Russians knew all about Titov's indiscretion. Mark Hughes was rightly furious and he fronted our appeals to UEFA, which were turned down twice. We were left to sit at home and watch the finals in Portugal on TV while the Russians got to play in them. Without Titov, of course: he was banned for twelve months and given a hefty fine, but that was no consolation to us.

Sparky moved on in 2004 to spread his managerial talent at club level. He would confirm his reputation as an outstanding manager at Blackburn. They were lucky to get him. One day he will progress to an even bigger club, and I am as certain as I can be that he will eventually be hailed as one of the all-time great managers. He is like a young Alex Ferguson and similar to Martin O'Neill in his approach. He's in that class and always manages to get the best out of his players. He turned Wales around, gave us back our professionalism. He himself had been brought up in a Welsh team full of first-class players. They had known how to enjoy themselves, just as we did, but they also knew what the limits had to be. So when he took over, Mark didn't stop us having an occasional drink, a little R and R, but it would always be on his terms. He had the stature to take command on the training field because he had been a great striker, but it was his ability to deal with players, to man-manage them and explain precisely what he expected of them that really won us over. His tactical knowledge – his footballing intuition, if you like – was near perfect. We played to a 4–5–1 system with me as his front man. I played that role for him in all but one game while he was in charge. Towards the end of his reign I had a very poor game against England in a World Cup qualifier at the Millennium when we lost to a Joe Cole goal. I paid the price by being left out for the next match in Poland. Sparky was right to drop me – I wasn't cutting it and my fitness wasn't what it should have been – and he was good enough to explain his reasons for leaving me out. To play two games in three days at international level is tough and requires a standard of fitness I simply didn't have at that moment.

Our best team would have Paul Jones in goal, Mark Delaney at right back, and Danny Gabbidon and Alan Melville as the two centre backs. There was a lot of experience there, as well as the younger legs of Gabbidon. Gary Speed was generally played at left back rather than in his usual Premiership position in midfield. The three central midfielders were Mark Pembridge, Robbie Savage and Simon Davis, who would have a certain amount of freedom to float. Then we had two sensational talents on the left and right wings: Ryan Giggs and Craig Bellamy. That left me up front, with the others coming forward to support whenever they could. So when we attacked it was 4–3–3 and when we defended 4–5–1. Sparky told me, 'Just get yourself on the halfway line and we will have ten people behind the ball, then they'll have to break us down.' When we attacked we threw men forward: Davis, Bellamy, Giggs, Savage and Pembridge supporting me. It was a great system for us because we had good players with height, physical presence and commitment. Sparky knew our strengths and knew how to play to them individually and to the benefit of the team. We trained hard, but he let us relax at the right times.

I thoroughly enjoyed my international career when Sparky was the boss and see it now as a great experience, especially in light of the way things had gone under the previous regime. The natural reaction is to say we didn't get what we deserved, particularly where Euro 2004 is concerned, but a more honest assessment would be that we got exactly that. I would never want to criticise Sparky, he's my hero and I love the man and his style, but perhaps tactically he could have done things a little differently. In the latter stages of some games I think we should have been more offensive, taken a few more chances. But who am I to criticise a man who took us so close? We should have done the business against the Russians in Cardiff, no matter who was in their team, and we failed.

When John Toshack took over in 2004 as manager for the second time, qualifying for the European Championships of 2008 was his target. I was prepared to give him my full commitment, and I did for a time, even though my personal life was in crisis. Representing Wales had always been a matter of considerable pride to me, so when I decided to quit in February 2006 I was very upset by all the criticism I received. I felt I had no option but to say I would not be available for the 2008 European Championship campaign because by then my marriage was in the process of unravelling completely and, at the age of thirty-one, I also had to consider how best to plan for what remained of my club career. I had been a regular in the Wales set-up since the age of fourteen and constantly since eighteen, when I was first selected for the Under-21s. I had won fifty-one senior caps and scored fourteen goals. I did it because of the honour of representing my country; and money certainly didn't come into it, because the Welsh FA is hardly the richest in the world. We were never on the sort of appearance money and bonuses England players receive. We turned up for the shirt and £300 in expenses per match. (Although, admittedly, we would have received more if we had qualified for the finals of a major tournament: if we had reached the European Championships in Portugal, for instance, the squad that had been rejuvenated by Sparky would have shared £1.3 million.)

Of course, my decision to leave international football was a big one, but I felt I had sacrificed a lot of my personal life to play for my country. I don't begrudge one second of that, but it irked me when, a few days after acknowledging and accepting my reasons for standing down, Toshack went public and said that I was more or less past it anyway. There was no need for that. I had played up front for five years on my own. Ask any centre forward what that's like: it's the hardest job in football to have your back to goal and battle for every ball with defenders who are taking it in turns to batter you. You basically give yourself up for the team in every match. Mark Hughes had asked me to do that for him and appreciated that I did it while never once complaining. I was disappointed not to receive similar respect from John Toshack.

I don't consider myself to be finished with Wales. My retirement was official and it was accepted, but there is nothing to stop me changing my mind. I would like to play for another three years at the highest possible level. I think I can achieve that with my club side, and if I am in good enough physical shape I could do so for Wales, too. I decided to stand down because I felt I would be incapable of devoting enough time to international duties because of my family situation. I didn't want to lose any more quality time with my children now that they are living with their mother in Cardiff. International football often extends far beyond the domestic season, leaving the players with only the shortest of summer breaks and I was worried there would be too little time for me to share with Rebeca and Joni. That is no longer a concern.

chapter 12

One of the Bhoys

My knowledge of Glasgow in the summer of 2001 was restricted to one experience with Rangers that I wouldn't inflict on a dog. But that was before I signed for Celtic, and before I got to know how things work and what the people would expect of me in this great city on the banks of the River Clyde. When you come to terms with that, and accept Glasgow's pace of life, then you are hooked.

I spent five amazing, bizarre, sad, funny, occasionally fearful but mainly hugely enjoyable years in the middle of it all. I can't think of too many cities that I could call my ideal, but Glasgow is. Football stems from the working class, and there is no city on earth that is more so than Glasgow. But it's working class with style, panache. To use a word that's not heard much these days, it's chic. It has outstanding restaurants and fashion boutiques (some of them miles ahead of London when it comes to innovation), fantastic art collections and museums, stunning buildings when you look up instead of down at your feet. There is a dignity about the place which makes it enormously impressive: it is a city of distinction. But it still has that hard edge, and it took time for me to learn the art of survival without too much confrontation. Once it's learned, though, it's never forgotten.

Glasgow has a reputation as a violent city, which I am told dates back to a more depressing, deprived age. I have never seen it as any more dangerous than other places I know – my home town of Swansea, Cardiff and London, for example – but there are some other elements that are unique for a British city. For a start, there is a verbal aggression that takes strangers by surprise; it is a trait that reminds me of Paris or New York. The Glaswegian does not hang back when it comes to the verbals, and he has the voice for it – when raised in anger it can sound very harsh, to my Welsh ears at least. If you are looking for trouble, you will surely be able to find it in Glasgow; and I imagine even if you aren't looking for it, you might be unlucky and it might still find you.

But the main reason why Glasgow is so different to other British cities is the continued importance of religion. You just can't avoid it: you are either Catholic or Protestant, and that determines whether you follow Celtic or Rangers. What I knew about religion before I joined Celtic was restricted to visiting church as a child, at my mother's insistence, probably about two or three times a month to sing a few hymns. I am not a Catholic, and I didn't even know the difference between the two religions until I signed for Celtic. I learned very quickly! In Glasgow, when you play for the Old Firm, you are either an 'Orange bastard' or a

'Fenian bastard'. Like everyone else who lives or works in Glasgow, I now know exactly what these terms mean. When I first went shopping in the city centre (I rarely did latterly), I was astonished to be greeted by shouts of 'Fenian bastard' or, alternatively, a thumbs-up and the cry of 'Stick it up those dirty Orange bastards'. And these were probably the least offensive words you heard. I am not making a judgement on either faction, merely describing what I, as a Welshman who was initially ignorant of Glasgow's great divide, have seen and heard over the last few years.

It is difficult for new players. First, you don't believe it; then you don't understand it; and finally you learn to cope and perhaps even comprehend a little of what makes up such a vital part of life for some people in the city. The irony is that, football apart, it does not impact greatly on most of the city's population. Catholics work with Protestants every day in Glasgow; Catholics sometimes even marry Protestants. But for a sizeable minority on both sides there is a very real animosity. It exists and it can't be disguised, although I am told it is much less pronounced than it was in the past. Still, if you walk to Celtic Park or Ibrox on an Old Firm match day, you certainly never have the feeling that the opposing fans are wishing each other good hunting.

This extreme form of rivalry has affected me and my family, as well as my team-mates, some of whom have received threats that have led to a lot of stress. But I don't want to paint a picture of constant harassment, because that has not been the case. Any tension has always been sporadic, and I have had many good meetings with fans from the other side. For instance, on the night I scored the goal against Hearts that clinched the title for Celtic in 2006, I was out celebrating with some friends and we met many Rangers supporters in the various bars and clubs we visited. I would say that 90 per cent of them wished me luck and congratulated me. The other 10 per cent said nothing. None of them would have enjoyed Celtic's title success, but they had the good grace not to acknowledge that in my company. I have two friends who are 'Rangers mad' but who wouldn't think of verbally abusing any Celtic player they happened to meet, although I am sure they are far more vociferous at Old Firm matches. That's the way it is in Glasgow, for the majority.

Alex McLeish, the former Rangers manager, once told me that if he had been in charge of the club when I failed the medical for them, he would have gone ahead and signed me anyway. I appreciate him going out of his way to tell me that. I have no hatred of Rangers, although the way the regime that was in charge at the time treated me over my so-called bad knee still rankles. I just happen to like putting one over them because they are Celtic's main rivals. It's not my style to try to rile any of my fellow professionals, no matter who they play for. I always try to be as pleasant as I can be to everyone, but that can be difficult when you sense the anger, the bitterness, that comes across when you meet certain people. When it happens you must just turn away.

When I arrived in Glasgow to start my career at Celtic, I suppose you could call me naïve. I wasn't interested in religion and I didn't give a damn about what the city and its citizens demanded of me. All I was concerned about was playing football and rebuilding my career with a manager in Martin O'Neill, who I liked from the outset, at a club I knew to be one of the greatest in world football. I was installed in a hotel in the West End of Glasgow for the signing. The official date for that was 2 August 2001. The transfer from Coventry had cost Celtic £6 million and I was determined to repay every penny with goals. As I said earlier, Martin and the team were in Manchester for Ryan Giggs' testimonial and I watched the match on television. It was the first occasion I had been able to concentrate on Celtic both as a unit and as a team of individuals, and I was impressed: they beat United 4–3, which was a fair indication to me that I had joined a team of resolve and considerable ability. The anticipation and excitement that have remained with me ever since began that night.

I was joining a team that already had a potent strike force in Henrik Larsson and Chris Sutton. They had scored sixty-six goals between them the previous season, when Celtic had lifted the domestic treble of Premiership, League Cup and Tennant's Scottish Cup. It was a fabulous season, particularly as it was Martin O'Neill's first in charge. He had turned his back on a successful career in English football to take over at a club that had been languishing in the wake of Rangers for far too long. It would have been acceptable had he demanded time to settle in, but that is not Martin's way: if he wants it, he goes for it right from the off. But even so, winning all three domestic honours in his first season was a fantastic, almost freakish, achievement. The main ingredient of success was Henrik's record-breaking fifty-three goals. Chris weighed in with thirteen, despite suffering a series of injuries. These two formidable players were to be my partners.

My arrival confused many of our supporters, who were asking, 'Why the hell do we need him?' The majority Celtic opinion was that I would hardly get a game, so why pay so much money for me? I suppose it didn't make much sense to them as they had seen Henrik and Chris in such brilliant form, scoring almost at will all season. But if the fans were dubious, there was no trouble from the players, who made me feel very welcome. That was the kind of support I needed, because the media applied pressure on me from the start. They looked at me as a player with a history of joining clubs and moving on quickly, but that was definitely not my mentality when I joined Celtic. They seemed to forget I needed Celtic, I needed goals, I needed to be a winner. It was important for me to fit into the team quickly, seamlessly, to win over the fans and show I was a major-club player. To achieve all that, first I had to cement my place in the team. Fortunately Martin O'Neill had guaranteed me a run in the side, which had been a vital assurance to me, but something that most managers would never be prepared to offer a new signing. It was my first experience of Martin O'Neill's single-mindedness: he did everything his way. I hadn't joined a club where the strikers were ordinary, run-of-the-mill, so I needed to know I would be given a reasonable opportunity to claim a position in the team. Basically, I had to outperform one of two top-class international strikers who were treated like gods by the Celtic support; particularly Henrik, who was an exceptional player back then and, judging by his brilliant performance as a sub against Arsenal in the 2006 European Champions League final, is still a wondrous talent.

I did not get off to a flying start: it would be eleven appearances before I scored my first goal, after making my debut at Kilmarnock on 4 August 2001. That dry period led to considerable frustration and I started to feel that I was letting the fans down. The newspapers never let me forget I was having trouble finding that first goal, and I thought their attitude was unfair. They would count a ten-minute run-out as a sub as an appearance, which technically it is, but it hardly gives you much of a chance to get on the score sheet. Only a small proportion of those first ten appearances were starts, so although I felt disappointed for the fans, I never once lost confidence in my own ability. I knew the goals would come and I was not prepared to let self-doubt eat into my psyche. My failure to find the net certainly wasn't through lack of trying. I came to the conclusion that I was just in one of those spells that come to all strikers sooner or later: it just wasn't my time to score. On one occasion, playing against Aberdeen in September, I hit a great half-volley which inched past the post. That sums it up: I was either unlucky or the goalkeeper played a blinder against me.

The drought ended spectacularly when I hit a hat-trick at Celtic Park on 20 October against Dundee United. We won 5–1 and the stadium went wild that day. It was a remarkable experience for me. I had seen our fans in action at previous matches, but this was a real celebration and I felt like an important part of it, the focal point perhaps; although over time I learned that the club, not any individual, is everything for Celtic fans. Those three goals were the turning point. I had started to feel the pressure, but Martin O'Neill had kept faith in me, and this was the reward for our persistence. He had watched me score in training, where I was doing everything he asked of me, and now I was starting to pay back his investment where it really mattered.

By the end of the season I had established a significant relationship with Henrik and Chris, as well as with Neil Lennon, Alan Thompson and the rest of Martin O'Neill's Premiership-winning side. But there were a couple of glitches on the way to my first title. One that I still remember vividly was a penalty I missed in the League Cup semi-final against Rangers; and it was also Rangers who blocked our classic double of SPL and SFA Cup. When you miss a spot kick and you are on the losing side, the feeling of inadequacy hits you like a hammer blow to the head. When it happens and Rangers are the opposition it's nothing short of a catastrophe. That was my fate on 5 February 2002. All I needed to do was strike the ball with accuracy and power and we would be on level terms, and would probably take the tie to a replay. I wasn't Celtic's regular penalty-taker, that was Henrik's job, but he had been out for a few games and I had been nominated in his absence. I half thought he would take over for this one, but Henrik being Henrik, he threw me the ball to me and said, 'You take it, John.' That is a generous gesture, striker to striker: he was guaranteeing me a goal that he could have added to his own tally . . . or so he would have thought. Unfortunately, I blew it. When it comes to penalties I believe there should only ever be one outcome – a goal scored. You should never miss the target or give the goalkeeper *any* chance of saving your shot. It should always be past him, out of his reach. So why did I miss on this occasion? I have no idea. But I can tell you one thing: I felt rotten.

We had fancied ourselves for another treble, but now that was gone. However, the main prize, the Premiership title, would be ours in time to relax and prepare for the Scottish Cup final, another chance to put one over Rangers. They say the Scottish Cup is a poor second to England's FA Cup, but it is no less important to the teams who take part. It is always good to win, as a national cup can set you up for a European campaign the following season if you haven't already secured that with your league position. Celtic generally finish high enough in the SPL (often winning it) for that not to be a factor, but this time we were chasing the double, and with it confirmation of our complete mastery of the Scottish game. That was still open to some debate, because we had not dominated Rangers as we had hoped we would that season. The final would be our sixth meeting, but we had won just two and lost one of the previous five. In these circumstances, and pride being the best possible incentive, all the indications were that this last meeting of the season, on 4 May 2002, would be special. I scored to put us in front, but the Dane, Peter Lovenkrands, equalised. Bobo Balde gave us the edge again, but this time Rangers' captain Barry Ferguson got them back into it. Lovenkrands then finished us off as cruelly as possible with a winner right on the final whistle. The neutrals say it was a great match to watch, much better than the average Old Firm clash, which is generally played at a frantic pace as the players react to the emotion and demand for victory that emanates from the supporters. That was no comfort to us, though, and the disappointment was intense, as it always is when we lose to Rangers – which, thankfully, was a rare occurrence in my time at Celtic Park. It doesn't matter to me if I score and we are beaten: I suffer with everybody else because there is no compensation for defeat, no adequate excuses that can be offered.

Setting aside those two matches – and wouldn't I like to! – I had begun to feel I had sprouted wings again, that I was capable of achieving my target, which was to win every prize on offer at home and in Europe. My Wales career was back on track since Mark Hughes had taken charge, and I was performing week in, week out in front of an audience that I am certain is second to none. I was also part of the European scene and loving it. We played ten European ties, winning five and losing five. We beat Ajax, José Mourinho's Porto and Rosenborg; even more impressively, we overcame Juventus 4–3 in a super tie at Parkhead that I missed. But I was back for our 1–0 win against Valencia in Glasgow. Although these were enjoyable victories, we didn't have the all-round consistency that was required to progress in the Champions League and we failed to qualify for the final stages. However, we had established a base camp for the next season, and we would go all the way to the UEFA Cup final and another meeting with Mourinho's team in Seville.

Those European nights provide some outstanding memories for me, but the one I savour most was the win at Parkhead that clinched my first title. The crowd produced an atmosphere that can genuinely be described as 'electric'. We beat Livingston 5–1, with Henrik scoring a hat trick and me getting the other two. We had gone through the entire season with just one SPL defeat – the 2–0 loss at Aberdeen in Christmas week – which gave us an eighteen-point gap to Rangers, in second place. I wanted that title, I wanted to be able to say I was part of a championship-winning squad, and we were so good that I saw no reason why we couldn't go on and on for the foreseeable future. My personal tally was twenty-four goals in all competitions, nineteen of them in the SPL. (Henrik scored twenty-nine in SPL games.) We felt formidable, almost unbeatable, although I could have done without the red cards which came late in the season: against Aberdeen, when I scored in a 2–0 victory; and in our 1–1 draw against Rangers, after which I was told my clashes with their Italian defender Lorenzo Amoruso created the same ghoulish interest as you often see at a road crash. At the time of writing, though, that is the last red card I have received.

More than anything else, the season highlighted Henrik's quality and the positive influence Martin O'Neill had on everything to do with the team. It might not have been conventional, but his management style was incredibly effective. Working with Martin also meant working with his right-

hand men – John Robertson, his friend from their Nottingham Forest days, and coach Steve Walford. Steve and I had
both played for Arsenal and West Ham, though not at the
same time. From the very first moment I met him, Martin
was full of fun and down to earth, just the sort of man I had
expected him to be. And I'd always liked Wally, as he was
easy to talk to and work with. We had similar backgrounds.
We would laugh about the Chicken Run at Upton Park, that
part of the ground where fans would stand and seemingly
do nothing but shout abuse at the players. None of us fancied having a bad game because the boys in the Chicken
Run would give you hell. I think Julian Dicks is just about
the only Hammers player who has never received stick from
that lot at some point. Partly because of that shared history,
I probably got on with Wally better than I did with Robbo.
That's not to say I disliked Robbo – I thought he was a good
man and his input with the manager was second to none.
They were very, very close, and I'm certain that Martin
trusted Robbo's judgement over anyone else's and took in
everything he said. Personally, though, I always felt more
comfortable talking to Wally on a one-to-one basis.

There were a lot of laughs and joking at Celtic, which
probably surprises those who see Martin as a manager who
rules by fear, is difficult to deal with, hard to talk to, a
strange fellow who can act like a madman on the touchline.
Well, the last part is undeniable, but for all his antics I can't
remember them ever having any effect on me when I was on
the pitch. It was only when I watched replays of matches on
television that I realised what people were talking about

when they referred to the dervish on the bench.

My first year at Celtic was a season of great achievement for me. I didn't know it at the time, but it would be my best season with the club. In subsequent years we would go on to win many more trophies, but I never enjoyed myself or was more satisfied than during my first ten months as one of the Bhoys.

chapter 13

Glory and Despair

We felt the tremors from Ibrox warning us that Rangers had regrouped and were going to be dangerous rivals as we prepared for the start of the 2002–03 season. They had both domestic cups on display in their trophy room across the city and would now consider themselves on a winning run. They no doubt expected their cup victories to provide the platform from which to launch their counter-attack to recover the SPL title. That said, we were the champions, and not just by a single goal or a single point, but by a considerable margin. There was no complacency as we prepared for the new season – that would have been unthinkable in a squad managed by O'Neill – but there was also no shortage of self-confidence and self-belief among the players. I was fit, 100 per cent fit, and as usual had spent a couple of weeks doing my pre-season fitness preparation with Tom Walley down in Watford. The nonsense about my bad knee – or was it knees? – was all behind me. Everything seemed good in my world and I was ready to take on all comers.

I foresaw a season of magnificent highs, but I did not

anticipate such gutting lows. It would be a season when we destroyed two of England's top teams, Blackburn and Liverpool; a season when I scored what I consider to be the best goal of my career; but a season which ended with me breaking down because of a back problem that could have finished my career. That bad back – which was not so much an injury as a medical condition, although in all probability partly caused by wear and tear on the football field – led to two major operations and would haunt me through this season and the next. It would develop in the months ahead, but I had no cares in the world as I began my second campaign as a Bhoy and scored in my first match of the season, our 5–0 drubbing of Dundee United. I had missed the opening matches against Dunfermline, Aberdeen, and FC Basle, whom we defeated 3–1 at Parkhead in the Champions League.

Our first setback came in the return against the Swiss club, led by the former Tottenham manager Christian Gross, when they beat us 2–0. That meant we failed to qualify for the Champions League proper (Basle went through on away goals) and had to settle for the UEFA Cup instead. The result was depressing for Celtic, but of more immediate concern to me was how bad my back was now feeling. I can't be certain when it started, but after a while it was always there, after every game. It didn't stop me playing, but it was a constant worry. I spoke to Doc Macdonald about it on numerous occasions, but it didn't manifest itself in a way which suggested to him that I needed surgical attention, at least not in the early stages. It still made me nervous, though, because it was one those problems that you just know will need an operation sooner or later. Nevertheless, I continued to meet all the physical demands that were made of me, albeit at times with considerable difficulty. I kept scoring, which put a smile on my face. But to give an idea of the state I was in before there was anything officially 'wrong' with me, I remember one occasion in the dressing room after a match when I turned to the doc and said, 'Do you mind undoing my bootlaces?' He looked shocked. 'Are you serious, big man?' he asked. 'You just scored. You've just played ninety minutes.' I was deadly serious. I couldn't bend far enough to take off my own boots!

After the disappointment of Basle we won five successive UEFA Cup ties. First we trounced FK Suduva 8–1 and 2–0, then we faced Blackburn Rovers in what was billed the 'Battle of Britain' or something crazy like that. With Graeme Souness, the former Rangers manager, now in charge at Ewood Park, the tie was given an extra spice it scarcely needed. I have to admit that they outplayed us at Parkhead, but through a bit of good luck we still managed to win 1–0. After the match Souness said it had been like 'men against boys', even though the boys had come out on top. Saying that was a serious error of judgement, and not only because it was unsporting. He had rattled our bars and we absolutely flattened them in the return leg at Blackburn. I had been an admirer of Souness as a player – remember, the Liverpool of his era were my team when I was a lad – but we all felt he shouldn't have said anything like that.

We had some momentum going now, and Celta Vigo

were next in our line of fire. Again we sneaked a 1–0 win at Parkhead, and in the return we lost 2–1, but that meant the away goals rule worked in our favour this time. In the next round I missed the first leg against Stuttgart, which we won 3–1 in Glasgow. Despite then losing 3–2 in Germany, we had once again done enough to progress. Now we were up against Liverpool. It is important, vital, for a club like Celtic to test itself outside domestic competition. It is hard to imagine a greater occasion than an Old Firm match, but when you take on the English that takes it into another dimension. Blackburn had earned their place in the UEFA Cup and we had comprehensively beaten them, tactically and through our pace and endeavour. We ripped them apart, murdered them, at Ewood Park, but in spite of that once again we were the underdogs against Liverpool, unrated. The message coming up from England was that we would be put in our place this time. That turned out to be another error of judgement.

We drew 1–1 in Glasgow and headed for Anfield and our 'inevitable' elimination. Well, it wasn't inevitable if you were a Celtic fan, if you were steeped in the club and its tradition. We accepted that overcoming Liverpool on their home turf was going to be a massive obstacle. Think of all the great European matches that have been played in front of the Kop and then work out how many teams have played there and come away with a win. We didn't need the exact statistics – we knew that very few had been good enough to do it. There would be 45,000 inside the ground and the Kop would be swaying. Celtic normally take at least 15,000 to matches in England, but we were restricted to an allocation of 2,700 for this one. Undoubtedly a few more than that managed to get inside the ground, but they were still vastly outnumbered by the Liverpool support. It didn't matter: they sounded like 50,000 to us.

Emile Heskey had scored at Parkhead, and although Henrik had kept us in the tie with his goal, Liverpool still had the advantage of an away goal. They would be at full strength, minus El-Hadji Diouf, who was dropped from the firing line after disgracefully spitting at one of our fans in the first match. But that hardly dented their quality: they still boasted Heskey, Michael Owen, Jamie Carragher, Dietmar Hamann, Steven Gerrard – the list went on and on. Yet we beat them on their own patch in front of their own fans. It has to be one of the greatest results in Celtic's history.

For me personally, it was also the stage where I scored the best goal of my career (so far). There are times when you do things on a football field that give you immense satisfaction, even though nobody else notices them. It could be something like a different role agreed between just yourself and the manager that turns out to benefit the team. He sees that you have carried out his instructions to the letter and is happy, even while everyone else is asking what the hell you were doing. On other occasions, though, your contribution is more obvious. Those are the times when everything just clicks, and it clicked for me that night at Anfield. Alan Thompson had already given us a deserved lead. We had taken the game to them and Tommo had made victory a very real possibility. But Liverpool were digging ever deeper for an equaliser, so without being reckless we needed to look for a second, knowing that would surely finish them off. The chance came when I went to collect a long ball from our keeper, Rab Douglas. I was fouled by Sami Hyypia, but the foul wasn't recognised by the referee, so when it wasn't given I played a quick one–two with Henrik. Getting the return pass, I dropped my shoulder and touched the ball past Dietmar Hamann. I thought it was rolling perfectly for me, so I just cracked it as hard as I could and watched it fly into the top corner. I must have been about thirty yards out. It was some feeling. My mum and dad were in the crowd, behind the goal. They told me later that people were picking them up and shaking their hands; that they wanted my dad's autograph and for both of them to pose for pictures. They were like, 'Bloody hell, we don't want any of this – we've just come to watch our boy play.' But that's the esteem they were held in on the night; that's how good these fans of ours are.

Alan Thompson and I were interviewed after the game for television. I said Liverpool had always been my club and mentioned that I was friendly with their former manager Roy Evans. Roy has a place in Spain that's on the same development as mine and we had worked together with Wales. He has known of my allegiance to Liverpool from way back when, and as I mentioned earlier, he came close to signing me when he was in charge of the Reds. My links to the club only increased the satisfaction I derived from the goal. You could say that the match against Liverpool was just another game, but to all of the Celtic players that night, and to me in particular, it was much more than that. Aside from anything else, we had taken Celtic to the semi-final of a major European competition for the first time in years. The disappointment of losing to Basle was finally erased.

We were to face Boavista of Portugal in the semis. Once again we could only draw 1–1 at Parkhead, making it difficult for ourselves in the return leg. In European competition, with the away goals rule coming into play so often, it is usually vital that you do not let your opponents score on your home turf. If they do, you know you face an uphill battle. But I suppose an eternal optimist would say that the result at Parkhead simplified matters for us: if we won in Portugal, we knew we were through. And that was exactly what we did. Henrik Larsson scored and we beat them 0–1. It was a fabulous victory.

European nights are great for the players and the fans of every football team, and they make a big contribution to clubs' finances. But our supporters' reaction to European competition was extraordinary by anyone's standards. If you are brought up in Glasgow then I suppose you are used to the fanaticism, but for a newcomer like myself it took my breath away. Even when the team was in a slump, as Celtic were when Rangers were winning title after title in the nineties, the fans kept coming. They made every game an occasion with their vast numbers and incredible enthusiasm. For the players, they are like a massive green-and-white back-up squad. There is a direct link between supporter and player, which is why we spent so much time with them. We owed it to them. When we went overseas to play a European

tie there were always hundreds of fans at the airport alongside the press and TV people. It jolts you, makes you realise
exactly what your responsibility is. It is often said that fans
can be an extra man to a team, and with Celtic that is no
exaggeration. The stadium itself can be an asset, too.
Footballers are brought up on tradition, and most will have
a strong connection with certain stadiums. It may be a childhood memory, such as the way I was awestruck by Anfield:
the noise, the celebrations, the intensity of watching
Liverpool play on television left an indelible impression on
me. It could have been the Nou Camp, the Maracana, the
Nep in Budapest, the Olympic Stadium in Munich, the
Bernabeu, the Millennium Stadium in Cardiff, Wembley,
Hampden or Ibrox. When you play in these theatres you
expect to be involved in something above the norm, and that
applies even when the clubs who call them home are less of
a force than they once were. Parkhead is Celtic's citadel, and
I can confirm from speaking to opposing players that they
have great respect for all it stands for. They respect the club's
tradition and count it as an honour to perform in the stadium. I have no experience of what it was like in the days of
the great Jock Stein and his Lisbon Lions, but although the
stadium has been modernised, the fans remain the same. I
was told from the beginning that they would expect 100 per
cent effort from me in every match, and that they would
hound out anybody who did not try hard enough for their
team. I don't think I could ever be accused of that, but the
very thought of a Parkhead crowd turning against a player
should have them shaking in their boots.

Parkhead is a prime example of how to improve a great old stadium by transforming it into a modern one without spending millions. In mid-season, when the cold creates a mist, the floodlights are on and the crowd is singing, it is spectacular. If you can play and you are confident, there is no finer stage to create good memories. Mark Hughes came to watch me once at Parkhead when he was manager of Wales. It was his first experience of an Old Firm clash. He was invited to make the half-time draw on the pitch, and afterwards he told me, 'I had butterflies, John, I really did.'

I replied, 'You're Mark Hughes! You have played for Manchester United and Barcelona and you still have butterflies?'

'I know,' he said. 'It was just the atmosphere. Unbelievable.'

That kind of atmosphere played its part in pushing us onwards in the UEFA Cup. There is no doubt it helped us make the final against Porto in Seville.

By the time that match came around, though, my back problem – now diagnosed as a classic disc rupture – was so serious that the alarm bells were clanging in my head. It wasn't so much what the surgeons told me (they were nearly always positive), but a self-imposed pessimism which would have overwhelmed me if I had succumbed to it completely. A disc problem is bad enough to deal with for the man in the street. For a professional sportsman, it is like a death sentence on your career. It won't kill you, but it can destroy your life as a footballer and therefore your lifestyle. At its worst, it can reduce locomotion to a shuffle. I have seen players who couldn't beat it and were constantly on painkillers, which alleviated the pain momentarily, but didn't effect a cure. It had been niggling away at me virtually all season. The medical men couldn't be certain how it had started because it may have been any form of movement, perhaps even something that at the time had seemed relatively minor.

Doc Macdonald had kept me in his sights to see how it would develop and had talked me through it. When it had been no more than an inconvenience there had been no need to panic – a question of 'just keep taking the tablets', which in my case were anti-inflammatories. I can't say I struggled through our early and mid-season programme, nor do I consider myself a hypochondriac, but it was constantly in my thoughts. In football, like the theatre, you are expected to perform virtually no matter what the cost, but while 'the show must go on' theory is fine, there eventually comes a point when you have to say 'enough is enough'. With a bad back, the symptoms leave you in little doubt when you have reached that point. When you can't walk, you can't play; when you cannot stand up, you know drastic measures have to be taken.

I had played in our win against Boavista on 24 April 2003. Henrik's brilliant goal had sent Celtic into the club's first European final since 1970, when they were beaten in the final of the old-style European Cup by Feyenoord. We were delirious that night in Portugal and now all of us should have been able to enjoy the run-up to the final. We knew we would meet Porto, difficult opposition but not insurmountable, but first we had to work our way through a few domestic matches that would go a long way to deciding the Premiership between Rangers and ourselves. We believed it should have been ours, but Rangers kept going, kept hanging in there, and we were their visitors at Ibrox three days after the Boavista match. I scored in our 1–2 victory and was subbed after seventy-five minutes. There were no special problems, just the usual back niggle, which anyway had been numbed a bit by the joy of scoring. My dad had travelled up from Wales for the match and we went for a couple of beers afterwards. Neither of us had any idea what was about to happen next. I didn't have a late night, but when I woke up in the morning I couldn't move, literally. I felt like I was nailed to the mattress. If I tried to move, I immediately went into spasm and the pain was intense. It was as if some torturer was sticking a needle into a nerve in my spine and twisting it every time I tried to turn. I managed to phone Roddy Macdonald and he began the process that would lead to an operation.

The easiest way of explaining it without the medical jargon is to say a disc in my spine had 'burst' – it was leaking. The disc was poking out of my back and touching the top of my spinal cord. This had been going on for quite some time and gradually, over the months, it had developed to the excruciating, agonising moment when it floored me. The problem was fully explained to me and I was told that I would need surgery, which was to be undertaken at Ross Hall Hospital in Glasgow, with Professor Robin Johnson acting as my surgeon. He talked me through the procedure and said there was no way I could avoid the knife. That meant my season was over, that there would be no UEFA

Cup final appearance for me, no fulfilling end to a competition in which I had played such a big part since the start of the season. Reluctantly I accepted the inevitable and agreed to the operation. The only compensation was that I would finally be cured and the medical team would have me fit and ready for the new season. At least, that was the plan.

But before I went under the knife I was determined to see the lads take on Porto in Seville. I am usually not comfortable watching my team, even from the best seats. Like most footballers, if I'm not playing, I would almost always rather be anywhere else. Seville would be different. Martin O'Neill asked me if I wanted to travel, be part of the team, and I said 'yes' without hesitation. In addition to the match, it would be a little holiday for me, Lowri, Rebeca and my mum and dad. I could lay out by the pool and have a few beers while the lads prepared for the big day.

No one knows for certain how many Celtic fans made it to the game on 21 May 2003. The capacity at the Estadio Olimpico was 52,000, but one estimate claimed there were something like 80,000 Scots, all wearing green-and-white hooped shirts, in the city. It has to be the biggest travelling support for a club side in history. It was extraordinary, mind-blowing. They were like an invading army, but an incredibly good-natured one. If a little drinking took place, then that was understandable in the searing heat of the region of Spain they call the 'frying pan', and I never saw any trouble, none whatsoever. I know that UEFA were stunned by the turnout, an unparalleled invasion by air, land and sea that had begun to arrive in Seville several days before the match, and I don't know how the city authorities coped, but they did. Luckily, because I doubt there were enough hotel beds in the city for all of them, the heat of the Andalucian spring meant that it was no hardship to sleep under the stars, and that's what many of them did.

We were staying in Jerez, where the team had their HQ. It was within easy reach of Seville, but far enough away from the hustle and bustle to give a degree of privacy and allow for some relaxation. Things were much more frantic in Seville itself as the hunt for tickets stepped up with kick-off time fast approaching. On the day of the match they were selling for upwards of three hundred pounds a piece. The Celtic fans must have cajoled almost all of the locals to sell their allocation, because when we arrived at the stadium it looked like Parkhead. Some 35,000 Bhoys managed to get into the ground, and the unlucky ones watched the game on big screens erected around the city.

I went on the team bus with the lads and the heat was oppressive. My thoughts were with the players, who were bound to suffer physically, although I would gladly have suffered with them if I could have done. We were entitled to feel good about our chances against the Portuguese, having beaten them the season before. Their manager, José Mourinho, was relatively new to the big time, but he had secured considerable success for Porto domestically and was now aiming to make a mark in European competition. He came across even then as different, and not always in a good way. The impression I have of him as a manager is that he is more disdainful of the opposition than respectful towards it. Obviously the game would have been more memorable for me if we had won rather than lost 3–2. And it would have been a more honourable win for the Portuguese and Mourinho if his team had concentrated on playing good football, which they were certainly capable of, rather than employing what seemed to me to be a totally unacceptable, cynical approach in such a prestigious match. But they wasted time and they play-acted, and that worsened the deep scars we carried back to Glasgow. If Martin O'Neill had believed the result was achieved by fair means, if he thought the opposition deserved to lift the cup, he would have been gutted, but he would have lived with it and would have accepted defeat graciously. But it wasn't like that against Mourinho's team, so Martin was incandescent at the end, and he had every right to be. Mourinho can win all the titles he wants, be a multi-millionaire, use someone else's money to buy the best players in the world, but I will always hold against him the way his team played against us that night.

The shining light for us in the final was Henrik's perform-ance. He scored twice with two great headers. Henrik was always assiduously professional, and managed to produce something that surprised you no matter how often you lined up alongside him. There is no aspect of the game he hasn't mastered, and his goalscoring record – he brought his Celtic total to two hundred in Seville – is astonishing. They say I might have made a difference, but I'm not so sure because I don't like playing in the heat. Maybe people were being kind and what they were really saying was that I deserved to play, as I had been instrumental in Celtic making it to the final.

After Seville there was one last hurdle to be cleared before the surgeon could attend to my back. It would be the most dramatic of weekends to round off the season, and again I could only be part of it as an onlooker, although I would be heavily immersed in the drama. The situation was this: Rangers and ourselves were neck and neck for the title with one game apiece to play. Rangers faced Dunfermline and we were up against Kilmarnock. When I say neck and neck, I mean there wasn't the width of a piece of tissue paper between us. We won 4–0, which was an exceptional result after the exhausting UEFA Cup final. But Rangers beat Dunfermline 6–1, which meant they recovered the title by a single goal. We just had to say 'well done', although Chris Sutton found that too hard to do. He is not usually the type to go out on a limb through the press – it's generally me who does that! – but this time he gave it both barrels by accusing Dunfermline of lying down to present Rangers with the title. A lot of people agreed with him, and still do, but Chris' outburst caused ructions and ended with him being suspended and eventually apologising (although some time after his agent and Martin O'Neill had apologised for him). I reckon if you believe it, say it, and then take the consequences. Chris did that, and if he is never forgiven in Dunfermline, then I don't think that will give him many sleepless nights.

The operation went ahead in June, which gave me six weeks to recover before the start of the next season. The medical people were delighted with how it went. They told me it had been successful, very successful, in fact. If only . . . As soon as I started walking again I knew it wasn't right. I was still in pain and the realisation that I had made no progress depressed me. My disc problem had won its first battle with me and I could not believe my misfortune. I had missed the big parade with Celtic in Spain and had been a useless bystander as Rangers had beaten us to the title and clinched the treble. A few weeks before it had all been so promising, yet by the end we were potless in Glasgow. Ultimately, it was the end of a season made in hell.

chapter 14

Losing the Plot with Martin

If you had caged me and thrown away the key, I couldn't have felt much worse than I did as my third season loomed. My bad back was officially 'uncooperative'. The op had left me in the same stressed condition as before, so I faced a dilemma: do I play on or do I put myself in the hands of the surgeon again? The trouble with most back problems of this type is that you appear normal. I was walking upright, not stooped, and it was only occasionally, during physical activity, that I was in any sort of pain. To the outsider, I must have looked like I was in good condition. It was always there, though, ready to flare up again at some time in the future. Nobody was forcing the issue at Celtic: they were sympathetic, even though my back must have been as perplexing to them as it was to me. I decided to play and see what happened, having been advised that it was unlikely I would do any lasting harm. That wasn't much comfort.

The team travelled to the United States for pre-season, and while there I was worked into a lather by the club physio, Brian Scott. He spent hour after hour with me in an effort to get me ready, if not for the very start of the season, then for as soon as possible after it. I did a lot of running, a lot of pounding in the sort of high temperatures that didn't suit me. I did my best, but I was still disturbed by the condition of my back. It was a strange situation to be in: I generally felt good and it was assumed that I was 'A OK' and fit for a full campaign, but I knew I wasn't, that there was still something seriously wrong. It was a long way from being straightforward, but I went ahead with my training and prepared to play as quickly as possible.

My first match of the season came on 27 August 2003 in a Champions League qualifier against MTK Hungaria. In many ways I was glad to be back, but it wasn't without some trepidation. Thereafter I went through a series of games in quick succession for club and country, including a European tie against Bayern Munich in Germany in mid-September. We lost 2–1, and I was still looking for my first goal of the season at domestic, European or international level. I was less than comfortable, very uncomfortable sometimes in fact, but at least I knew everything that could be done was being done on my behalf. Men of my size are particularly susceptible to back problems, and when you consider the amount of punishment I had given my spine over the years since my teenage days, mine was understandable. Nobody was forcing me to play, but once again I was haunted by the fear that there might never be a proper cure for this particular problem, so I went on to play in many important games until 31 January 2004. In that time I scored twelve goals in total – eleven for Celtic and one for

Wales. The goal for my country came in a disappointing 2–3 home defeat against Serbia and Montenegro. Another disappointing defeat occurred when Celtic were beaten 3–2 in Lyon by a side that was developing into a formidable unit. But we hammered Hibernian 6–0 just before Christmas (I scored two goals) and destroyed Rangers 3–0 in our first game of the new year. I managed to play out another four matches after that until, for the second time in under a year, I had to say 'enough is enough'. My last match of the season was at Parkhead when we beat Kilmarnock 5–1, but at least I finished on a high with two goals.

I sought out Roddy Macdonald after the game and told him I was in no doubt that I needed another operation. That was easy to say, but there were problems connected with the surgery. It was emphatically pointed out to me that a second operation could be career threatening. As they were explained to me, the complications would make most people queasy. The surgeons told me they would have to enter through the scar they had made last time, and once I had listened to them going on and on about 'angles of access' and other technical issues I was asked whether I still wanted to go ahead. But really I had no choice: I had to risk finishing my career at twenty-eight. I just couldn't play on while my back was reacting so badly to the physical demands of the game. I could risk the operation now or simply play on until my back gave in completely. As no one could tell me when that would happen – it could be two years; it could be a month – I had to go for surgery.

When something as persistent as this happens, the medics

handling your case tend to become friends, and that's the way it was for me. Before I went into hospital I had a number of conversations with Robin Johnson. When he had been working on my first disc he had told me there was a chance another would bulge because there was so much pressure on my back. But two operations in the space of a few months is far from ideal for a professional sportsman. There was talk of 'fusion', but I didn't want that, as it seemed unnatural to me. I put all my faith in the surgical procedure favoured by Robin. I remember coming round in post-op and feeling initially disorientated, but when my brain started to function properly again I immediately tried to assess how my back was feeling.

To my delight and huge relief, for the first time in ages it felt amazingly good. As I said earlier, I knew as soon as I woke up after the first operation that I still had a problem, but this time everything seemed to be as it should be. The difference between how I felt after the first operation and how I felt after the second was like night and day. As I lay in bed I knew the problem had been solved, that my career had been prolonged thanks to Roddy Macdonald, Robin Johnson and the surgical team. In moments like that you realise how lucky you have been; you think of all the players you have come across over the years who have been crippled by injury and were unable to make it back into football. I missed half a season, but that is nothing if you can return fit for a new campaign. It was the end of a highly traumatic period in my professional life. All I needed to do now was rest, recuperate and be available for selection in August 2004.

By now I was well acquainted with Martin O'Neill's management style and tuned in to the way he operated with Robbo and Wally. He is an intriguing operator, single-minded and effective. The fact that he stayed out of football until August 2006 was bad news for the game, but hardly unexpected for those of us who know him well. He has always been very family-orientated and is especially close to his wife Geraldine, so when she fell ill it was no surprise that he resigned from Celtic to spend more time with her. Geraldine has always been delightful company, full of fun and charm. She has supported him throughout his career and he needed to do the same for her.

I am sure that he had no problem saying 'no' to any of the clubs he was linked with after he decided to quit Celtic in the summer of 2005, until he finally accepted the Aston Villa job. But one thing that has surprised me recently is England's apparent failure to offer him the role of national coach. He certainly would have been my first choice. By saying that I am not taking anything away from Steve McClaren, who many will think deserves his chance because he has been Sven-Göran Eriksson's understudy for a number of years. And he has done a great job at Middlesbrough, taking them all the way to the UEFA Cup final in 2006. But I think the English FA made a mess of it, and my opinion is based on the four years I spent listening to, learning from and obeying the instructions of Martin O'Neill. It is staggering to me that the Football Association in London didn't go flat out and pull out all the stops to try to secure Martin's appointment. I am sure that every player who has worked with him would agree that it should have been a one-manager race.

What is it about the man and his way of working that consolidates the talent in his squad and turns them into a team of champions? Some might patronisingly say, 'So he won some titles in Scotland. So what?' But he was also a highly successful manager at Leicester: winning promotion to the Premiership and guiding them to two League Cup finals, which are considerable achievements for a club of Leicester's size in an era when the Chelseas, Arsenals and Manchester Uniteds have cornered the transfer market and buy all the best players who come up for sale. Martin was also a winner earlier in his career with Wycombe Wanderers, taking them from non-league football into the Football League and then to further promotion.

Of late there has been a lot of talk of player power in the England set-up under Sven-Göran Eriksson. If that's true, it's unhealthy. It is sure to backfire sooner rather than later, and perhaps it has already had an impact on the team's performance, given England's failure to reach the latter stages of the World Cup finals in Japan and Germany, and the European Championships in Portugal. Martin O'Neill would never tolerate any player, no matter how talented, telling him, the boss, what to do. The merest hint of that sort of behaviour would finish him in the team: Martin would simply leave him out and never bring him back. And he wouldn't given it a second thought, either. I have seen him talk to players of the calibre of Neil Lennon, Henrik Larsson and Chris Sutton and tell them exactly what he thinks of them. They were all left in no doubt about who was in charge. But if you give him the respect he deserves, he is loyal.

When I went through my first ten games without scoring at Celtic there was a lot of outside pressure calling for him to drop me; but he didn't, and that encouraged me to go on and score twenty-four goals that season. That is a significant point to make. If I might speak on behalf of all goalscorers, it is vital that we are given the chance to prove ourselves. The first season after Henrik left, 2004–05, I scored twenty-eight goals for my club, and the next season I netted twenty as the number-one striker. If someone says to you, 'There's the jersey, it's yours,' it brings out the best in you because you don't think you are in anybody's shadow. I had Martin's assurances, he stood by them and I scored many goals for him. Remember, my best season came after Henrik had left. I see that as a point proved. The onus was on me, I had full responsibility, and I delivered. At Arsenal I felt I was in the shadow of Dennis Bergkamp and Ian Wright, but when I was given the shirt as the main man it brought out the best in me.

There is a similar situation in England right now. If Darren Bent from Charlton was given a chance, a run of six or seven games, and was told that he would be playing come what may, then I am sure he would produce his club form and become a very valuable player for England. But if you put him on the bench and then throw him on for Michael Owen for the last ten minutes, he will never feel like an England player; and if you don't feel it, you can't be it. At the start of my career I was in Darren's position. When I was behind Rush, Hughes and Saunders for Wales I was average in terms of goalscoring, but as soon as I knew I was the main striker it transformed me. When Mark Hughes took over from Bobby Gould he told me I was going to be his number-one striker and that made all the difference to me. When you are entrusted with the task of scoring goals, you feel obliged to supply them. Under Mark I won twenty-eight caps in five years and scored twelve goals, for the other managers I played twenty-three times and scored just twice. That sort of form can only come from a sustained run in the team.

When I look at the England set-up and I think of Theo Walcott being selected for the 2006 World Cup finals squad as an untried kid I ask, 'Why?' Not because he is only seventeen, but because he hasn't been tested in the Premiership. We are not talking about Under-21 football but catapulting him straight into the senior squad. Again I ask, 'Why?' I am not knocking the lad because clearly he is a very talented footballer with the potential to have a great career, but how could he be preferred to a player like Darren Bent, who was England's top domestic scorer with twenty-two goals in the 2005–06 season. That was three more than Wayne Rooney managed, so surely Darren deserves a chance. If Eriksson was determined to gamble, why didn't he gamble on a mature player we know can score goals at Premiership level? For me, no matter what happened in Germany, the manager made the wrong decision by selecting Walcott ahead of Bent because it must have been offensive to the far better-qualified player.

Martin O'Neill is very quick witted and knows how to laugh with his players. He and Alan Thompson would always feed off each other in training. Tommo is a Geordie and constantly cracks jokes on the training ground. Usually Neil Lennon or I were on the receiving end. Tommo would slaughter me with lines like: 'How many crocodile sandwiches did you eat last night, John?' The lads would burst out laughing and I'd go bright red. I don't know why, but in spite of being a high-profile sportsman in the public eye, I still blush really easily. I am all right one-on-one, full of confidence, but if I am shot down in front of others I go crimson and can feel the ground opening up to swallow me. Or I *want* the ground to open up.

Martin was always a regular at training, contrary to rumours that he rarely attended the sessions and left that side of the game to his staff. He oversaw everything, and if he wasn't there in body you still felt his presence. But nine times out of ten he would be at the ground. We used to start at 10.30 a.m. when Jim Hendry, our fitness coach, would take the warm-up for half an hour. Steve Walford would be in charge of the session for the next hour or so, and after twenty minutes Martin and John Robertson would turn up to analyse the training. Then Martin would make any points he felt were necessary. We never did much in the way of heading practice, but we hardly needed to as we had several great headers of the ball: Chris Sutton, Johan Mjallby, Bobo Balde, Henrik and myself. Henrik was supreme with his head: he could get up, leap and he was brave. By the time I arrived, Martin had already brought in some first-class players: Tommo, who could deliver the ball as well as anyone; and Neil Lennon, who was like the team's heartbeat. They were so gifted that we never felt the need to do a lot of work on set-pieces, either in attack or defence. If we conceded a goal to a set-piece at the weekend, Martin would identify the problem and put it right over the course of about half an hour on the Monday morning, just to make sure it didn't happen again.

He always liked big, strong players. If you look at his Leicester and Wycombe days, he had a few towering players in his side, and that's how it was at Celtic, too. First of all he wanted his centre halves to be able to head the ball. If they could come out and play as well, even better, but their heading ability was paramount, and he wanted them to be able to do it in both boxes. He liked his front men to get hold of the ball and keep it. He regularly told me not to have two million things in my head when the ball came to me. The point he was making was that sometimes I would already be thinking of what I was going to do with the ball before I had it under control and I'd give it away as a result. He would shout at me, 'Put your foot on the ball and stand there. Let us get up with you and let's play from there.' He would have a go at me for not doing that, but he knew what I was good at, and that if the lads got the ball in the appropriate areas that I'd score goals for him. I managed to net ninety during his time at Celtic.

Wally had the authority to make decisions, but I suppose you could say the philosophy was pure Martin O'Neill, although they must have thought the same way 99 per cent of the time. Martin liked to keep the training very bubbly and buzzing, which helped me get through it because I've never been a brilliant trainer. But he could still be strict when he needed to be. As I mentioned earlier, I've never liked the running element in training, so if Martin wasn't happy with my fitness, if he felt I had been lazy at the weekend or had lost my edge through not working as hard as I should have done in the gym, he would organise runs around the pylons at the training ground. I've got butterflies now just thinking about them. He would say to me, 'Right, you've got forty seconds to get round the pylon and back.' That would cripple me, but then he would give me only thirty seconds for the next three. Once I'd done them, and was out on my feet, he would say, 'Right, you've got thirty-two seconds for one more. If you don't get in on time you are going again.' It wasn't a request but a demand, and he made similar demands about discipline during games. When he told you to do something on a Saturday, you fought to do it for him. I used to hate these runs. I had nightmares about them. Martin O'Neill knew that, but he also knew they kept me right.

Since he left Celtic I have talked with Neil Lennon, Alan Thompson and all the rest of the boys about Martin, and we are all in agreement: we all loved him; we all thought he was fantastic. He just had a good way about him, and he is always very honest. He is also not the type of manager who hangs people out to dry. He commands tremendous respect because he knows the game inside out. I've got only good things to say about him. He treated me brilliantly and I will always be thankful to him for bringing me to Celtic and helping my career progress. The buck stopped with him, which was evident when he took the chance of signing me when Spurs, Rangers and West Ham had all backed away because of the doubts about my knee. Martin just said, 'Give him the contract.' And when I recovered from my back operations, he gave me a two-year extension on my contract on a very good salary. I think his faith in me has been justified, and that pleases me immensely.

Having said all that, and although I've got enormous respect for the man, we still had a couple of bust-ups in our time. Once I swore at him in a very offensive and explosive manner. I would not recommend that approach to anyone else. It was one of the biggest mistakes of my life and it could have finished my career at Celtic, but fortunately, while Martin can flare up with the best of them (including me), there is also a forgiving side to him.

I hadn't played since the win at Kilmarnock in January 2004, but my operation had been successful, my rehab had gone well, and I was preparing for the forthcoming season. Without me for the last few months of the season, the team still regained the Premiership title, finishing a highly impressive seventeen points ahead of Rangers. And they made it a classic double when they won the Scottish Cup with a 3–1 win against Dunfermline at Hampden. Henrik was again Scotland's top goalscorer with a supreme tally of thirty, but we had all known he would be leaving at the end of the season, and throughout my rehab I had been spurred on by a determination to make his departure as painless as possible.

Satisfyingly, I did just that by matching him the following season, scoring twenty-three league goals in 2004–05 to finish as Scotland's top goalscorer. But it was in this season that I fell out with Martin, when he brought me off in the semi-final of the Scottish Cup against Hearts.

I admit I had not been on brilliant form, but I had set up our opening goal for Chris Sutton, and we were coasting after Craig Bellamy had given us a two-goal lead. Then Martin decided to replace me with Aiden McGeady. I wasn't happy and walked straight down the tunnel in one of my petulant moods. I really had nothing to complain about. Martin had brought me back immediately after a two-match absence through injury, which most managers wouldn't do. He felt I'd earned my place and that I'd performed well enough in the previous cup ties to come straight back into the team. But the red mist was dictating to me. I walked into the changing room and smashed three plates of sandwiches before the rest of the lads arrived. I should have been happy because we had just beaten Hearts to reach the final, but instead I was raging that I'd been substituted.

When Martin came in I told him to 'fuck off'. It was the worst thing I could have done. He just stood there for a moment as I unloaded on him. Now industrial language is very common in football, both in training and during matches. Footballers are not mealy-mouthed when it comes to swear words. But what you should never do is direct them with venom at your boss, especially if your boss is Martin O'Neill. He came right up to me, his finger pointing in my face, and absolutely nailed me in front of the whole team. They had been in mid-celebration, but by then their eyes were popping at the confrontation. If I had been raging, Martin really was now: 'Don't you ever, *ever* tell me . . . Don't *ever* talk to me like that,' he shouted. I wouldn't say we nearly came to blows because I had too much respect for him for that, even in that furious moment, but there was more finger-pointing on both sides, and I was still shaking when I sat down on the bus. The celebrations of the rest of the team were cut short and they all just showered and changed in a deathly quiet.

Martin didn't speak to me for four or five days after the incident. That was a very disturbing period for me because there was no way to minimise the seriousness of my position. I had to accept that it was dire – I had crossed the line. I spoke to John Robertson about it, seeking his advice, which was to go immediately to Martin's office and apologise, if that's what I wanted to do. I faced up to Martin, admitted that I had been out of order and said that I was sorry, really sorry. He told me not to worry, it was over. And he was true to his word. That was the last I heard about it. There was no fine, no club punishment, even though he was not shy about going down that route if he thought it was necessary. He had fined me once before, when I had turned up late for training in my first season. He hated that type of behaviour, hated his players being lazy or not concentrating on what we were being told. When Jackie McNamara and I arrived a little late, that was enough for him to fine both of us £2,000. In retrospect I can see that it was another useful wake-up call for me. Although it has to be said that I doubt Martin himself has ever been early for anything in his life!

Sometimes I have been an innocent bystander when Martin has lost his temper in the dressing room, but it's not a pleasant sight, even when you are not the one on the receiving end. At times Neil and Tommo argued their case against the boss, but there was only ever one winner. Martin was always right. That's not to say he was a super-disciplinarian. He was never ultra-strict. There were just rules and regulations, and you either obeyed them or paid the price. But if he wasn't happy with you, he would give you the cold shoulder. Another tactic he used if he thought you weren't putting in enough effort was the 'shame' of the yellow jersey, which was handed out to the worst player in training. It came my way a few times, but not enough, according to some of my team-mates.

As a senior player you expect to be treated as an adult, and by and large most managers do this; it was how Martin acted towards us. You abused that relationship at your peril, as I had done with my outburst against him. You could take the occasional liberty, which would be ignored, but only if it didn't cut into planning or performance. Ninety-nine per cent of team curfews were observed, but one that wasn't happened in the USA during a summer trip there. We used to love our pre-seasons in the States and Seattle was a favourite. Martin used to allow us to go out for meals and have a few beers. There was no problem; if we were on a leash it was a long one.

On this particular night, Robbo and Wally told us there would be an eleven o'clock curfew. Several of us enjoyed ourselves so much that we went past that time by a distance. We were all over the place when we returned to the hotel and were last on the bus in the morning. Martin had sat at the front as usual and we had to pass him. If we breathed normally he would have smelled stale beer off us, so the plan was to hold our breath for the six or seven seconds it took to climb on to the bus and make our way to the back where we let it all out to pleas of 'put the blowers on'. We got away with that one which made it an occasion in itself.

I always found the team spirit at Celtic to be first class. The joking was never deliberately cruel but it could be naughty, as it was when we had some fun at the expense of the diminutive Brazilian Juninho. We set him up at his first meal with the team at the Glasgow Hilton hotel. We would sit at our various tables, senior players on one, foreign players on another, the younger players on yet another table. It was all very normal to us. When Juninho came down there was no obvious seat for him. Well, actually there was. We had told one of the waiters to find a baby seat and place it in the middle of the floor. When Juninho asked where he could sit, we all pointed to the high chair with the straps and the holes for tiny legs. Some of the lads were worried it would humiliate him, but he saw the joke and laughed with us.

Martin always wanted us to enjoy our football, to enjoy everything about the training, the preparation, the matches

and the success. He was at his entertaining best at an end-of-season reception with the wives and girlfriends present. He wasn't a big drinker, but after a couple of glasses of wine, he would take the microphone and give players like me, Lenny, Sutty and Tommo a bit of a tousing – all in good spirits. He didn't hang back and people would nudge you and whisper that he is only saying that because he likes us. We took the full force of the verbals.

I suppose overall the 2004–05 season could be called bittersweet. I had to be happy with my goalscoring contribution, and after beating Hearts in the semi-final we went on to win the Scottish Cup, but we missed out on the main prize, the Premiership, which again was snatched from us by Rangers. This time the circumstances were not as controversial as they had been two years before, but it was no less sickening. We lost by a single point, which was bad enough, but what made it even worse was that in March we had been five points clear with just four games to play. Somehow we lost two of those matches to gift the title to Rangers.

Our final game was at Motherwell and we knew that if we won it, we won the league, no matter what Rangers did at Hibs. But we managed to lose 2–1 after we had been leading with just two minutes remaining. Scott MacDonald, who calls himself a Celtic fan, scored both of Motherwell's goals. I couldn't understand what happened at the time and it is no clearer in my mind now. We were all devastated. We had been all over them throughout the match, and although we led by Chris Sutton's goal we really should have been four or five up and out of sight. Both Craig Bellamy and I had a couple of good chances saved, and then we were stunned not once but twice right at the end. Meanwhile, Rangers held on to their one-goal lead in Edinburgh against a Hibs team that had come to Parkhead and shocked us by winning 1–3 three weeks earlier. Everything happened so late in our game that the helicopter carrying the SPL trophy had to be diverted from Motherwell to Easter Road. It was all so surreal. The fans started to file out of the ground while Martin just sat numbly with his head in his hands. It was awful, a desperately sad way to say goodbye to the boss.

When I think about it now, it was weird being named Scottish Professional Footballers' Association Player of the Year near the end of a season which brought us so much heartache as a team. I shared the title with Rangers Dutchman Fernando Ricksen, and it was an honour for both of us. When you are acknowledged by your fellow pros (the Scottish football writers later voted me their Player of the Year), then it is with great satisfaction and real pride that you accept these awards. That is how I felt on the morning the SPFA award was announced, and I am sure Fernando felt the same.

I never had any concerns about it being shared. I'd had a good season and so had Fernando. It was the first time in the history of the award that it was a split vote, but in no way did that diminish the honour as far as I was concerned. What it did do was lead to a remarkable telephone conversation on my way home from training after the joint award had been announced. The call came through on my car mobile. The number was withheld. I pushed the speak button.

'Hi, John, this is Fernando Ricksen.'

'Hi, Fernando, how are you?'

He continued, 'Oh, I got your number from Celtic Park, delighted to say that we share the award.'

I said, 'Yeah, great. Yeah.'

It was the first time I had spoken to him and then he went on to say in a thick Dutch accent, 'I can't believe we've shared this award because I felt I was the much better player throughout the season.'

The arrogant way he talked took me by surprise and I could only think of saying 'Well, I wouldn't completely disagree with you, but I scored thirty goals, Fernando.'

Then he said, 'I'm going to be in Holland next year for quite a lot of time. Can I have the trophy for ten months and you have it for two months.'

'No problem,' was my reply and I went on. 'Look, if it means that much to you just keep it for twelve months.'

But that didn't satisfy him and he went on, 'John, the bottom line is . . .' and he started to swear and added: 'It is an absolute joke that we are sharing this award. I can't believe it, I'm a much better player than you.'

I thought I'd been generous to him, but this was too much. I was raging by now: 'Do me a favour, why don't you just eff off. I can't wait to play against you, I'm going to kick you all over the pitch when we meet.'

I went on and on in similar vein, and then there was a massive burst of laughing. It was Alan Thompson who had me on the loudspeaker of his car. Tommo had phoned me up pretending to be Fernando and he had me hooked for ten minutes on the phone.

chapter 15

Divorce – A Fateful Decision

For a whole year I had been living a double life, and on 18 September 2005, Lowri's birthday – a date seared in my brain – Lowri, my beautiful wife, friend and soul-mate for twelve years, found out about my affair. It was over; for both our sakes our marriage had to end. I think it took her completely by surprise, and the hurt, the terrible hurt, I created that day has barely subsided in the months since, with the introduction of lawyers and the hellish decisions that have to be made when two people decide they can no longer live together. The discovery prompted a period of unrelenting misery, and I am entirely to blame. I take full responsibility for my actions. I have no defence other than to say I didn't mean it to end like this and that until the last couple of years I felt we would see out our lives together and watch our children grow up as a family.

Ideally all of this should have been conducted in private, if for no other reason than because young children are involved, but unfortunately footballers have to accept that very little they do can be kept private. So, unsurprisingly, what was a dreadfully difficult situation for us both became headline news in Scotland and Wales. There were occasions when I felt our privacy was being invaded on a daily basis. It was unhelpful, it led to more lies and it became increasingly unbearable.

The split had nothing to do with football, or pressure, but was simply the erosion of my feelings for Lowri, the mother of my children. She did not, and does not, deserve to be scorned by me. She is the most fantastic-looking woman, a stunner, and it was always a bit of a mystery why she was attracted to me in the first place. I wasn't a name in the game when we first met, when she was seventeen and I was nineteen. I might never have made it, so she could never be accused of gold-digging. She followed me to Luton, quit her college course to be near me, and then was with me through every step of my career as lover, homemaker, mother and friend. She stood by me when life was difficult and asked nothing of me other than, I presume, my loyalty. There were never any restrictions; she never told me what to do. If I wanted to go out for a beer or two with the lads then Lowri didn't object. And if I stayed out all night there was not automatically a row about it. I am not saying she was in any way docile or subjugated by a macho lifestyle. It wasn't like that. I always had the utmost respect for her and that will never dim. She was a brilliant wife. So why did it all go wrong?

I had been seeing a girl, Sarah McManus, for the best part of a year. We saw each other regularly, even though I knew it was wrong. I was telling a lot of lies to my wife and she would say I was also neglecting the children. I would disagree with that, because my children are my life and I always found time for them. I never stopped taking them out, and always sat and read stories to them, watched videos with them. I would and will do anything for my children. But I *was* deceiving Lowri. I probably felt invincible, that I would never be caught, which eventually was completely ridiculous as we were walking out together hand in hand. Friends would tell us we couldn't do that in public, not in a city where I was easily recognised, but when you are happy – I want to say in love – then you want to express it, don't you?

It was a coincidence that it all came out on Lowri's birthday. I certainly hadn't planned it that way. We broke up that very day and have not lived together since, although we have met up, cried a lot and even been hysterical on occasion. We spoke about getting back together, but I couldn't do that because I had decided the lying had to end. It was time for me to start being honest, which meant I had to tell Lowri that I was sorry but it couldn't happen. Our hearts were breaking; we were crying together and cuddling each other. But we both knew it was over.

The stories started to appear in quick succession in the *News of the World*, the *Sunday Mirror* and other newspapers. I can't be certain who leaked them. They all claimed I had asked Lowri back, that I had wined and dined her and bought her a special necklace. They had one basic fact correct: I *had* asked her back, but only because I couldn't cope with seeing her so distressed. Even given the circumstances, it didn't seem normal. The way she spoke shocked me.

It wasn't just Lowri and me, of course. I also had Rebeca and Joni to think of. They were shielded from it to some degree because of their age and because they were moved down to Cardiff, but it was still a scandal and it distracted everybody. Apart from anything else, the stories demeaned Lowri.

I could only tell Lowri that I was deeply sorry. We have been all over the world, we have two of the most amazing children, and it kills me now not seeing them every day. I am saving as much as I can, and when the time is right – and that will depend on my career – I will try to move closer to where they live. One day I also hope to have the chance to explain why it happened.

There have been a few crises in my life, but none as intense as the break-up of my marriage. I feel as if my heart has been ripped out and stepped on. It has taken its toll physically, too. I have come out in a rash, hardly a medical problem to rank alongside a ruptured disc, but it indicates the tension I have felt. It stems from living a lie, having to admit it and then facing the consequences. Maybe someone will be able to tell me why I did what I did, why I lost that precious feeling for my wife.

A major deception makes you act strangely because you are constantly covering up. I would get up in the middle of the night in my own home and go and sleep downstairs. It wasn't healthy, and of course I should have been sleeping happily with my beautiful wife. Instead I would be downstairs trying to work out what was wrong with me. I was so depressed and I'd just stay there thinking about what was happening. In the morning I couldn't find the energy to get up and bounce around as I previously did. I came to the conclusion that I'd got into a rut with Lowri, and in the end it was a case of I don't want to – or at least I shouldn't – be in her life. I know this sounds cruel and very harsh and hurtful, but it's the truth: I would look forward to spending time with our children, but it wasn't intense for me any longer. We would go on holiday and have ten days in one of the most beautiful places in the world. We could look out over the marina at the incredible boats and the sunset. It should have been magical, but it wasn't because I was there with the wrong person. I told Lowri it wasn't her, it was me, and that was absolutely true. It wasn't what she was doing, how she was acting, how she looked: everything about her was still fantastic. She couldn't have been better as a wife and mother, but at some point a stage was passed and I couldn't deal with it.

We had been together for twelve years, since we were kids, and when we were married I was so in love. We met at my sister Hayley's twenty-first. My folks had laid on a barbecue in our back garden and my brother James brought along his girlfriend, Lowri's elder sister. It was James who suggested that Lowri should come along and meet me. As soon as I set eyes on her I thought she was gorgeous and we got talking. We went to a club after the barbecue and our relationship developed pretty quickly from then. I was really shy, so although I had an eye for the girls I never had many girlfriends at school. I was also a bit freckly with orange hair, so I didn't see myself as the best-looking kid in school. That didn't seem to bother Lowri, though, and within a year she moved in with me at Luton. The next year I was off to Arsenal and in the big-money league, and she came along with me. We had enough to buy a little house together and were blissfully happy.

After a while we moved to Brookmans Park, where we stayed for four years. It was an upmarket house in an upmarket location. That's where we got married, in the back garden of our house, with a massive marquee and two hundred guests. It was a memorable day for both of us. As I mentioned earlier, living in Brookmans Park meant a long commute when I was transferred to Wimbledon and an even worse one when I moved to Coventry, so we couldn't have been happier when I moved on to Celtic at the age of twenty-six.

Most importantly, we have our two children to protect. My daughter is now at the age when kids at school can be quite nasty. They poke fun if they see a weakness, anything they can latch on to, something out of the ordinary. I don't want that for Rebeca or Joni. I want them to be proud of their mum and their dad, but I think Lowri sometimes forgets how important that is because she feels she has been so badly let down and is so upset and hurt. I don't know if she now really feels badly towards me, but it can't be good for our kids. There were periods when we didn't talk or even text each other.

The most depressing day of all was the one I spent with my lawyers disclosing absolutely everything: how much I spend on clothes, food, petrol, holidays, how much I've got in my bank account, how much I've got in property, how much I give away, the value of my pension, how much I save. I had to disclose everything other than the colour of my pants. That then went off to Lowri's lawyer and she did the same, disclosed everything, what her demands are, what she would like. That was then returned to my solicitor. When you spend three hours in a lawyer's office going over details like these it is a horrible experience. At that point the seriousness of the situation finally hits home, although sometimes I still have to remind myself that I am not with her any more and we are not together as a family, despite having been so happy for so many years. It was only when I reached thirty that I suffered what might be called my first trauma, my first breakdown.

My parents were less than happy when they heard about the divorce plans. They took it badly and there was quite a long period when I wasn't talking to either of them, although that is resolved now. Another regret is that obviously I have soured my relationship with Lowri's dad, Aaron, who is a gentleman, a cracking guy. We used to go to the pub together as drinking partners, but I haven't spoken to him since the break. While I am now on better terms with my own dad, he is still gutted. When we first got together, he and Mum didn't really take to Lowri, but looking back I can see that was just a typical parents' reaction. They would have been worried no matter who I started seeing because they thought

I should be concentrating on my career as a footballer. But as we got older together they came to realise how important she was to me and what a nice girl she was. When we got married they could see how special she was to me, and from then on they were great with her. They eventually became quite close, and they still are now, which is great, because my children can go and visit their grandparents in Swansea, which makes me feel a lot happier. In a way, it keeps them close to me. When I talk to my father on the phone he says Joni sounds like him, which makes me smile. No disrespect to Lowri's family, but I want my children to pick up things from both sides of the family. Dad takes the kids down to the local park, and everybody says they are 'Johnny's children, John's little girl and boy' and makes a fuss of them. I like the fact that they are still hearing that, if only occasionally.

There is a terrible sadness about all of this, but also a realisation that some relationships just don't survive. When that happens, surely the best thing to do is admit to it and break up in the most civilised way possible, then get on with your life. I don't pretend that this has been anything other than a nightmarish experience for Lowri and me. It affects all the people involved in so many ways. It has certainly had a dramatic effect on me and I know Lowri has suffered a great deal of pain and anguish, too. But you live on in the belief and hope that something good will come out of it all, even when, in the blackest of moments, that seems impossible.

In the midst of the blackest depression you find extreme kindness from all sorts of people. The divorce proceedings ate into my whole being, but the children were paramount in my thoughts. As I approached my first Christmas Day on my own, because Rebeca and Joni were staying with their mother in Wales, I was faced with a truly terrible prospect. I reported to the ground on Christmas morning with the rest of the lads, played in a five-a-side and then we all shook hands.

Gordon Strachan came over to me: 'What are you doing, big man?' he asked.

'Nothing,' I replied. 'I'm on my own.'

'Come home with me,' he said. 'Spend the day with my family.'

It was a kind offer, typical of him. He knew I was having a difficult time, but I couldn't impose, so I thanked him and said no. It is the time of year to be with your own family and, as I didn't have one in Glasgow, I didn't want to force myself on anyone else's, however thoughtful the invite.

You need friends. Giovanni was another really good one of mine from L'Ariosto restaurant in the city centre. I took a call from him and he asked me to go round to his place. When I got there he said he had a surprise for me; he had prepared a marvellous packed meal to take back to my apartment. It was the full Christmas dinner – pudding included.

During what was a personal crisis for me, not forgetting the others involved, I also received considerable and desperately needed help from Dennis, a great friend of Sarah's. I was so grateful to him and the compassion he showed us. The only way I could think of repaying him in some way was to allow him to use my VIP family tickets for a Celtic match. These were three acts of kindness I will never forget at a time of utter misery.

You try so hard to keep the children apart from the obvious tensions that arise in any separation. However, when the final divorce papers come through as well as the sadness there is also a sense of relief that a new life is opening up. Of course Lowri has been upset with me: I was the one who had the affair and walked away from the marriage. She's a great mother and our kids dote on her; and I hope that with time we can be good friends again, as we know that it will help our children if we get on. By law she was entitled to 50 per cent of all I own, and that is what she has for herself and our children. It is important to me that I give them a good lifestyle, however much difficulty it causes me. The option of retiring from football and not providing for them was not one I could take. I have pride, and the money is for my children's future as well as for Lowri. And I will keep working to do my best for them, and for my own future.

I constantly tell Rebeca and Joni that Lowri and I still love each other but just can't live together any more. It is so difficult to explain, but I have found it best to stick with the truth, after all the lies.

chapter 16

The New Boss –
Rising from the Ashes

The 2005–06 season began so dramatically in our favour that we were the favourites for the league title long before Christmas. That was fortunate, because I don't think our nerves would have stood another last-minute championship decider. There was virtually no chance of that this time. We were so far in front of the two-club chasing 'pack' that our meeting with our closest rivals, Hearts, at Parkhead on 5 April 2006 could guarantee us the Premiership at a ridiculously early point in the season. As I relaxed in Glasgow's city-centre Hilton in a day-room booked by Celtic overlooking the River Clyde on the afternoon of the match, all my senses told me this should be the perfect occasion. Thinking about it is easier than having to do it in front of 60,000 demanding supporters, but it was also my thirty-first birthday and I saw that as a good omen. I was convinced everything would finally work out in my favour after a year that had been a nightmare of my own making through the collapse of my marriage. I admit my concentration had wavered under the strain of the break-up during the season, but that afternoon my mind was focused on Hearts and scoring a goal.

I was relaxed thanks largely to it being my birthday: I was busy receiving cards and trying to sort out tickets for my mates (there are never remotely enough to satisfy the demand, especially when they are all up in Glasgow to help me celebrate). So initially I wasn't worrying too much about the game, which was a good thing because I didn't have a great record against Hearts. I had scored a hat-trick against them two seasons earlier in Glasgow, but Tynecastle remained the only SPL ground on which I hadn't scored. A couple of friends, Tommy and Wayne, had arrived from Wales for the match and a birthday celebration my girl-friend Sarah had organised for afterwards. So win, lose or draw, I could look forward to a few beers, good food and some chat with my old mates.

Only very rarely does a dream materialise, but it did for me that day, even though it came from a misjudgement. The game was only four minutes old when Artur Boruc, our Polish goalkeeper, aimed a long kick upfield. There was a swirling wind that night and it affected the flight of the ball so much that I lost its track and had to spin round quickly as Maciej 'Magic' Zurawski, my Polish partner up front, headed it into my path. Nine times out of ten I would just have taken a touch and laid it wide, but for some reason it bounced beautifully for me and I thought, Just hit it! I caught it cleanly, but it wasn't one of those shots that go forty yards and fly into the top corner. It was weird because the Hearts goalkeeper, Craig Gordon, seemed to have it covered, but it took an awkward turn in the wind and he couldn't get across in time. GOAL! The celebrations could begin and they continued for the rest of the night because there was no more scoring for the remainder of the match. Dream fulfilled. Craig had had a great season, winning the Scottish Football Writers' Award, a prize I had lifted previously, and he will be Scotland's first-choice keeper for the foreseeable future, but I am certain he was disappointed with that goal. From my point of view, though, it was a brilliant moment that no doubt led to thousands waking up with hangovers in the morning.

I wouldn't claim it was my best goal, that remains the one I scored at Liverpool, but it gave me a tremendous amount of satisfaction because of its importance. It rarely happens that your goal seals a championship, and it is even more rare that all the threads come together at home in front of a packed stadium against one of the two teams that could conceivably beat you to the title. In my years at Celtic, I have always fancied myself to score on the big occasion – in Europe, during Old Firm matches – and I can't think of a bigger occasion than this. Undoubtedly we would have gone on to win the title at some point, but to win it on that night was extraordinary. My family watched it all at home in Swansea on TV, and I could imagine what it must have been like for them and my old mate Colin Payne, seeing me score the goal to win the SPL with six matches still to play.

Sarah had arranged for us all to meet at L'Ariosto. We got there about 10.45 p.m. when the city was buzzing with supporters. My mate closed the doors so it was a private party, and we had a brilliant time until there was a power cut when we were eating and drinking at about one o'clock in the morning. We just lit candles and continued to enjoy ourselves until some security men showed up and demanded that we had to leave. There's a nightclub called the Tunnel right next door, so when we filed outside there must have been 2,000 people milling about, having just been chucked out of the club because of the power cut. Someone recognised me and, before you knew it, everybody was singing my name in the street. It was incredible – everybody was shaking my hand, wishing me 'happy birthday'. Well, most of them seemed to be doing that, anyway. I suppose the ones that weren't must have been Rangers fans, but for once I didn't even get any abuse off them. Rangers knew the championship race should have been tighter, but, credit to them, they had a great run in Europe in what was Alex McLeish's last season as manager. It would have been very shallow if their fans had given me stick on the night we won the league. I didn't think it would happen, and I was happy to be proved right.

From there we went on to the Corinthian, a wine bar, about a mile away, in a part of Glasgow where there was no problem with the electricity. Then we headed to the Piano Bar, where I ended up singing. I don't normally dash out to buy the papers, but going home at about quarter to three in the morning I said to Sarah, 'Stop at the garage. I want to buy the papers.' Predictably, I was all over the back page . . . but I was also on front page – only this time for a good reason!

Losing the title at Motherwell ten months earlier had left the Celtic team in a variety of moods, ranging from fury to disbelief. Personally, it made me feel physically sick, but it also left me with a determination to be a champion again in 2005–06. I had learned very quickly that the demand for success at Celtic was never-ending, as it should be for a club of their size and support. With Martin's departure we had a new manager in Gordon Strachan, who had my complete support, not merely because he began the process that saved my career, but because I had first-hand experience of how good he was at the job. They say that for a player to succeed he must have talent, but just as importantly a desire to work hard for his success. It is just the same for a manager. And that was how I saw Gordon: highly knowledgeable in every area of the game and devoted to the job. Players generally wait to see how things develop and whether a new manager is going to be the type who inspires them before making a decision on him. To those who asked, I gave my opinion. I knew Gordon would introduce his own way of working, which would be very different from Martin's, but I believed he had every chance of being equally successful.

I sensed that not everyone agreed, and here I am talking about some of the fans. Gordon had no history with Celtic: he wasn't a former player, and coming from Edinburgh he had no association with the Glasgow scene other than as an opposing player in his Aberdeen days. He would make changes that would have to be accepted, and he would probably also need time to bed in to the job. A winning start would be a big advantage, an offering to those who doubted him, a result which said, 'There you go. We can move on from here.'

Europe was his first port of call in one of those dreadful July ties that come far too early in the season, but which are a necessary evil these days if you have failed to win the league title. Our opponents had no history of European competition, but as they were from Slovakia we suspected they would be very physical, skilful and therefore potentially dangerous. Their name – Artmedia – didn't trip off the tongue like 'Juventus' or 'Barcelona', but that was irrelevant. A lot of big money had begun to finance clubs in Eastern Europe, so new names were appearing all the time and could not be discounted simply because they had no pedigree. Neverthe-less, what happened to us when we met Artmedia in Bratislava on 27 July 2005 was so unbelievable that it made headlines throughout the footballing world, and I suspect was greeted with particular relish in England. We were hammered 5–0 by a team no one but anoraks knew existed. It was the worst possible start for the new boss.

We couldn't believe it and neither could Gordon, but there was nowhere to hide. It was defeat shrouded in humiliation. We had reeled at Motherwell a couple of months earlier and it seemed we were still in a daze, but there was never an attempt by anyone at Celtic to make excuses for a defeat that was truly devastating. *Artmedia*, for heaven's sake! We had beaten far bigger and far better teams in my four seasons at Parkhead, yet we were turned over and spanked by a bunch of anonymous Slovakians. We could only profusely apologise to the fans and say we would try to reverse the score at the return in Glasgow. The one crumb of hope we could take from the game in Bratislava was that we had at least created plenty of chances. The conclusion we drew from that was that they were nothing like five goals better than us. And even after our thrashing I didn't rate them as a good side so much as a lucky one. We had just been terrible, and as the game had progressed we couldn't find a foothold to enable us to climb out of the hole we had dug for ourselves. There have been suggestions that we took them too lightly, that we weren't ready. I don't agree. We viewed them as a considerable obstacle that had to be cleared. But we defended poorly and we didn't take our chances. Another factor against us, and certainly one that affected me, was the extreme heat. I always struggle to play in conditions like that: after an hour I am usually blowing a gasket, my face is red and blotchy and I am out of breath. It is one of the reasons I have never contemplated playing abroad.

We had suffered similar setbacks in Europe in my time at Celtic, but coming on the heels of the Motherwell disaster, the Artmedia result was particularly worrying. The new boss had to face the criticism, mainly from those who didn't like him and wanted him out before he had been given a chance to prove himself – there were even ludicrous calls for his sacking there and then. We could only try to claw our way back into the tie at Parkhead – but first we had some domestic commitments. Within three days of our return from Bratislava we were back at the scene of our earlier crime at Fir Park. The pressure was really on Gordon –

mocking headlines, whispers; all outside the club, though – but if it weighed heavily on him he never made us aware of it. I scored a hat-trick at Motherwell and we were leading 3–1 at half time. But astonishingly, after the interval, just as we had done a couple of months before, we let them back into the match. They took a 4–3 lead, which they held until Craig Beattie came on as sub to score the equaliser for us one minute from the end. So we scrambled a draw, but we had conceded nine goals in two matches – not good news.

The fans must have been wondering what the hell was going on, but they produced yet another example of their amazing loyalty when the Slovaks came to Parkhead. Maybe they sensed we had a chance, but I think they would have been there, supporting their club, even if they believed we had none whatsoever. The reception they gave us was superb, which was precisely what we needed to hear: the team already believed that an aggregate win was possible, but now that we knew the fans believed it too we were determined to give it everything. We hit Artmedia for four and I scored one. We needed another to force extra time, but it just wouldn't come. We recovered a little of our credibility but we were still out of Europe, which was hard to take.

Back in the SPL, we continued our winning ways for a while with two victories at home against Dundee United and Falkirk. Next was the first Old Firm match of the season, at Ibrox. We lost 3–1, Alan Thompson was sent off during the match, and Neil Lennon was dismissed after the final whistle for laying in to the referee. It could hardly have been worse, but you can bounce back from setbacks if you have the proper attitude and a leader. We had both, and we reacted. After that Ibrox match in mid-August we didn't lose again until Dunfermline beat us 1–0 at Parkhead at the end of November. In that time we played thirteen, won twelve and drew at home to Hearts. The Edinburgh club had had a fantastic start to the season themselves and were still setting the pace in the SPL, but we were right behind them and our confidence was sky high. Gordon had turned our season around by focusing on defence, which he feels is the bedrock of the team, and by November we had a great back four.

A truce, albeit an uneasy one, seemed to have developed between the gaffer and those who didn't see him as the right person to consolidate our position as Scotland's number-one club. But some fans still wanted him out. There were two reasons for their attitude: first, Martin O'Neill is so revered in Glasgow that he's a hard act to follow; and second, our elimination from Europe still rankled. Some of our fans might even have welcomed the Artmedia result because it gave them a golden opportunity to savage Gordon.

The Dunfermline defeat was a blow, and we had another one shortly afterwards when we suffered a spectacular collapse against Clyde, who knocked us out of the Scottish Cup. It was Roy Keane's debut, and I am sure he now wishes he had signed a week or two later. There are very few matches in my career in which I would call our performance appalling, but this was definitely one of them.

Of course, this was all happening in the period when my private life was in turmoil. And while I was upset by the occasional banana skins that tripped up Celtic during the season, I must say they paled into insignificance when set against what was happening with Lowri. I felt I had to devote as much time as possible to Rebeca and Joni, so when Lowri and the kids moved out that meant regular trips to Cardiff to visit them. Fortunately, although my mind was elsewhere for much of the time, my form was good: I was still knocking in the goals, fifteen by January, which kept the pressure off. Gordon Strachan also kept my spirits up and turned a blind eye to me missing a few of my club responsibilities, allowing me the time to see my kids, attend legal meetings, and see to the many other things that are involved in a divorce.

In the new year, as if I didn't have enough to worry about already, I was horrified to be caught up in what was described on television as 'a sectarian row'. It had been sparked off by Stephen Pearson and me singing the Irish folk ballad 'The Fields of Athenry' with some Celtic supporters in Dublin during Jackie McNamara's testimonial dinner. The song itself could hardly be described as 'sectarian', but while Stephen and I were singing there were shouts in the background of 'IRA!' and 'Sinn Fein!' Of course, they didn't come from us, but we were accused of chanting along with the fans when an amateur video of the event became public. And in Glasgow, stirring up sectarianism is the last thing that will be tolerated of any player from the Old Firm because the fallout can be considerable, to put it mildly. Here is an example of the stories that I awoke to in the first week of 2006 in the *Daily Record*:

TWO Celtic stars were at the centre of a sectarianism row last night after they were filmed taking part in a singalong at a fans' function. Shouts of 'IRA!' and 'Sinn Fein!' were heard as John Hartson and Stephen Pearson joined in a chorus of club anthem 'The Fields of Athenry'. But both players angrily deny that any of the shouts came from them. The singing was filmed on a mobile phone camera. The clip has been circulating widely on the internet since last week and was shown on TV last night.

Both Stephen and I were appalled. To be associated with the IRA in such a way was more than serious – it could have been damning enough to make our positions with the club untenable. Yet we had done nothing wrong. I have sung 'The Fields of Athenry' for as long as I can remember. I used to sing it in my Arsenal days, and I have never associated it with sectarianism. I have always loved it, have known all the words to it for years, and when I came to Celtic I didn't even realise it was like an anthem at Parkhead. I had always liked Irish songs, and I am a bit of a singer, you see. When I have a few beers and there's a microphone going I'll always get up and do a bit of Tom Jones singing 'Delilah'. The next morning I'm absolutely beside myself, thinking, Why the hell have I got to do that? Why can't I just sit down? But at the time it seems great when everybody's singing and chanting and you think you're Robbie Williams for five minutes.

I never really tried to get my head round the religious side of things in Glasgow. I didn't talk about religion to people and I didn't get involved in any big functions. Jackie's testimonial was different: it was a night for singing, which was all Stephen and I did.

There were about thirty people at Jackie's party. When I was singing some of them were shouting, '. . . and the IRA' between the verses, but HTV (who I haven't spoken to since) and BBC Scotland said that we were chanting, too. It caused a lot of embarrassment to me and my family. Happily, though, a lot of supporters from both sides of Glasgow have told me they didn't believe I had done it for a second. Celtic set up an investigation led by Ronnie Hawthorn, the head of security at Parkhead. He got hold of the tape and analysed it closely, which neither of the TV companies had bothered to do. The TV people also hadn't asked any questions, hadn't come to me or Stephen for an explanation, but had simply run the video as soon as they had got hold of it. Ronnie was asked to confirm our innocence, confirm the truth, but unfortunately, by the time he did that, it was too late to stop the embarrassment or the damage that had already been done. We were due an apology from the TV companies, but it never came. They had exposed us to the possibility of threats and abuse, but they denied all responsibility. I think their behaviour was disgraceful. It brought the religious stuff out for an airing which everybody could have done without. Of course I meant no offence to Protestants. Of course I wasn't having a go at Rangers. I loved to score goals against them – I got nine – but it's not a religious thing. I don't think about religion, I don't talk about it, I really have no opinion about it. I haven't looked deeply into the sectarian stuff either, and I have no idea what happened hundreds of years ago.

You can count on one hand the number of serious incidents that have happened to me during my time in Glasgow, although I have lost count of the number of times I've had 'Fenian bastard' shouted at me. All you can do when that happens is shrug and turn away. If they called me 'fat Welsh bastard' it would probably hurt my feelings a lot more. And I certainly had a few run-ins with cabbies. Sometimes a taxi would pull up, the driver would have a quick look, then he'd stick up two fingers and carry on driving. But that was balanced out by cabbies who supported Celtic, who dropped you off and refused to accept your money. If you got one of the less intense Rangers-supporting cabbies, one who actually let you inside his taxi, you would definitely know which team he supported by the time he let you out.

I was used to all of that, but some people take their obsessions too far. One night a guy got into my flat when I was asleep in bed. This was during the collapse of my marriage, and I had been living in the apartment for four or five months. Ninety-nine times out of a hundred I lock the door, but on this particular night I jumped straight into bed at about a quarter to ten and went to sleep without doing so. At half past two in the morning I heard somebody walking into my flat. Now it doesn't matter who you are or how big you are, if you are in bed, it's the early hours of the morning, it's pitch black, you are half asleep and you hear your door going, you shit yourself. So I jumped up and shouted, 'Hello, who's there? Who's there?' I ran to the stairs, but he had already gone.

Two months later something similar happened, and it was

just as frightening. Again it was early in the morning, one o'clock this time, and I was woken by the sound of my door handle being worked. I looked through the peephole and there was a man out there who looked like he was trying to rip the handle right off. I could make out that there was someone with him, too. When I shouted they ran away and got into the lift. In the morning, when I took the lift down to the ground floor, I noticed they had engraved 'Fat Hartson' on the wall and had spat all over the mirror. They had also peed outside the door. I didn't bother telling the police because then it would have ended up in the papers, which was probably exactly what the thugs wanted. I did change the locks, though, and have had a twenty-four-hour CCTV camera installed right outside my door.

Neil Lennon has been the main target for the hate squad almost since the day he joined Celtic. He has had to suffer everything from death threats to being physically attacked. Thankfully, though, he is very single-minded, a very strong character, and crucial to the team every season. Perhaps because of that, sometimes it's overlooked that he has feelings. I like Neil, he was one of my best mates at the club, and when you ask him a question you are guaranteed to receive an honest answer. He's not aggressive, he doesn't go round kicking people; in fact, he's a fantastic footballer, and very underrated. It's only when you play alongside him that you realise what a great job he does. He very rarely gives the ball away, and he's one of the fittest players in the team. Unfortunately, he had an awful time when a very personal situation surfaced in public, as they tend to for all of us footballers. It couldn't have been easy for his missus, either, as she had just had a baby when the papers ran the story. Happily, they came through it together and Neil lifted two trophies as our captain. He was certainly my player of the year for 2005–06.

Despite my own upsets I battled on and ended the season with twenty goals, which, considering how I felt for most of it, was an acceptable return. I could not have survived that season without the support of the gaffer. Gordon has the experienced manager's knack of knowing what to say and when to say it for maximum effect. He coaxed me through the campaign, and we even managed a few laughs.

This is one typical example. In one of his first team meetings he got us all together in training and started explaining, principally for the benefit of the young players, what he expected from stamina training. In a twelve-minute run he demanded eight laps which would work out at ninety seconds per lap. It was achievable for most, but in that time I would do only six and a half laps. It was not my scene.

'Look,' he said. 'There are freaks you come across in life.' He turned to me and continued: 'Big John, you are a freak. You score thirty goals a season and you've done it all your career. Some of these players haven't come anywhere near that and they dream of doing what you're doing and having the career you've had. You're just a freak. So I'm talking to all you other kids and all you other players, I'm not talking to the big man.'

Everybody just started laughing. It had broken the ice. Jim Hendrie, the Celtic fitness coach, maintained Gordon's theme. He didn't call me a freak, but he did say I defied logic because my body fat ratio was always greater than that of every other player. They brought in a life-sized photograph of a magnificent male athlete to explain to the players what went on in the body. The model, whoever he was, had the perfect physique with the most amazing pecs and six pack. Arrows pointed to where the food went, where the water went and how the body burned calories; that sort of detail. As a joke the lads cut the model's head off and replaced it with one of me. Jim wasn't very happy, but it stayed like that for a month, right in the middle of the first team changing room.

Gordon had a nice dry sense of humour – unless you were on the receiving end. He liked quiz nights and in one organised for me to be on a table with the foreigners who hardly spoke a word of English. Did he do it on purpose? I don't know, but I have my suspicions. There was Mo Camara, whose English is just about passable but who doesn't understand anything about our culture. Bobo Balde's English is worse and he knows even less about the UK. Gordon added the two Polish lads, 'Magic' Zurawski and Artur Boruc, who at that stage had difficulty saying hello and good morning. The last member of my quiz team was Shansuke Nakamura, the Japanese forward whose interpreter speaks worse English than Boruc and he's from Edinburgh. We ended up with four points and the winners had ninety-five. There was even a question about which Japanese stadium was voted the best in 2005. I turned to Shansuke and said, 'Surely you must know the answer?' But he didn't.

Managers always seem to know every detail about their players, their habits, good and bad, what they eat and drink, the way they behave off and on the field. But although Gordon was well aware of how much I loved my food, I never felt comfortable eating certain things in front of him. Sometimes it couldn't be avoided and that would be embarrassing for me. There was one of these red-faced occasions in Newcastle, after I had scored my last goal for Celtic against United in Alan Shearer's testimonial at St James'. In the morning we had to be in the hotel reception at six o'clock for a flight to Ireland. I awoke early and starving, as I hadn't eaten the night before. I went downstairs to order a couple of bacon sandwiches only to find the kitchens weren't open, but a waitress said she would make me up a couple of rolls with bacon and meet me on the ground floor.

While she was doing that, I returned to my room to finish my packing. The hotel girl phoned my room to say 'Mr Hartson's rolls are ready', so I knew she would be waiting for me. I called the lift but, instead of going straight down to the girl, the bacon rolls and the bus, it went to the penthouse suite where Gordon Strachan was waiting for it.

'Morning, big man.'

'Right, boss.'

'How did you get on, did you have a good night? Did you have a couple of beers after the game? Good goal last night. Brilliant, let's go over to Ireland now and have a bit of a celebration.'

'Yeah, gaffer.'

I'm thinking, I can't believe my luck, I just cannot believe my luck.

'Have you had any breakfast?' he said

'No, gaffer, no.'

'Don't you fancy one this morning?'

By now I was praying the lift went to the bottom floor, but it stopped at the restaurant. The door opened, and there stood the girl: 'Mr Hartson, there you go, there's your two bacon rolls.'

'I knew it wouldn't be too long big man,' the boss said and repeated. 'I knew it wouldn't be too long.'

I was less happy about another aspect of the game, though: the referees. I understand they have a difficult job, and I know we have the benefit of watching replays, slowing things down and using different camera angles whereas they have a split second to make a decision, but sometimes they drive me to the point of rage with their inconsistency. I know I sound like an old record, but I think it's a valid point. I also think that some of them get personal. I feel a little bit singled out, and I'm sure that defenders get the decision against me more often than they should. I'm not looking for any favours. It's just that I think some referees haven't got a clue about the game. They have never played football at a high level, have never been shoved in the back by a sixteen-stone centre half and then had to get up off the floor and see a referee waving his arms in the air. He's not exactly calling you a cheat in front of 60,000 people, but he is treating you like a kid, telling you to get up and play on when you know you'll have a massive bruise in the morning.

In situations like that I want to run over and shout, 'Couldn't you see that was a blatant foul? Sixty thousand people saw it but you didn't, and you are being paid to do a job and you're only ten yards away. Now, please, blow your whistle next time!' Eventually, after it has happened time and again, I crack and retaliate. But when I push the defender it's a foul and a yellow card, and the crowd must be thinking, Why doesn't the big man keep his arms down and stop fouling?

Most people are surprised that I have been red-carded only twice since joining Celtic, and one of those was rescinded on appeal. That occasion highlighted just how badly wrong a referee can get it. It was in my first season at the club and I was pulling Rangers' Bob Malcolm out of a mêlée in an Old Firm game, but as I dragged him he ducked and my arm went around his neck so it looked as if I had him in a headlock. The referee came over, completely lost control of the situation and sent off me, Johan Mjallby and one of the Rangers players. It was madness.

Martin O'Neill would always ask what had happened before talking to the media and even before he had watched a video of the incident. This time he asked me, 'What do you think, John?'

'Gaffer,' I said, 'that was a disgrace. I was trying to pull him out of a crowd of players.'

Martin replied, 'Fine, that's what I'll go with.'

Credit to the Scottish FA, they looked at the tape, listened to evidence from some of the Rangers players, then overturned the ref's decision.

chapter 17

Reflections

Marbella in June. It was blisteringly hot in the early afternoon as I lay beside the swimming pool. I was more at ease with myself than I had been for some time. My relaxed mood was mainly due to my decision to remain with Celtic, see out my contract and hopefully have the opportunity to score a few more goals for the club. The simple act of making a decision had helped clear my head.

The feeling abruptly ended when I returned to my apartment for a cold drink, switched on the television and read to my utter shock at the bottom of a Sky Sports report that Celtic had agreed a fee for me with West Brom. The club had not contacted me, they had not warned me – I was in the dark. It is an unfortunate way to find out your employer has decided you are no longer wanted.

West Brom had been in my thoughts earlier in the year when they showed an interest in signing me. I had thanked their manager Bryan Robson for that interest, but, like Portsmouth who also wanted to sign me, it was in the hands of Celtic, and as far as I knew at the time they were not prepared to sell me. The least you would expect when something like this happens is for the club to have made more effort to keep either myself or Jonathan, my agent, in touch with the situation. They did not and now I had to deal with it. My immediate reaction was to phone Celtic Park and find out exactly what had happened. I also wanted to talk to Gordon, but he was on holiday and I didn't think it was right to interrupt that. Anyway the decision had been made; it was quite obvious that they wanted me out.

In the end, I did nothing. I contacted neither the club nor Gordon, and it was only on the third day that anyone from the club spoke to me. It was the gaffer calling me from Barbados. His first words were: 'I thought I'd give you a couple of days to calm down.'

'I'm OK,' I said and added: 'I'm calm, it's no problem.'

He went on: 'I've read the stories on Teletext and in the papers. It's just to let you know, John, you have a year left on your contract. You can come back next season if you want and we'll use you as a player. But what I am saying to you is if you want to go and secure yourself a two-year contract elsewhere feel free to do so.'

That was my manager, my friend, someone I respected telling me that if I wanted to move on I could now do so. Gordon didn't have to spell it out, neither did Celtic. They had made their plans for 2006-07, and I wasn't part of them. From that second I knew my time with Celtic was over and it would be down to Jonathan and me to finalise a deal with West Brom, though I had other options: one from a Scottish Premier League side, one from the English Premiership and two from abroad.

Bryan Robson was, like me, on holiday, so I made contact with his assistant Nigel Pearson and then club chairman Jeremy Peace. The negotiations went ahead over a ten-day period and in secrecy. I wanted it kept out of the media as much as possible. I'd had too many bad experiences conducting big transfers deals in public only to see them collapse about my feet and I was determined that would not happen this time. It was known West Brom wanted me, but no more than that. Nothing was leaked about the extent of the talks, which is to the credit of my new club.

I returned to Celtic and completed four days' training with them before finalising my contract with West Brom. It gave me time to have long chats with Gordon and Celtic's chief executive Peter Lawwell, who shook my hand and told me: 'You'll always be a legend at Celtic. You've been fantastic for five years. When you come back here in years to come your picture will be on the wall. You have been a great servant to this club. I wish you well.' They were kind words at the parting of the ways. I left with no bad feelings about anyone at a great club. The circumstances concerning the way I found out their intentions were odd, but that's football.

I think you can instantly tell if you are going to enjoy working for a particular club. I had said to Bryan Robson that West Brom would be my choice if I was to leave Celtic. When the opportunity materialised, I stood by that decision. I have taken a pay drop of £10,000 a week to join Bryan at the Hawthorns. I hope that is seen as a declaration of my intent. They wanted me, they pursued me and that warmed me to their cause. It means playing in the Championship for at least a season, and not the Premiership; there will be no more European football when I could have been playing in the Champions League with Celtic.

Moving south to the Midlands has created a new lease in my life. The prospect excited me and the more I saw of this area and the club, the more excited I became about the potential here with the team and the lifestyle it offers. Sarah has joined me and we spent the first few weeks house-hunting while we stayed in the Springs health resort near Ashby, which is part of the Champney's chain owned by a great friend of mine Stephen Pardew. Staying there contributed to the fitness I needed and, I have to say, was unfortunately missing latterly at Celtic because of the stress of the divorce. Glasgow was, in some ways, like a prison, because everywhere I went I was recognised, and as I have explained before, it made you reluctant to risk what would turn into a public appearance. I am not complaining, it was part of the job and often a pleasure; you were never left in any doubt about what it meant to be part of a club as massive as Celtic. But there's no doubt I have found freedom in my new surroundings. Sarah and I can stroll through Stratford, take in the shops, visit a quiet pub beside the River Avon or a little restaurant without being stopped and asked for an autograph or abused because of the club I represent. It has been complete bliss.

Living here has also represented a major turning point in

my life. It was in Ashby I took the decision to stop gambling at the level the money I earned allowed me to. I had been trying to stop for years and have already explained the damage it can and does cause. I have stopped because I want to, but it is also a cost-cutting exercise. My divorce settlement means that my finances are considerably reduced, so I can't afford to gamble as I used to. I haven't found it difficult to stop and I am also aware of having more time for people now I'm not engrossed by who won what, where and at what odds. I have always enjoyed the social atmosphere of a race track and I did not ban myself from that, but from July 2006 only the occasional flutter was permissible.

For me the priority was success with my new club. It was expected of me. Bryan never said that I must score twenty goals a season for him, there was never a goal target as such. He just wanted me to be a success; he wanted me to storm through the Championship. That's all. Expectation should not be a burden to a professional sportsman. It signifies confidence in you and to me that is important. My memory of West Brom when I played against them was of a strong club with a marvellous fan base and always a tough, well-balanced team playing attractive football. That tradition remains. Bryan wanted nothing less than a return to the Premiership as quickly as possible. And when I had studied the quality of the players in the squad, I saw that as a very reasonable request. The fact that a quality player like Curtis Davies re-signed for the club prior to the 2006–07 season was good for squad morale. He is a young player of considerable ability who is being constantly assessed by other clubs, yet he saw enough in West Brom to want to stay. It was so important to me I wanted to congratulate Curtis as soon as I was told the news. The club have recovered their equili-brium after the disappointment of relegation and I would not have joined them if I didn't feel I could contribute to their successful future. Time will tell.

I experienced all the emotions in my first run of matches for the Albion. It was a bit like the British weather, all the seasons in a few days. In my first three matches, I scored twice on my debut against Hull, helped set one up in my second match at Cardiff and just missed with a header to score in my third at Southampton: there was the exceptional warmth and emotional support of the Albion fans in contrast to the abuse directed at me when I, a Swansea lad remember, appeared in Cardiff.

The support a team receives can determine the outcome of a season. It can be the driving force that propels you through matches without which you might lose. In my first appearance, it was obvious there was no apathy emanating from the crowd, and you assume they would never accept a hint of it from the players. That is a perfect understanding to have. The crowds are bigger at major Premiership clubs and at Celtic than they are at the Hawthorns, but with Albion you feel you are representing a special area of the country. I was surprised at the intensity of their support. I was told it would be fulsome, but I wondered if they would blame the players for relegation, and feel they had been badly let down, thus leaving a hangover from dropping out of the top league. No doubt the disappointment will linger with some, but the vast majority obviously looked at it as a new season and therefore a new start. 'Let's go for it' was the attitude that came across to me and that is exactly how we as players, through our manager, wanted to react with our performances in the Championship.

It is my job to score goals and to score twice on my debut was hugely satisfying. You are told, as an experienced player, you do not have to prove anything, but you do. I might not have been set a target, but Albion would not have wanted me playing for weeks without a goal. If it had happened that way, then I am sure everybody would have been good about it. But as the player involved, I'd have felt the pressure of letting down the manager and the fans, knowing that they in turn would feel bad for you. The manager would have been on the back foot having to ask questions about why I wasn't scoring game after game. So, scoring twice so soon cut out all the potential for that early embarrassment. I felt considerable pleasure at making my mark, confirming my commitment to the fans and taking the pressure off Bryan Robson – and myself. I had decided on joining Albion to give it all I could to play a part in helping this club, with its tradition, back to the Premiership.

I felt good about myself, physically, in every way. I was told I looked happier than I had done for a while. So, in the second week of August 2006, I even phoned Bryan and told him I would like to play again for Wales if the opportunity arose, without using up all my energy, but in an agreed way, when my experience would be most beneficial to my country.

After a year of despair, my mind had cleared and I could focus again on football. I could plan again and think seriously about the future. I like the idea of moving into coaching when my playing career ends. I could realise my ambition of returning to my part of Wales and managing Swansea. That is the impact West Bromwich Albion has had on me.

Until I was forced to think otherwise, my focus in Marbella had been on what I could achieve at Celtic. I knew that Gordon would not be happy to tread water, and would want to drive the club further forward, pushing the players to the limit of their ability. I had actually set a target to score forty goals in the two years I thought I had left on my contract. That would have brought my club total to 150, and very few of the club's renowned goalscorers have managed that. I also knew that to achieve that I would have to follow a fitness routine that would ensure I could survive and flourish at the highest level. My fitness was criticised in the 2005–06 season, and I concede it was not what Gordon would have demanded if it had been a normal season for me. But he knew that while I may have been physically on the training ground, my mind was elsewhere. I was worrying about the divorce and lawyers when I should have been concentrating fully on the club.

Celtic are lucky that after Martin O'Neill they found Gordon Strachan to step into the breach. His success must have impressed many and even pacified those who vehemently opposed his appointment. I will always like him as a person: he is very honest and he loves the game, he knows players, how they work, what they want. And he certainly knows me. He never gave me a particularly hard time, and he has been very encouraging towards me, but while he can be your friend and put his arm around you, he's also the manager of a major football club and a man with very high standards.

A certain stigma has followed me throughout my career, mainly because of petulance in my early years and some silly sendings-off. Fortunately, with just a couple of exceptions, my managers have been able to see past that, because they know I have ability and can play. Other managers have not been so open-minded, and have refused to sign me, either because of my reputation or because of my supposed knee problem. I sometimes reflect on how different my career might have been if they had given me a chance. Don't get me wrong, I have played for some great clubs, and none greater than Celtic. I was a champion with Celtic – three times in five years as well as various cups. I have also made over fifty appearances for my country, so I haven't done too badly for someone who is a past master at talking himself down. But I feel I should have looked after myself as the likes of Frank Lampard and Rio Ferdinand do – those lads who haven't got an ounce of fat on their bodies. If I had watched what I ate and drank, who knows what I might have achieved? But that wouldn't have been me. When I was thirteen I was picking up pint glasses to make a few bob. I'm from a council estate where you go out at the weekend for a couple of beers and a game of pool. That's what my dad did. That's what my mates do to this day. And

I'm no different. But perhaps, given my job, I should have been.

At my first club, Luton, I would go for a couple of pints in London on a Sunday night, and I did exactly the same at Arsenal, West Ham and Wimbledon. I still do it now when my mates come up to Glasgow from Wales. I like to socialise with them because they are a big part of my life, really big. A while ago my dad told me: 'Don't mix with this one, don't mix with that one. Don't go here with him, don't go there with him,' but my mum interrupted him and said, 'Cyril, you're telling him off, but you loved your mates.' And he did – they meant everything to him. And mine mean the same to me. I've got a group of five or six lads who I would stake my life on. We are very close, and I think that's so important. If I'm in trouble, I just have to pick up a phone and they can talk me through it.

I hope my mates would tell you that the money and the fame haven't changed me, but I *have* changed in some ways: I now eat the right things and I watch my weight. When I go to the south of Spain each summer I relax, but I also train every day. I was determined to keep playing and make an impact with Celtic in the Champions League, but now that applies to success with West Brom. I even follow the dieticians' advice these days. You get to an age when you have to.

Who knows, though, maybe the excess weight sometimes helped me. I spoke to Paul Gascoigne about this once after watching him in a match when he was about half a stone overweight. At one point he held up his arm to hold off a defender, and the guy didn't have a chance of getting the ball off him. I've used that tactic many times myself: if my arm comes across the defender there is no way he's going to get the ball because I'm so strong. Wayne Rooney does it, too. If I was a couple of stones lighter I might not have had that strength.

Gazza is a legendary drinker, and there is no way I am in his league. I enjoy a pint, but I'm no more than a social drinker. I've certainly never been kicked out of a team for turning up drunk for training. At those times I go out for a drink, I really enjoy it, though! Over the last two or three years I've thought, Well, I've worked my bollocks off during matches, I get kicked, I get elbowed, I try for every header that comes to me, I battle with these monster centre halves all round the country, I'm thirty-one years of age, I'm a father, I've got hard-earned money, I'm going to have a pint if I want one. Maybe that attitude has led to me over-doing it a bit, and I now realise that I'm at the stage where I have to start thinking about how to extend my career. So I've got to watch it. There have been occasions when I have been enjoying a few lagers with my mates and I have known exactly what the other people in the bar are thinking: What's he doing drinking? He's meant to be a footballer. That can annoy me. After all, why shouldn't I have a drink?

We all know the dangers of alcohol, not just in terms of reducing fitness levels, but the certainty that too much booze will push your behaviour beyond what is acceptable. This message was further rammed home during the summer of 2006, when Fernando Ricksen of Rangers, the man who had shared the SPFA Player of the Year award with me a year before, was sent home from the pre-season tour to South Africa following an incident on the flight out. He subsequently sought help from the Sporting Chance Clinic. I sent him a text message to wish him all the best, and he then texted back to say he was doing well. In these circumstances, it can be important to know others are thinking of you.

Once my career is over, I feel I could have a career in the media, as a pundit on television. I have always been able to pick out the strengths and weaknesses of players and explain how they can improve their game. Or I might go down another route and stay more closely involved in the coaching side, but I plan to play on until I lose my usefulness. Then it will be a question of what I am offered, but I am sure football will play a large part in whatever I do.

That's it. I have told my story. I'm proud of my Swansea roots, proud of what I've achieved, proud of being associated with Glasgow, and particularly proud of my children.

Career Record

John Hartson's Career Record (to start of 2006–07 Season)

Club Career

Season	Club	League Apps	Goals	FA Cup Apps	Goals	League Cup Apps	Goals	Other Apps	Goals	Champions League Apps	Goals	UEFA Cup Apps	Goals	Cup-Winners' Apps	Goals
1993–94	Luton	21+13	6	2+3	1	0+1	–	2*	–	–	–	–	–	–	–
1994–95	Luton	11+9	5	1	1	–	–	–	–	–	–	–	–	–	–
1994–95	Arsenal	14+1	7	–	–	–	–	2#	–	–	–	–	–	4+1	1
1995–96	Arsenal	15+4	4	1	–	1+2	1	–	–	–	–	–	–	–	–
1996–97	Arsenal	14+5	3	1+1	1	1+2	–	–	–	–	–	2	–	–	–
1996–97	West Ham	11	5	–	–	–	–	–	–	–	–	–	–	–	–
1997–98	West Ham	32	15	5	3	5	6	–	–	–	–	–	–	–	–
1998–99	West Ham	16+1	4	2	–	1	–	–	–	–	–	–	–	–	–
1998–99	Wimbledon	12+2	2	–	–	–	–	–	–	–	–	–	–	–	–
1999–00	Wimbledon	15+1	9	1	–	3	–	–	–	–	–	–	–	–	–
2000–01	Wimbledon	19	8	–	–	2	4	–	–	–	–	–	–	–	–
2000–01	Coventry	12	6	–	–	–	–	–	–	–	–	–	–	–	–
2001–02	Celtic	26+5	19	4	2	3	3	–	–	1+1	–	1+1	–	–	–
2002–03	Celtic	8+9	18	1+1	2	4	2	–	–	0+1	–	9+2	3	–	–
2003–04	Celtic	14+1	9	1	1	–	–	–	–	6+1	1	–	–	–	–
2004–05	Celtic	38	23	4	3	1	1	–	–	6	1	–	–	–	–
2005–06	Celtic	29+6	18	1	–	2+1	1	–	–	2	1	–	–	–	–

Key: * = Anglo-Italian Cup; # = Super Cup; figures after + sign denote substitute appearances

Totals

	Club	League Apps	Goals	FA Cup Apps	Goals	League Cup Apps	Goals	Other Apps	Goals	Champions League Apps	Goals	UEFA Cup Apps	Goals	Cup-Winners' Apps	Goals
	Luton Town	32+22	11	3+3	2	0+1	–	2	–	–	–	–	–	–	–
	Arsenal	43+10	14	2+1	1	2+4	1	2	–	–	–	2	–	4+1	1
	West Ham Utd	59+1	24	7	3	6	6	–	–	–	–	–	–	–	–
	Wimbledon	46+3	19	1	–	5	–	–	–	–	–	–	–	–	–
	Coventry City	12	6	–	–	–	–	–	–	–	–	–	–	–	–
	Celtic	125+21	87	11+1	8	10+1	7	–	–	15+3	3	10+3	3	–	–
	English football	192+36	74	13+4	6	13+5	7	–	–						
	Scottish football	125+21	87	11+1	8	10+1	7	–	–						
	European football							4	–	15+3	3	12+3	3	4+1	1

International Career (Wales)

Cap	Date	Opposition	Venue	Result	Goals	Tournament
1.	29/3/95	Bulgaria	Sofia	1–3		ECQ
2.	26/4/95	Germany	Dusseldorf	1–1		ECQ
3.	7/6/95	Georgia	Cardiff AP	0–1		ECQ
4.	6/9/95	Moldova	Cardiff AP	1–0		ECQ
5.	24/4/96	Switzerland	Lugano	0–2		Friendly
6.	9/11/96	Holland	Eindhoven	1–7		WCQ
7.	14/12/96	Turkey	Cardiff NS	0–0		WCQ
8.	11/2/97	Rep of Ireland	Cardiff NS	0–0		Friendly
9.	29/3/97	Belgium	Cardiff NS	1–2		WCQ
10.	27/5/97	Scotland	Kilmarnock	1–0	1	Friendly
11.	11/10/97	Belgium	Brussels	2–3		WCQ
12.	25/3/98	Jamaica	Cardiff NP	0–0		Friendly
13.	3/6/98	Malta	Valletta	3–0	1	Friendly
14.	6/6/98	Tunisia	Tunis	0–4		Friendly
15.	31/3/99	Switzerland	Zurich	0–2		ECQ
16.	5/6/99	Italy	Bologna	0–4		ECQ
17.	9/6/99	Denmark	Liverpool	0–2		ECQ
18.	9/10/99	Switzerland	Wrexham	0–2		ECQ
19.	7/10/00	Norway	Cardiff MS	1–1		WCQ
20.	11/10/00	Poland	Warsaw	0–0		WCQ
21.	24/3/01	Armenia	Erevan	2–2	2	WCQ
22.	28/3/01	Ukraine	Cardiff MS	1–1	1	WCQ
23.	2/6/01	Poland	Cardiff MS	1–2		WCQ
24.	6/6/01	Ukraine	Kiev	1–1		WCQ
25.	5/9/01	Norway	Oslo	2–3		WCQ
26.	6/10/01	Belarus	Cardiff MS	1–0	1	WCQ
27.	13/2/02	Argentina	Cardiff MS	1–1		Friendly
28.	27/3/02	Czech Rep	Cardiff MS	0–0		Friendly
29.	14/5/02	Germany	Cardiff MS	1–0		Friendly
30.	21/8/02	Croatia	Varazdin	1–1		Friendly

Cap	Date	Opposition	Venue	Result	Goals	Tournament
31.	7/9/02	Finland	Helsinki	2–0	1	ECQ
32.	16/10/02	Italy	Cardiff MS	2–1		ECQ
33.	20/11/02	Azerbaijan	Baku	2–0	1	ECQ
34.	12/2/03	Bosnia	Cardiff MS	2–2	1	Friendly
35.	29/3/03	Azerbaijan	Cardiff MS	4–0	1	ECQ
36.	6/9/03	Italy	Milan	0–4		ECQ
37.	10/9/03	Finland	Cardiff MS	1–1		ECQ
38.	11/10/03	Serbia-Montenegro	Cardiff MS	2–3	1	ECQ
39.	15/11/03	Russia	Moscow	0–0		ECQ
40.	19/11/03	Russia	Cardiff MS	0–1		ECQ
41.	18/8/04	Latvia	Riga	2–0	1	Friendly
42.	4/9/04	Azerbaijan	Baku	1–1		WCQ
43.	8/9/04	Northern Ireland	Cardiff MS	2–2	1	WCQ
44.	9/10/04	England	Manchester	0–2		WCQ
45.	*13/10/04*	*Poland*	*Cardiff MS*	*2–3*	*1*	*WCQ*
46.	26/3/05	Austria	Cardiff MS	0–2		WCQ
47.	17/8/05	Slovenia	Swansea	0–0		Friendly
48.	3/9/05	England	Cardiff MS	0–1		WCQ
49.	8/10/05	Northern Ireland	Belfast	3–2		WCQ
50.	12/10/05	Azerbaijan	Cardiff MS	2–0		WCQ
51.	16/11/05	Cyprus	Limassol	0–1		Friendly

Abbreviations: AP = Arms Park; ECQ = European Championship qualifier; MS = Millennium Stadium; NP = Ninian Park; NS = National Stadium; WCQ = World Cup qualifier. Appearances *in italics* are substitute appearances.

Career Hat Tricks

1.	29/9/97	West Ham U (H)	Huddersfield	3–0	3	League Cup
2.	20/10/01	Celtic (H)	Dundee United	5–1	3	SPL
3.	3/11/02	Celtic (H)	Aberdeen	7–0	4	SPL
4.	26/12/02	Celtic (H)	Hearts	4–2	3	SPL
5.	13/4/05	Celtic (A)	Livingston	4–0	3	SPL
6.	30/7/05	Celtic (A)	Motherwell	4–4	3	SPL

Index

Aberdeen FC 195, 199, 203, 252
AC Milan 95
Adams, Tony 91, 94, 95, 99–101,
  109, 114, 118, 120
Advocaat, Dick 14, 24
Afan Lido FC 28–8
Ajax FC 198
Albertz, Jörg 12
Amoruso, Lorenzo 199
Arsenal FC 5, 85–128, 224
Artmedia FC 253, 255
Aston Villa FC 109, 157, 222
Azerbaijan 181, 182

Baggs, Gary 158–9
Balde, Bobo 198, 226, 263
Ball, Alan 67, 68
Barnett, Jonathan 5, 6, 7, 8, 9, 10,
  11–12, 13, 19, 22, 137, 138, 139–
  40, 141, 151, 159, 163, 164, 268
Bassett, Dave 156–7
Bayern Munich 219
Beardsley, Peter 70, 73, 74–5
Beattie, Craig 255
Beckham, David 114
Beech, Cyril 43–4
Belarus 10, 15

Bellamy, Craig 20, 181, 185, 230,
  234–5
Benjamin, Ian 62
Bent, Darren 224–5
Bergkamp, Dennis 105, 106, 108,
  109, 112, 126, 224
Berkovic, Eyal 132, 144–9
Best, George 177
Bishop, Ian 127, 132
Black, Kingsley 57
Blackburn Rovers FC 131, 184, 203,
  204, 205
Blake, Nathan 170, 171, 172
Boavista FC 208, 211
Boer, Ronald de 12, 24
Bolton Wanderers FC 65
Boruc, Artur 249, 263
Bosnia-Herzegovina 182
Bould, Steve 91, 96, 114
Bowyer, Lee 89
Bradford City FC 156
Bright, Mark 94
Brittain, Vince 48
Brown, John 12
Burrows, Frank 132
Burton, Terry 10, 18, 157, 160, 162,
  163

Butt, Nicky 114

Camara, Mo 263
Cambridge United FC 55
Campbell, Kevin 91
Cantona, Eric 83, 114
Cardiff City FC 78–80, 153, 272
Carragher, Jamie 206
Carrick, Michael 132
Cascarino, Tony 83
Celta Vigo FC 204–5
Celtic FC 3, 19–20, 26, 148,
    189–269, 275
  defeat by Artmedia 253–4
  fans 208–9, 213–14
  managers *see under* O'Neill;
    Strachan
  pre-season US tours 232–3
  Scottish Premier League 199, 202,
    216, 229, 235, 248–50, 255–6
  sectarianism 190–2
  UEFA Champions League 205–15,
    219
Charles, John 180, 182
Charlton Athletic FC 3, 8–9, 24
Chelsea FC 80–3, 142
Chettle, Steve 57
Church, Charlotte 31
Claridge, Steve 50, 51
Clark, Frank 55
Clough, Brian 59, 82
Clyde FC 256
Cole, Andy 73
Cole, Joe 80, 132, 185
Coleman, Chris 64, 170
Cort, Carl 156, 163
Coventry City FC 3, 16–18, 93, 130,
    163–5
Cross, Roger 132
Crossley, Mark ('Big Norm') 57, 58,
    174, 175
Crystal Palace FC 64

Cunningham, Kenny 163
Curbishley, Alan 8, 9, 10
Cyprus 62–3, 166

Daily Mirror 107
Dalglish, Kenny 67, 175
Davies, Curtis 271–2
Davies, Simon 181, 185
Davies, Steve (agent) 98, 107, 126,
    129
Davis, Kevin 77
Dein, David 120
Delaney, Mark 185
Derae, Tibius 148–9
Derby County FC 44, 130
Dicks, Julian 127, 132, 200
Diouf, El-Hadji 206
Dixon, Kerry 49, 62, 72, 81, 82,
    83–4, 85
Dixon, Lee 91, 114
Douglas, Rab 207
Dowie, Iain 132, 134
Dreyer, John 49, 83
Dundee United FC 195, 203, 255
Dunfermline FC 203, 216, 229, 256

Earle, Robbie 163
England national team 68, 69, 183,
    185, 222, 223, 224–5
Eriksson, Sven-Göran 222, 223, 225
European Championships 10, 178,
    179, 180–1, 183, 186, 223
European Cup (old-style) 209, 211
European Cup-Winners' Cup 102–3
European Super Cup 95
Evans, Roy 67, 207
Everton FC 93, 131

FA Cup 197
  Arsenal FC 93, 110, 128
  Luton Town FC 53, 70–83
  West Ham FC 133, 149

Wimbledon FC 152, 168
FA (Football Association) 148, 222
Falkirk FC 255
Faulkner, John 60
FC Basle 203
Ferdinand, Rio 80, 127, 132, 275
Ferguson, Sir Alex 113, 175
Ferguson, Barry 198
Ferguson, Duncan 93
Finland 181, 182
Fitzgerald, Carl 35, 37
FK Suduva 204
Flo, Tore Andre 24, 156
Flynn, Brian 167
Foster, Steve 44
Freeman, Mick 7
Friar, Ken 120

Gabbidon, Danny 185
Gallagher, Peter ('Pinto') 37
Gascoigne, Paul 121, 276
Gayle, Marcus 156, 163
Gerrard, Steven 121, 206
Gier, Rob 157–8
Giggs, Ryan 22, 114, 124, 169, 176,
    185, 193
Glasgow 189–91
Glover, Paul 45–6
Goodfellow, Scott 45
Goodfellow, Steve and Joan 45, 47
Gordon, Craig 249–50
Gould, Bobby 166, 168, 169–78, 225
Graham, George 5, 10, 86, 87, 88,
    92, 93, 94, 100, 101, 114
Gross, Christian 203

Hall, Eric 81
Hamann, Dietmar 206, 207
Hammam, Sam 4, 152, 153–4, 155,
    162, 163
Harford, Mick 44, 49, 50, 151, 154
Harford, Ray 44

Hartson, Cyril (father) 30, 159
Afan Lido FC 27–8
Arsenal transfer 90
footballing advice 29, 33–4
and grandchildren 245
JH's divorce 244
JH's football trials 41, 42
JH's gambling addiction 36
JH's lifestyle 123–4, 141, 276
Rangers transfer 11, 12, 13, 14
watching JH play 207, 212
Hartson, Diana (mother) 30, 31, 32,
    207, 244, 276
Hartson, Hayley (sister) 30, 31–2, 37,
    242
Hartson, James (brother) 30, 31,
    32–3, 38, 136, 242
Hartson, John
football career
    arguments with managers 156–7,
    229, 230–2
    back problem 203, 210–11,
    212–13, 216–17, 218, 219–21
    career record 280–2
    disappointments of 183
    disciplinary record 65–7, 94, 100,
    126, 149, 156, 157, 266, 275
    on 'diving' 74–5
    failed medicals 5–7, 8–9, 10–16
    first proper game of 28–9
    football trials 40–2
    future plans 278
    high points of 76–7, 206, 235,
    249–50
    international 10, 15, 62–3,
    166–88, 198, 219–20, 225, 273
    kicking incident 144–9
    missed penalties 183, 196–7
    on referees 265–6
    and Rioch 104–12
    sectarianism 257–61
    tackling 63–4

teams
    Arsenal FC 85–128, 224
    Celtic FC 19–24, 189–269, 275
    Coventry City FC 16–19, 163–5
    Luton Town FC 42–52, 71–83,
    276
    West Bromwich Albion FC
    267–74
        West Ham FC 126–50
        Wimbledon FC 152–63
    television appearances 51
personal life
    divorce 31, 238–47, 257
    drinking 135–8, 143–4
    family life 30–2, 38
    first meeting with Lowri 242–3
    gambling addiction 34–6, 34–9,
    35–6, 39–40, 45, 50, 51, 60, 96,
    119, 121–5, 138–43, 271
        golfing 7, 16
        greyhound-owning 158–9
        smoking 34
        social life 111, 276, 277–8
        stealing 34–5, 45, 77–8
        taking speed 96–9
Hartson, Joni (son) 188, 241, 245,
    247, 257
Hartson, Keith (uncle) 134–5, 136
Hartson, Lowri 21, 22, 31, 77, 90,
    111, 124, 125, 141, 149
    divorce 238–47, 257
    first meeting with JH 242–3
    greyhounds 158–9
    JH's gambling addiction 118–19,
    121–2
Hartson, Rebeca (daughter) 153, 188,
    241, 243, 247, 257
Hartson, Victoria (sister) 30, 31, 37
Hauge, Rune 94
Hawthorn, Ronnie 259
Hearts FC 192, 230, 234, 248–50,
    256

Hendry, Jim 226, 262–3
Henry, Thierry 114
Heskey, Emile 206
Hibernian FC 220, 235
Hill, Dean 42
Hill, Michael 37
Hill-Wood, Peter 120
Hillier, David 91
Hislop, Shaka 132
Hoddle, Glenn 113
Holland 177
Holyfield, Evander 96
Hooper, Mike 74, 76
Hoppe, Spencer 37
Horne, Barry 178
Houston, Stewart 94, 101–2, 103,
    104, 110, 112
Howard, Ron (scout) 47
Howells, Barry 37
Howey, Steve 73
Hughes, Ceri 42, 64, 78
Hughes, Mark 10–11, 94, 127, 169,
    171–2, 175–6, 178, 180, 183–7,
    198, 210, 225
Hull FC 272
Hyypia, Sami 207

Italy 181, 182

Jenkins, Chris 37
Jenkins, Nicky 37
Jensen, John 91
Johnson, Andy 174, 175
Johnson, Professor Robin 212, 221
Jones, Gareth 37
Jones, Marcus 37
Jones, Paul 185
Jones, Vinnie 170
Jordan, Joe 66
Juninho 233
Juventus FC 198

Kamara, Chris 51
Kanchelskis, Andrei 12
Keane, Roy 121, 256
Keegan, Kevin 73, 77
Kemp, David 155
Kennedy, Mark 159–60
Keown, Martin 92, 114, 120–1
Kilcline, Brian 76
Kilmarnock FC 195, 216, 220
Kimble, Alan 158, 163
King, Andy 151
Kinnear, Joe 152, 154, 155, 158, 162, 163
Kitson, Paul 129, 130, 132, 134

Lampard Jnr., Frank 80, 132, 275
Lampard Snr., Frank 132
Larsson, Henrik 193, 194, 195, 196, 199, 206, 208, 211, 215, 223, 224, 226, 229
Lawwell, Peter 269
Lazaridis, Stan 127
League Cup
  Arsenal FC 109
  Luton Town FC 55
  West Ham FC 133, 145
Leeds United FC 41, 128
Leicester City FC 223
Lennon, Neil 196, 223, 226, 227, 228, 232, 255, 261–2
Linighan, Andy 92
Linton, Des 83
Liverpool FC 67, 145, 168, 203, 205–8, 209
Livingston FC 199
Ljungberg, Freddie 114
Lomas, Steve 132, 134
Lonlas Boys' Club, Skewen 28–9
Lovenkrands, Peter 197–8
Luton Town FC 36, 42–52, 276
Lyon FC 220
Lyttle, Des 57

McClaren, Steve 222
Macdonald, Roddy 23, 24, 203, 204, 211, 212, 220
MacDonald, Scott 234
McGeady, Aiden 230
McGrath, Paul 175
McLeish, Alex 192, 251
McManus, Sarah 239–40, 249, 250, 270
McNamara, Jackie 231, 257, 259
Malcolm, Bob 266
Malta 177
Manasseh, David 137, 139, 159
Manchester City FC 42
Manchester United FC 83, 106, 114, 193
Maradona 121
Marshall, Dwight 62
Melville, Alan 185
Melville, Andy 170
Merson, Paul 91, 95, 96
Middlesbrough FC 126, 222
Millwall FC 93
Mjallby, Johan 226, 266
Moncur, John 127, 132, 134, 146
Moore, Bobby 121
Morrow, Steve 110
Motherwell FC 234, 252, 255
Mourinho, José 173, 198, 199, 214–15
MTK Hungaria 219
Murray, David 11, 12, 13, 14

Nakamura, Shansuke 263
Nayim, Mohammed Ali Amar 103
Neville, Gary and Phil 114
Newcastle United FC 70, 73–7, 264
Nogan, Kurt 46
Nogan, Lee 46, 171
Northampton Town FC 145
Nottingham Forest FC 55, 56–9
Oakes, Scott 62, 64, 72, 78, 80

Olsen, Egil 155–6, 157, 162
O'Neill, Geraldine 222
O'Neill, Martin 3, 19, 22–3, 59, 177, 193, 194, 196, 199–200, 213, 215, 216, 222–4, 226–34, 256, 266
Owen, Michael 133, 206, 224

Palmer, Carlton 23
Pardew, Stephen 270
Parkhead Stadium, Glasgow *see also* Celtic FC 210
Parlour, Ray 91, 100
Payne, Colin 250
Peace, Jeremy 269
Peacock, Gavin 83
Peake, Trevor 49, 76, 83
Pearce, Stuart 56
Pearson, Nigel 269
Pearson, Stephen 256, 257–9
Pelé 121
Pembridge, Mark 42, 43, 185
Petit, Emmanuel 114
Petrescu, Dan 94
Pires, Robert 114
Pleat, David 5, 6, 43, 46, 47–8, 49, 50–1, 55, 57, 60, 66
  FA Cup run (1993–94) 72, 79, 81, 82, 83
  JH's transfer to Arsenal 85, 86–7, 89
Porto FC 198, 199, 210, 211, 213–16, 214–15
Portsmouth FC 267
Preece, David 78–9, 81
Purdew, Steven 82

Queens Park Rangers FC 67

Rangers FC 3, 23, 24–5, 199, 208, 212, 235, 266
  2002-3 season 202
  JH's failed medical for 10–15, 192

JH's missed penalty against 196–7
  Old Firm clashes 198, 220, 229, 234, 255
  Scottish Premier League title 216
Real Zaragoza 102–3
Redknapp, Harry 126, 127, 128, 129, 130, 131–2, 133, 136, 145–7, 155
Redknapp, Jamie 132
Rees, Jason 42
Rice, Pat 117
Richardson, Brian 17, 21, 164
Ricksen, Fernando 235–6, 277–8
Rioch, Bruce 65–6, 104–12, 114, 156, 160
Rioch, Greg 105
Roberts, Andy 163
Robertson, John ('Robbo') 59, 177, 200, 222, 226, 231, 233
Robson, Bryan 175, 267, 269, 271, 273
Robson, Stewart 157, 158
Rooney, Wayne 121, 124, 142, 225, 277
Rosenborg FC 198
Ruddock, Neil ('Razor') 146
Rush, Ian 67, 127, 169, 171, 175, 176, 180, 225
Russia 183–4
Ryan, Jim 47, 60

Saunders, Dean 127, 169, 171, 175, 176, 180, 225
Savage, Robbie 170, 174, 185
Sawyer, Kevin 140, 141
Scholes, Paul 114
Schwarz, Stefan 91
Scotland 183
Scott, Brian 218–19
Scottish Cup 2, 197–8, 229, 230, 234
Seaman, David 91, 103, 114
Selley, Ian 91
Serbia-Montenegro 182, 220

Sexton, Dave 69
Shearer, Alan 121, 264
Sheffield United FC 110
Sheffield Wednesday FC 93–4, 130
Sky television 146–7, 156, 267
Smith, Alan 88, 91, 94
Smith, Mike 169, 180
Sommer, Jurgen 64, 74
Souness, Graeme 204
Southall, Neville 170, 174, 175
Southampton FC 67, 93, 157, 272
Southend United FC 72
Speed, Gary 170, 173, 177, 178, 185
SPL (Scottish Premier League) 2, 199,
    202, 216, 229, 235, 248–50, 255–6
Stein, Brian 44, 50, 151
Stein, Jock 209
Stenson, Tony 107
Stone, Steve 57
Storrie, Peter 131
Strachan, Gordon 3, 4, 16–21, 23,
    26, 160, 163–5, 246, 252–4, 256,
    262–5, 268, 274–5
Stubbs, Alan 65, 67
Stuttgart FC 205
Sullivan, Neil 163
Sutton, Chris 144, 193, 194, 196,
    216, 223, 226, 230, 234
Swansea City FC 41, 78, 80, 149

Telfer, Paul 64, 72
Thatcher, Ben 160, 163
Thompson, Alan ('Tommo') 196,
    206, 207, 226, 227, 228, 232,
    236–7, 255
Thorpe, Tony 74
Titov, Egor 183–4
Todd, Colin 65, 66
Toshack, John 94, 169, 186, 187
Tottenham Hotspur FC 3, 5–7, 24,
    25, 107, 130
Tunisia 177

Turkey 173, 174, 177
Turner, Wayne 60
Tyson, Mike 96

UEFA Champions League 198–9,
    199, 203, 204–15, 219, 222
UEFA (Union of European Football
    Associations) 183–4

Valencia FC 198
Veart, Carl 110
Venison, Barry 73
Vieira, Patrick 114, 121

Walcott, Theo 225
Wales, national team 2, 10–11, 15,
    62–3, 66, 69, 127, 128, 133, 144,
    166–88, 219–20, 225, 273
Walford, Steve ('Wally') 200, 222,
    226, 227, 233
Walley, Tom 159–60, 202
Warner, Stuart 56
Webb, Neil 57
Wenger, Arsène 113–18, 119, 120,
    126, 127, 148, 173
West Bromwich Albion FC 64–5,
    267–74
West Ham United FC 80, 84, 126–50
Westley, Terry 44, 47, 48, 55, 60, 159
Whiteside, Norman 57
Wilkinson, Howard 21
Williams, Martin 55
Wimbledon FC 4–5, 152–63, 168,
    173
Winch-wen Boys' Club, Swansea 42
Winterburn, Nigel 91, 96, 114
Woan, Ian 57
World Cup 68, 170–1, 173, 174, 177,
    179, 180, 223, 225
Wright, Ian 88, 91, 92, 93, 94, 104,
    110, 112, 115, 126, 148, 175–6,
    224

Wright, Jason 77
Wycombe Wanderers FC 223

Yeats, Ron 67
Yorath, Terry 166–7, 169, 180
Yorke, Dwight 109
Young, Eric 64, 170

Zurawski, Maciej ('Magic') 249, 263